History–Social Science Framework

for California Public Schools
Kindergarten Through Grade Twelve

2005 Edition with New Criteria
for Instructional Materials

Developed by the
History–Social Science Curriculum Framework
and Criteria Committee

Adopted by the
California State Board of Education
October 11, 2000

Published by the
California Department of Education

Publishing Information

On January 8, 2003, the California State Board of Education approved the modified *Criteria for Evaluating Instructional Materials in History–Social Science, Kindergarten Through Grade Eight.* The members of the State Board at that time were Reed Hastings, President; Joe Nuñez, Vice President; Robert J. Abernethy; Donald Fisher; Susan Hammer; Nancy Ichinaga; Marion Joseph; and Suzanne Tacheny. The new criteria are included in this edition of the framework.

When the *History–Social Science Framework for California Public Schools, Kindergarten Through Grade Twelve, 2001 Updated Edition with Content Standards* was adopted by the California State Board of Education on October 9, 2000, the members of the State Board were as follows: Monica Lozano, President; Susan Hammer, Vice President; Robert Abernathy; Marian Bergeson; Kathryn Dronenburg; Reed Hastings; Nancy Ichinaga; Carlton Jenkins; Marion Joseph; and Vicki Reynolds. The 2001 framework was developed by the Curriculum Development and Supplemental Materials Commission. (See pages vii–xiv for the names of the members of the commission and the names of others who made significant contributions to the framework.)

The 2001 publication was edited by Dixie Abbott, working in cooperation with Thomas Adams, Administrator, Curriculum Frameworks Unit, California Department of Education. It was prepared for printing by the staff of CDE Press. The original painting from which the cover illustration of this edition of the framework was reproduced was painted by Childe Hassam (see below). It was integrated into a cover design by Cheryl McDonald, who also created additional artwork and prepared the layout and design. Typesetting was done by Jeannette Huff.

The framework was published by the California Department of Education, 1430 N Street, Sacramento, California 95814-5901. It was printed by the Office of State Publishing and distributed under the provisions of the Library Distribution Act and *Government Code* Section 11096.

ISBN 0-8011-1598-1

Ordering Information

Copies of this publication are available for $17.50 each, plus shipping and handling charges. California residents are charged sales tax. Orders may be sent to the California Department of Education, CDE Press, Sales Office, 1430 N Street, Suite 3207, Sacramento, CA 95814-5901; FAX (916) 323-0823. Current information on prices, credit card purchases, and shipping and handling charges may be obtained by calling the Sales Office at (800) 995-4099. Prices on all publications are subject to change.

An illustrated *Educational Resources Catalog* describing publications, videos, and other instructional media available from the Department can be obtained without charge by writing to the address given above or by calling the Sales Office at (916) 445-1260.

Photo Credits

The California Department of Education gratefully acknowledges the following organizations and individuals for the use of the photos that appear in this framework:

The Sacramento Bee, photo by Michael Williamson, pp. 1, 2; Harvey Miller, pp. 9, 10, 17, 33, 37; The Bancroft Library, University of California, Berkeley, pp. 14, 42, 158; California Department of Parks and Recreation, pp.16, 56; Franz Jantzen, Collection of the Supreme Court of the United States, p. 19; Constitutional Rights Foundation, Los Angeles, p. 24; San Diego Historical Society Photograph Collection, *http://www.sandiegohistory.org,* p. 48; Donald Kairott, p. 86; National Archives and Records Administration, pp. 100, 125, 140; and Sally Ride, Director, California Space Institute, University of California, San Diego, p. 118

All images are used by permission.

About the Cover Illustration

This painting by Childe Hassam is entitled *Allies Day, May 1917.* It was a gift of Ethelyn McKinney to the National Gallery of Art in memory of her brother, Glenn Ford McKinney. Painted in 1917, the original of this work was done in oils on canvas and measures 30 1/4 by 36 1/2 inches. Copyright 1996 by the Board of Trustees, National Gallery of Art, Washington, D.C.

Contents

Foreword v

Acknowledgments vii

Introduction to the Framework 1

Goals and Curriculum Strands 9

Goal of Knowledge and Cultural Understanding 12

    Historical Literacy 12

    Ethical Literacy 14

    Cultural Literacy 15

    Geographic Literacy 16

    Economic Literacy 17

    Sociopolitical Literacy 19

Goal of Democratic Understanding and Civic Values 20

    National Identity 20

    Constitutional Heritage 22

    Civic Values, Rights, and Responsibilities 23

Goal of Skills Attainment and Social Participation 24

    Participation Skills 24

    Critical Thinking Skills 25

    Basic Study Skills 26

Course Descriptions 27

The United States and World History Courses 29

The Primary Curriculum, Kindergarten Through Grade Three 32

    Kindergarten—Learning and Working Now and Long Ago 33

    Grade One—A Child's Place in Time and Space 37

    Grade Two—People Who Make a Difference 42

    Grade Three—Continuity and Change 48

The Middle Grades Curriculum, Grades Four Through Eight 54

    Grade Four—California: A Changing State 56

    Grade Five—United States History and Geography:

        Making a New Nation 64

    Grade Six—World History and Geography: Ancient Civilizations 76

Grade Seven—World History and Geography: Medieval
and Early Modern Times 86
Grade Eight—United States History and Geography:
Growth and Conflict 100

The Secondary Curriculum, Grades Nine Through Twelve 116

Grade Nine—Elective Courses in History–Social Science 118
Grade Ten—World History, Culture, and Geography:
The Modern World 125
Grade Eleven—United States History and Geography:
Continuity and Change in the Twentieth Century 140
Grade Twelve—Principles of American Democracy
(One Semester) 158
Grade Twelve—Economics (One Semester) 169

Criteria for Evaluating Instructional Materials 179

Appendixes 191

Introduction to the Appendixes 192
Appendix A: Nationalism, Free Markets, and Democracy in the
Contemporary World 194
Appendix B: U.S. History and Geography 204
Appendix C: Religion and the Teaching of History–Social Science 207
Appendix D: The World History Sequence at Grades Six, Seven,
and Ten: Content, Breadth/Depth, and Coverage Issues with
Some Local Options 212
Appendix E: Examples of Careers in History–Social Science 215
Appendix F: Using Primary Sources in the Study of History 217
Appendix G: Bowling Alone: America's Declining Social Capital 221
Appendix H: History–Social Science and Service-Learning 233

Foreword

The *History–Social Science Content Standards for California Public Schools,* adopted in 1998, demonstrated our state's commitment to providing all students a world-class education. The increasing complexity of geopolitics reinforces the wisdom of that commitment as our state's role in the national and international arena expands constantly.

Shifts in historical trends, economic conditions, cultural exchanges, and demographics have created a greater need than ever before for understanding the foundational ideas and philosophy of our country. We want all students to become prepared to participate successfully in events of local, state, national, and international significance. To do so, they need a solid background in history, the social sciences, and the humanities.

This framework provides guidance for instruction through which students will understand historical trends and current social, political, economic, and cultural conditions. The framework will help students recognize reasons for optimism as well as reasons for concern. Students should comprehend ideas central to liberty, responsible citizenship, and representative government and how these elements have evolved into institutions and practices that guide their decision making as future voters and leaders.

The California Department of Education and its governing and policy-determining body, the State Board of Education, are pleased to present this 2005 edition of the *History–Social Science Framework for California Public Schools* to support these goals. This edition incorporates California's rigorous academic history–social science content standards, which are the basis for statewide instruction and assessment in history–social science. This edition also includes the evaluation criteria that will guide the primary adoption of history–social science instructional materials (for kindergarten and grades one through eight) to be conducted in 2005.

This framework reflects guidance, comments, and thoughts from scholars of history–social science, curriculum experts, and classroom teachers throughout California. Therefore, the document is an essential resource to ensure that all public school students have the opportunity to receive history–social science instruction that is world class.

The United States Supreme Court's 1954 decision in *Brown v. Board of Education* put in place an agenda for public schools: equality of education for all students. As we commemorate the fiftieth anniversary of this decision, we remain committed to that agenda and now recognize that standards-based education is a fundamental tool in creating equality. This framework (with the academic content standards) needs to be consistently implemented by educators at all levels so that students will be prepared to live knowledgeably, thoughtfully, and constructively within a promising yet uncertain world. Chief Justice Earl Warren's sentiments of 50 years ago apply equally well in our present day:

> . . . *it is doubtful that any child may reasonably be expected to succeed in life if . . . denied the opportunity of an education. Such an opportunity, where the state has undertaken to provide it, is a right which must be made available to all on equal terms.*

We are confident that this framework, along with the other standards-based frameworks, will serve as a basis for providing equal education to all students.

Sincerely,

Jack O'Connell

JACK O'CONNELL
State Superintendent of Public Instruction

Ruth E. Green

RUTH E. GREEN
President, State Board of Education

Acknowledgments

$\mathcal{W}$hen the *Criteria for Evaluating Instructional Materials in History–Social Science, Kindergarten Through Grade Eight,* were adopted by the California State Board of Education on January 8, 2003, the following persons were serving on the Board:

Reed Hastings, President, Los Gatos
Joe Nunez, Vice President, Stockton
Robert Abernethy, Los Angeles
Donald Fisher, San Francisco
Susan Hammer, San Jose
Nancy Ichinaga, Los Angeles
Marion Joseph, Menlo Park
Suzanne Tacheny, Los Angeles

Members of the Curriculum Commission serving at the time the Criteria were recommended for approval to the State Board were:

Sue Stickel, Chair, Elk Grove Unified School District
Leslie Schwarze, Vice Chair, Novato, California
Norma Baker, Inglewood Unified School District
Catherine Banker, Upland, California
William Brakemeyer, Fontana Unified School District
Mary Coronado Calvario, Sacramento Unified School District
Edith Crawford, San Juan Unified School District
Milissa Glen-Lambert, Los Angeles Unified School District
Lora Griffin, Sacramento City Unified School District
Sandra Mann, San Diego City Unified School District
Julie Maravilla, Los Angeles Unified School District
Veronica Norris, Tustin, California
Dale Webster, Los Angeles Unified School District
Karen Yamamoto, Washington Unified School District

Members of the History–Social Science Subject Matter Committee of the Curriculum Commission responsible for overseeing the development of the *Criteria for Evaluating Instructional Materials in History–Social Science, Kindergarten Through Grade Eight* were:

Karen Yamamoto, Chair, Washington Unified School District
Milissa Glen-Lambert, Vice-Chair, Los Angeles Unified School District
Norma Baker, Inglewood Unified School District
Edith Crawford, San Juan Unified School District
Dale Webster, Los Angeles Unified School District

Note: The titles of commission and committee members were current at the time the various editions of the framework were being prepared.

When the 2001 updated edition of the *History–Social Science Framework for California Public Schools* was adopted by the California State Board of Education on October 11, 2000, the following persons were serving on the Board:

Monica Lozano, President, Los Angeles
Susan Hammer, Vice President, San Jose
Robert Abernethy, Los Angeles
Marian Bergeson, Newport Beach
Kathryn Dronenburg, El Cajon
Reed Hastings, Los Gatos
Nancy Ichinaga, Los Angeles
Carlton Jenkins, Los Angeles
Marion Joseph, Menlo Park
Vicki Reynolds, Beverly Hills

Vicki Reynolds served as liaison for history–social science, providing leadership and guidance to the State Board on the *History–Social Science Framework.*

The 2001 updated edition of the *History–Social Science Framework,* which includes the adopted state standards, was developed under the guidance of the Curriculum Development and Supplemental Materials Commission. The Commission that unanimously recommended the framework in July 2000 included:

Marilyn Astore, Chairperson, Sacramento County Office of Education
Patrice Abarca, Vice Chair, Los Angeles Unified School District
Roy Anthony, Grossmont Union High School District
Catherine Banker, Upland, California
Rakesh Bhandari, Los Altos, California
Mary Coronado Calvario, Sacramento Unified School District
Ken Dotson, Turlock Unified Elementary School District
Lora L. Griffin, Sacramento, California
Viken "Vik" Hovsepian, Glendale Unified School District
Veronica N. Norrris, Tustin, California
Janet Philibosian, Los Angeles Unified School District
Richard Schwartz, Torrance Unified School District
Leslie Schwarze, Novato Unified School District
Barbara F. Smith, San Rafael City School District
Susan Stickel, Elk Grove Unified School District
Karen S. Yamamoto, Washington Unified School District

Commission members who also served on the History–Social Science Subject Matter Committee, which oversaw the development of the updated framework, included **Ken Dotson,** Chairperson; **Roy Anthony,** Vice Chairperson; **Rakesh Bhandari; Janet Philibosian; Barbara F. Smith;** and **Karen S. Yamamoto.**

Instrumental in providing guidance, helpful observations, and insightful comments to the History–Social Science Subject Matter Committee was **Marilyn Astore,** Chairperson of the Curriculum Development and Supplemental Materials Commission.

The Content Review Panel for Updating the History–Social Science Framework, which advised the Curriculum Commission on accuracy and current and confirmed research, included:

Stanley Burstein, History Department, California State University, Los Angeles

Ralph James Charkins, Department of Economics, California State University, San Bernardino

Charlotte Crabtree, Department of Education, Emeritus, at the University of California, Los Angeles

William Deverell, History Department, California Institute of Technology

Nicholas J. Entrikin, Department of Geography, University of California, Los Angeles

Mahmood Ibrahim, History Department, California State Polytechnic University, Pomona

Sheilah Mann, Education and Professional Development, American Political Science Association

Robert Platzner, Department of Religious Studies, California State University, Sacramento

Linda Pomerantz, Department of History, California State University, Dominguez Hills

Eileen Sunada Sarasohn, History Department, Sacramento City College

Richard Shek, Department of Humanities and Religious Studies, California State University, Sacramento

Clarence Walker, Department of History, University of California, Davis

Special appreciation is extended to the following scholars and commentators:

Rod Atkinson, California Department of Education

John Burns, California Department of Education

Tom Gibbons, Los Angeles County Office of Education

Richard Hovannisian, Department of History, University of California, Los Angeles

Diane Ravitch, Teachers College, Columbia University, New York

Andres Resendez, Department of History, University of California, Davis

Deborah Stipek, Department of Education, University of California, Los Angeles

For the 2001 framework, the overall process for taking feedback from the Content Review Panel, receiving public comment, incorporating the standards, and publishing the document were coordinated by the following individuals:

Thomas Adams, Administrator, Curriculum Frameworks Unit

Sherry Skelly Griffith, Director, Curriculum Frameworks and Instructional Resources Division, and Executive Secretary, Curriculum Commission

Contributions to the process of completion of the 2001 updated edition of the framework were made by the following staff members in the Curriculum Frameworks and Instructional Resources Division:

Judi Brown, Consultant
Miguel Cordova, Staff Services Analyst
Teri Ollis, Staff Services Analyst
Jean Sarino, Support Staff
Lino Vicente, Support Staff

The Curriculum Frameworks Unit wishes to express its gratitude to Dan Holt for his help in making full use of the Internet and Department Web site for public information and comment.

The 1997 edition of the *History–Social Science Framework,* which was updated with appendixes, was developed under the guidance of the Curriculum Development and Supplemental Materials Commission, particularly the History–Social Science Subject Matter Committee:

Kirk Ankeney, Chairperson, History–Social Science Subject Matter Committee, and Vice Principal, San Diego City Unified School District
Geno Flores, former Chairperson, Curriculum Commission, and Administrator, Assessment Program, Long Beach Unified School District
Michele Garside, Assistant Superintendent, Butte County Office of Education
Lisa Jeffery, Teacher and Magnet School Coordinator, Los Angeles Unified School District
Jerry Treadway, Chairperson, Curriculum Commission, and Professor, San Diego State University
Jean Williams, Area Assistant Administrator, Fresno Unified School District

Much of the material that appears in the appendixes was developed from studies and surveys conducted in the field. For their work in compiling and articulating this research, appreciation is extended to the following writers:

Edward Berenson, Professor of History, University of California, Los Angeles
Diane L. Brooks, Administrator, Curriculum Frameworks and Instructional Resources Office, California Department of Education
Jan Coleman-Knight, Teacher and Department Chairperson, Fremont Unified School District
Amanda Podany, Executive Director, California History–Social Science Project
Diane Ravitch, Professor of History, Teachers College, Columbia University
Margaret Rose, Professor of History, California State University, Bakersfield
David Vigilante, Retired Teacher, San Diego Unified School District

For the 1997 framework, the overall processes for field input, completion of appendixes, and document publication were coordinated by the following managers:

Diane L. Brooks, Administrator, Curriculum Frameworks and Instructional Resources Office, California Department of Education

Glen Thomas, Assistant Superintendent, Elementary Teaching and Learning Division, California Department of Education

Contributions to the process of completion of the 1997 edition of the framework were made by the following staff members in the Curriculum Frameworks and Instructional Resources Office:

Christine Bridges, Staff Services Analyst
Larry Dunn, Staff Services Analyst
Vickie Evans, Support Staff
Ken Gardella, Support Staff
Lorna Winter, Consultant

In 1996, when this updated version was approved by the State Board, its members included the following persons:

Yvonne W. Larsen, President, San Diego
Gerti B. Thomas, Vice President, Albany
Kathryn Dronenberg, Member, El Cajon
Jerry Hume, Member, San Francisco
Elaine Lokshin, Student Member, Claremont
S. William Malkasian, Member, Sacramento
Marion McDowell, Member, San Carlos
Janet G. Nicholas, Member, Sonoma
Sanford C. Sigoloff, Member, Santa Monica
Robert L. Trigg, Member, Elk Grove
Marina Tse, Member, Monterey Park

When the original edition of the *History–Social Science Framework for California Public Schools* was adopted by the California State Board of Education on July 10, 1987, the following persons were serving on the Board:

Perry Dyke, President, Redlands
Francis Laufenberg, Vice President, Orange
Joseph D. Carrabino, Member, Los Angeles
Agnes Chan, Member, San Francisco
Gloria Hom, Member, Palo Alto
Angie Papadakis, Member, San Pedro
Kenneth L. Peters, Member, Tarzana
Jim. C. Robinson, Member, Long Beach
David T. Romero, Member, Hacienda Heights
Armen Sarafian, Member, Glendora

The original framework, published in 1988, was developed by the History–Social Science Curriculum Framework and Criteria Committee:

James H. Bell, Teacher, Poway High School, Poway Unified School District
Joyce A. Buchholz, Program Director, World Affairs Council of Northern California

Gary W. Cardinale, Curriculum Coordinator, Corona-Norco Unified School District

Pedro G. Castillo, Associate Professor of History, Oakes College, University of California, Santa Cruz

Todd Clark, Education Director, Constitutional Rights Foundation

Jean T. Claugus, Social Studies Consultant, Sacramento

Jan E. Coleman-Ghilarducci, Teacher and Chairperson, Social Science Department, Thomas Junior High School, Fremont Unified School District

Charlotte Crabtree, Professor of Education, Graduate School of Education, University of California, Los Angeles

Matthew Downey, Professor of History, Graduate School of Education, University of California, Berkeley

Patricia K. Geyer, Teacher, West Campus, Hiram W. Johnson High School, Sacramento City Unified School District

Jack N. Hoar, Consultant, History–Social Science, Long Beach Unified School District, and Framework Committee Chair

Michael A. Hulsizer, Curriculum Consultant, Office of the Kern County Superintendent of Schools

Milton A. Kato, Teacher, Thomas Jefferson Upper Elementary School, Madera Unified School District

David L. Levering, Professor of History, California State Polytechnic University, Pomona

Cosetta E. Moore, Social Studies Specialist, Los Angeles Unified School

Diane Ravitch, Professor of History, Teachers College, Columbia University

Linda K. Reeves, Teacher, Patricia Nixon Elementary School, ABC Unified School District

David I. Reinstein, Principal, Beverly Vista Elementary School, Beverly Hills Unified School District

Alvieri M. Rocca, Teacher, Sequoia Middle School, Redding Elementary School District

Christopher "Kit" Salter, Professor of Geography, University of California, Los Angeles

Jo-Ann L. Wells-Foster, Coordinator, Elementary Education, Inglewood Unified School District

The principal writers of this document were **Charlotte Crabtree,** Professor of Education, Graduate School of Education, University of California, Los Angeles; and **Diane Ravitch,** Professor of History, Teachers College, Columbia University.

The compiler of the first draft was **Matthew Downey,** Professor of History, Graduate School of Education, University of California, Berkeley.

Appreciation is extended to members of the Blue Ribbon Advisory Committee for History Scope and Sequence, which was established by Superintendent of Public Instruction Bill Honig. The committee members met in January 1986 to discuss then-current research and needs in history–social science education and to present suggestions for consideration to the Curriculum

Framework and Criteria Committee. The members of the advisory committee were as follows:

Zoe Acosta, Director, History–Social Science Curriculum Implementation Center, Office of the Kern County Superintendent of Schools

R. Freeman Butts, Professor Emeritus, Teachers College, Columbia University

Henry Chambers, Professor of Ancient History and Humanities, California State University, Sacramento

Todd Clark, Education Director, Constitutional Rights Foundation, Los Angeles

F. Michael Couch, Teacher, Santa Barbara Senior High School, Santa Barbara High School District

Matthew Downey, Professor of United States History, Graduate School of Education, University of California, Berkeley

Paul Gagnon, Professor of European History, University of Massachusetts

Paula Gillett, Director, CLIO Project, Graduate School of Education, University of California, Berkeley

Joyce Harper, Teacher, Manual Arts Senior High School, Los Angeles Unified School District

Milton A. Kato, Teacher, Thomas Jefferson Upper Elementary School, Madera Unified School District

Carol S. Katzman, Director, Educational Services for Kindergarten Through Grade Eight, Beverly Hills Unified School District

David Kennedy, Professor, Department of History, Stanford University

Juan Francisco Lara, Assistant Dean, Graduate School of Education, and Assistant Provost, College of Letters and Science, University of California, Los Angeles

Carol Marquis, Teacher, Monte Vista High School, San Ramon Valley Unified School District

Page Miller, Director, American Historical Association, Washington, D.C.

Diane Ravitch, Professor of History, Teachers College, Columbia University

Christopher "Kit" Salter, Professor of Geography, University of California, Los Angeles

Ted Yanak, Teacher, Miller Junior High School, Cupertino Elementary School District

Participating directly in the preparation of the framework as members of the Curriculum Development and Supplemental Materials Commission were:

Carol S. Katzman, Chairperson of the History–Social Science Subject Matter Subcommittee responsible for developing the framework, and Director, Educational Services for Kindergarten Through Grade Eight, Beverly Hills Unified School District

Zoe Acosta, Director, History–Social Science Curriculum Implementation Center, Office of the Kern County Superintendent of Schools

Daniel Chernow, Pacific Theatres Corporation, Los Angeles

Charlotte Crabtree, Professor of Education, Graduate School of Education, University of California, Los Angeles

William Habermehl, Assistant Superintendent, Office of the Orange County Superintendent of Schools

Dorothy K. Jackson, Assistant Principal, One Hundred Second Street Elementary School, Los Angeles Unified School District

Bruce C. Newlin, Superintendent, Norwalk-La Mirada Unified School District

The overall processes of framework development were managed by:

Francie Alexander, Associate Superintendent, Curriculum, Instruction, and Assessment Division, California Department of Education

Diane Brooks, Manager, History–Social Science and Visual and Performing Arts Unit, Office of Humanities Curriculum Services, California Department of Education

California Department of Education staff members who contributed to the process of developing the framework were:

Ira Clark, Consultant, History–Social Science

Richard Contreras, Consultant, Curriculum Framework and Textbook Development Unit

Jerry Cummings, Consultant, History–Social Science

Tomas Lopez, Director, Office of Humanities Curriculum Services

Harvey Miller, Consultant, History–Social Science

Glen Thomas, Manager, Curriculum Framework and Textbook Development Unit

Support staff included:

Amy Hibbitt, History–Social Science

Jim Lane, History–Social Science

Patti Miller, Office of Humanities Curriculum Services

Linda Vocal, Office of Humanities Curriculum Services

Introduction to the Framework

Introduction to the Framework

By studying history–social science, students will appreciate how ideas, events, and individuals have produced change over time and will recognize the conditions and forces that maintain continuity within human societies.

*T*he children of California will spend their lives in the twenty-first century. As educators we have the responsibility of preparing these children for the challenges of living in a fast-changing society. Their lives, like ours, will be affected by domestic and international politics, economic flux, technological developments, demographic shifts, and the stress of social change. The only prediction that can be made with certainty is that the world of the future will be characterized by continuity and change. The study of continuity and change is, as it happens, the main focus of the history–social science curriculum. The knowledge provided by these disciplines enables students to appreciate how ideas, events, and individuals have intersected to produce change over time as well as to recognize the conditions and forces that maintain continuity within human societies.

As educators in the field of history–social science, we want our students to perceive the complexity of social, economic, and political problems. We want them to have the ability to differentiate between what is important and what is unimportant. We want them to know their rights and responsibilities as American citizens. We want them to understand the meaning of the Constitution as a social contract that defines our democratic government and guarantees our individual rights. We want them to respect the right of others to differ with them. We want them to take an active role as citizens and to know how to work for change in a democratic society. We want them to understand the value, the importance, and the fragility of democratic institutions. We want them to realize that only a small fraction of the world's population (now or in the past) has been fortunate enough to live under a democratic form of government, and we want them to understand the conditions that encourage democracy to prosper. We want them to develop a keen sense of ethics and citizenship. And we want them to care deeply about the quality of life in their community, their nation, and their world.

The object of the history–social science curriculum is to set forth, in an organized way, the knowledge and understanding that our students need to

We want our students to understand the value, the importance, and the fragility of democratic institutions . . . to develop a keen sense of ethics and citizenship, and to care deeply about the quality of life in their community, their nation, and their world.

function intelligently now and in the future. Those who prepared this framework believe that knowledge of the history–social science disciplines (history, geography, economics, political science, anthropology, psychology, sociology, and the humanities) is essential in developing individual and social intelligence; preparing students for responsible citizenship; comprehending global interrelationships; and understanding the vital connections among past, present, and future. Without the knowledge that these disciplines convey, our students will be buffeted by changes that are beyond their comprehension. But with a firm grounding in history and the related disciplines, they should have the capacity to make wise choices in their own lives and to understand the swift-moving changes in state, national, and world affairs.

In addition to the knowledge that our students will acquire by studying the human past, they should gain a deep understanding of individual and social ethics. This framework emphasizes concern for our students' ethical understanding in every grade. We want students to see the connection between ideas and behavior, between the values and ideals that people hold and the ethical consequences of those beliefs. Students should realize that tragedies and triumphs have resulted from choices made by individuals. They should recognize that ideas and actions have real consequences—that history, in other words, is not simply the ebb and flow of impersonal forces but is shaped and changed by the ideas and actions of individuals and governments. We study history to learn from the sometimes painful, sometimes exhilarating, often humdrum experiences of those who preceded us. We want our students to understand how people in other times and places have grappled with fundamental questions of truth, justice, and personal responsibility and to ponder how we deal with the same issues today. By studying the humanities and examining the ideas of great thinkers, major religions, and principal philosophical traditions, our students will reflect on the various ways that people have struggled throughout time with ethical issues and will consider what the consequences are for us today.

The 13 years of study in which our children are engaged from kindergarten through grade twelve are barely time enough for the educational tasks to be accomplished. Our highly complex society needs well-educated minds and understanding hearts; it needs men and women who understand our political institutions and are prepared to assume the responsibilities of active citizenship. The younger generation needs to understand our history, our institutions, our ideals, our values, our economy, and our relations with other nations in the world. It is commonplace to acknowledge that we live in an interdependent world and function in a global economy. Specifically, we want our students to learn about the cultures, societies, and economic systems that prevail in other parts of the world and to recognize the political and cultural barriers that divide people as well as the common human qualities that unite them.

> We want students to see the connection between ideas and behavior, between the values and ideals that people hold and the ethical consequences of those beliefs.

> We want our students to learn about the cultures, societies, and economic systems that prevail in other parts of the world and to recognize the political and cultural barriers that divide people as well as the common human qualities that unite them.

History, placed in its geographic setting, establishes human activities in time and place.

This framework represents an effort to strengthen education in the history–social science curriculum while building on the best practices contained in previous frameworks. The distinguishing characteristics of this framework are as follows:

1 **This framework is centered in the chronological study of history.** History, placed in its geographic setting, establishes human activities in time and place. History and geography are the two great integrative studies of the field. In examining the past and present, students should recognize that events and changes occur in a specific time and place; that historical change has both causes and effects; and that life is bounded by the constraints of place. Throughout this curriculum, the importance of the variables of time and place, when and where, history and geography, is stressed repeatedly.

2 **This framework proposed both an integrated and correlated approach to the teaching of history–social science.** The teacher is expected to integrate the teaching of history with the other humanities and the social science disciplines. The teacher is also expected to work with teachers from other fields, such as the language arts, science, and the visual and performing arts, in order to achieve correlation across subjects. Within the context of this framework, history is broadly interpreted to include not only the political, economic, and social arrangements of a given society but also its beliefs, religions, culture, arts, architecture, law, literature, sciences, and technology.

3 **This framework emphasizes the importance of history as a story well told.** Whenever appropriate, history should be presented as an exciting and dramatic series of events in the past that helped to shape the present. The teacher should endeavor to bring the past to life and to make vivid the struggles and triumphs of men and women who lived in other times and places. The story of the past should be lively and accurate as well as rich with controversies and forceful personalities. While assessing the social, economic, political, and cultural context of events, teachers must never neglect the value of good storytelling as a source of motivation for the study of history.

Studies of history are enriched with the literature of the period and about the period.

4 **This framework emphasizes the importance of enriching the study of history with the use of literature, both literature *of* the period and literature *about* the period.** Teachers of history and teachers of the language arts must collaborate to select representative works. Poetry, novels, plays, essays, documents, inaugural addresses, myths, legends, tall tales, biographies, and religious literature help to shed light on the life and times of the people. Such literature helps to reveal the way people saw themselves, their ideas and values, their fears and dreams, and the way they interpreted their own times.

5 **This framework introduces a new curricular approach for the early grades (kindergarten through grade three).** In recognition of the shrinkage of time allotted to history–social science instruction in these grades in the past, and the need for deeper content to hold the interest of children, this framework proposes enrichment of the curriculum for these grades. While the neighborhood and the region provide the field for exploratory activities related to geography, economics, and local history, the students will read, hear, and discuss biographies, myths, fairy tales, and historical tales to fire their imagination and to whet their appetite for understanding how the world came to be as it is.

This framework introduces a new curricular approach for the early grades (kindergarten through grade three).

6 **This framework emphasizes the importance of studying major historical events and periods in depth as opposed to superficial skimming of enormous amounts of material.** The integrated and correlated approach proposed here requires time; students should not be made to feel that they are on a forced march across many centuries and continents. The courses in this framework identify specific eras and events that are to be studies in depth so that students will have time to use a variety of nontextbook materials, to think about what they are studying, and to see it in rich detail and broad scope.

This framework emphasizes the study of major historical events and periods in depth . . .

7 **This framework proposes a sequential curriculum, one in which knowledge and understanding are built up in a carefully planned and systematic fashion from kindergarten through grade twelve.** The sequential development of instruction that proceeds chronologically through the grades will minimize gaps in students' knowledge and avoid unnecessary repetition of material among grades. Teachers in each grade will know what history and social science content and which skills their students have studied in previous years. At each grade level some time will be designated for review of previously studied chronological periods, with attention to differing themes, concepts, or levels of difficulty of understanding.

8 **This framework incorporates a multicultural perspective throughout the history–social science curriculum.** It calls on teachers to recognize that the history of community, state, region, nation, and world must reflect the experiences of men and women and of different racial, religious, and ethnic groups. California has always been a state of many different cultural groups, just as the United States has always been a nation of many different cultural groups. The experiences of all these groups are to be integrated at every grade level in the history–social science curriculum. The framework embodies the understanding that the national identity, the national heritage, and the national creed are pluralistic and that our national history is the complex story of many

The history of community, state, region, nation, and world must reflect the experiences of men and women and of different racial, religious, and ethnic groups.

peoples and one nation, of e pluribus unum, and of an unfinished struggle to realize the ideals of the Declaration of Independence and the Constitution.

9 **This framework increases the place of world history in the curriculum to three years (at grades six, seven, and ten), organized chronologically.** While emphasizing the centrality of Western civilizations as the source of American political institutions, laws, and ideology, the world history sequence stresses the concept of global interdependence. Special attention is to be paid to the study of non-Western societies in recognition of the need for understanding the history and cultures of Asian, African, and other non-Western peoples. At each grade level, the world history course should integrate the study of history with the other humanities.

10 **This framework emphasizes the importance of the application of ethical understanding and civic virtue to public affairs.** At each grade level, the teacher of history and the social sciences will encourage students to reflect on the individual responsibility and behavior that create a good society, to consider the individual's role in how a society governs itself, and to examine the role of law in society. The curriculum provides numerous opportunities to discuss the ethical implications of how societies are organized and governed, what the state owes to its citizens, and what citizens owe to the state. Major historical controversies and events offer an appropriate forum for discussing the ethics of political decisions and for reflecting on individual and social responsibility for civic welfare in the world today.

Opportunities should be available for participation and for reflection on the responsibilities of citizens in a free society.

11 **This framework encourages the development of civic and democratic values as an integral element of good citizenship.** From the earliest grades, students should learn the kind of behavior that is necessary for the functioning of a democratic society. They should learn sportsmanship, fair play, sharing, and taking turns. They should be given opportunities to lead and to follow. They should learn how to select leaders and how to resolve disputes rationally. They should learn about the value of due process in dealing with infractions, and they should learn to respect the rights of the minority, even if this minority is only a single, dissenting voice. These democratic values should be taught in the classroom, in the curriculum, and in daily life at school. Whenever possible, opportunities should be available for participation and for reflection on the responsibilities of citizens in a free society.

12 **This framework supports the frequent study and discussion of the fundamental principles embodied in the United States Constitution and the Bill of Rights.** In addition to the customary three years of United States history in grades five, eight, and eleven and the course in "Principles of American Democracy" in grade twelve, the history–social science curriculum places a continuing emphasis on democratic values in the relations between citizens and the state. Whether studying United States history or world history, students should be aware of the presence or absence of the rights of the individual, the rights of minorities, the right of the citizen to participate in government, the right to speak or publish freely without governmental coercion, the right to freedom of religion, the right to trial by jury, the right to form trade unions, and other basic democratic rights.

We must develop in students a continuing concern for democratic values in the relations between citizens and the state.

13 **This framework encourages teachers to present controversial issues honestly and accurately within their historical or contemporary context.** History without controversy is not good history, nor is such history as interesting to students as an account that captures the debates of the times. Students should understand that the events in history provoked controversy as do the events reported in today's headlines. Students should try to see historical controversies through the different perspectives of participants. These controversies can best be portrayed by using primary sources, such as newspapers, court decisions, and speeches that represent different views. Students should also recognize that historians often disagree about the interpretation of historical events and that today's textbooks may be altered by future research. Through the study of controversial issues, both in history and in current affairs, students should learn that people in a democratic society have the right to disagree, that different perspectives have to be taken into account, and that judgments should be based on reasonable evidence and not on bias and emotion.

Through the study of controversial issues, students should learn that judgments should be based on reasonable evidence and not on bias and emotion.

14 **This framework acknowledges the importance of religion in human history.** When studying world history, students must become familiar with the basic ideas of the major religions and the ethical traditions of each time and place. Students are expected to learn about the role of religion in the founding of this country because many of our political institutions have their antecedents in religious beliefs. Students should understand the intense religious passions that have produced fanaticism and war as well as the political arrangements developed (such as separation of church and state) that allow different religious groups to live amicably in a pluralistic society.

Students must become familiar with the basic ideas of the major religious and ethical traditions of each time and place . . . and the role of religion in the founding of this country. . . .

Activities in the school and the community enlarge the classroom learning environment and help students develop a commitment to public service.

15   **This framework proposes that critical thinking skills be included at every grade level.** Students should learn to detect bias in print and visual media; to recognize illogical thinking; to guard against propaganda; to avoid stereotyping of group members; to reach conclusions based on solid evidence; and to think critically, creatively, and rationally. These skills are to be taught within the context of a curriculum that offers numerous opportunities to explore examples of sound reasoning and examples of the opposite.

16   **This framework supports a variety of content-appropriate teaching methods that engage students actively in the learning process.** Local and oral history projects, writing projects, debates, simulations, role playing, dramatizations, and cooperative learning are encouraged, as is the use of technology to supplement reading and classroom activities and to enrich the teaching of history and social science. Video resources such as video programs and laser discs, computer software, and newly emerging forms of educational technology can provide invaluable resources for the teaching of history, geography, economics, and the other disciplines.

17   **This framework provides opportunities for students' participation in school and community service programs and activities.** Teachers are encouraged to have students use the community to gather information regarding public issues and become familiar with individuals and organizations involved in public affairs. Campus and community beautification activities and volunteer service in community facilities such as hospitals and senior citizen or day care centers can provide students with opportunities to develop a commitment to public service and help link students in a positive way to their schools and communities.

Goals and Curriculum Strands

Goals and Curriculum Strands

The three major goals
are interrelated; none is
developed wholly
independent of the rest.

*T*he goals of this *History–Social Science Framework* fall into three broad categories: **Knowledge and Cultural Understanding,** incorporating learnings from history and the other humanities, geography, and the social sciences; **Democratic Understanding and Civic Values,** incorporating an understanding of our national identity, constitutional heritage, civic values, and rights and responsibilities; and **Skills Attainment and Social Participation,** including basic study skills, critical thinking skills, and participation skills that are essential for effective citizenship.

None of these goals is developed wholly independent of the rest. All interact within this curriculum. Study skills and critical thinking skills, for example, are developed through challenging studies in history and the other humanities, geography, and the social sciences. Democratic understanding and civic values are enriched through an understanding of the history of the nation's institutions and ideals. Civic participation requires political knowledge and incurs ethical choice.

The learnings contained in this curriculum can be enriched in countless ways. However, teachers and curriculum developers should be aware that for each of the three major goals, some essential learnings are integral to the development of this history–social science curriculum. These basic learnings serve as curriculum strands, unifying this curriculum across all grades, kindergarten through grade twelve. These basic learnings are first introduced in the primary grades, in simple terms that young children understand, and then regularly reappear in succeeding years, each time deepened, enriched, and extended.

The curriculum strands are
a constant in every grade,
and each year these basic
learnings are deepened,
enriched, and extended.

These curriculum strands are a constant in every grade, not options to be added or dropped from one year to the next. In every grade teachers will be expected to integrate and correlate these strands as part of their teaching of the history–social science curriculum.

In the sections that follow, each of the three goals is presented, together with its basic learnings serving as curriculum strands.

History–Social Science
K–12 Goals and Curriculum Strands

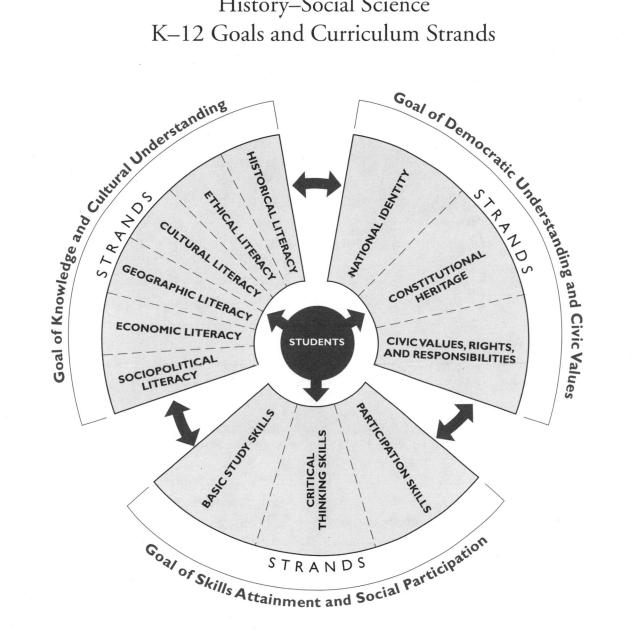

Goal of Knowledge and Cultural Understanding

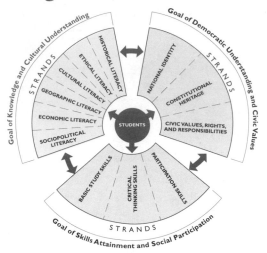

Developing literacy
in history, the other
humanities, and the social
sciences is essential to
this curriculum.

The goal of knowledge and cultural understanding is pursued by developing students' literacy in history and the other humanities (including ethics), geography, economics, sociology, and political science. Certain essential learnings are integral to the development of each of these literacy strands.

Historical Literacy

To develop historical literacy, students must:

Develop research skills and a sense of historical empathy. The study of history involves the imaginative reconstruction of the past. Ideally, students should have a sense of what it was like to be there, to realize that events hung in the balance, that people living then did not know how things ultimately would turn out. Through the use of primary sources, such as historical documents and artifacts, students will be able to reconstruct the past and the actions and thoughts of a people. As students become better readers and improve their research skills, they should learn to critique primary and secondary sources, looking for bias in the author's perspective, evaluating the credibility of the author, and distinguishing between fact and opinion. Students should also be able to distinguish between opinions based on intuition or impression and interpretations based on evidence. Through their analysis of primary sources, students will come to a deeper understanding of events and the people who experienced them. Historical empathy is much like entering into the world of a drama, suspending one's knowledge of "the ending" in order to gain a sense of another era and living with the hopes and fears of the people of the time. In every age, knowledge of the humanities helps to develop a keen sense of historical empathy by allowing students to see through the eyes of people who were there. Students should understand that each event in the past took place within its own historical context, and they should recognize that civilizations share common features across time and distance, yet also have their own unique aspects.

Understand the meaning of time and chronology. History inescapably deals with the dimension of time. Children must learn the meaning of such terms as decade, generation, century, and so on. As they grow more mature, students should learn not only when events occurred but also what else was happening at the same time in that society and elsewhere. To define a moment in time (and place) for study is to select a particular set of possibilities and constraints. Chronology defines relationships in time, and students should learn how major events relate to each other in time so that the past is comprehensible rather than a chaotic jumble of disconnected occurrences.

Analyze cause and effect. Integral to the study of history are efforts to understand why things happened and with what consequences; that is, to interpret causes and effects. Historical events usually have multiple causes and multiple effects, some of which are not recognized until long after the event occurs. Students should learn to tell the difference between a cause and a correlation. They also need to understand that the study of causes and effects does not yield cut-and-dried answers because historical interpretation is speculative and subject to change.

Understand the reasons for continuity and change. Most of the major events studied in history are examples of change, but it is no less important to recognize why things do not change; in other words, students should understand the sources of continuity. In retrospect certain changes appear to have been inevitable, but students will miss the drama of history if they do not realize that things might have turned out otherwise. What ideas, traditions, and values explain the absence of change? What combination of ideas and events explains the emergence of new patterns?

Recognize history as common memory, with political implications.
Throughout recorded time, societies have used their history as a vehicle for maintaining their identity as a people and a nation. The study of history allows people to explain and transmit their ideas and traditions to the younger generation. In tightly controlled societies the historical record may be altered to redefine public consciousness of the past and to regulate the public's loyalties; in democratic societies the historical record is open to debate, revision, conflicting interpretations, and acknowledgment of past mistakes.

Understand the importance of religion, philosophy, and other major belief systems in history. To understand why individuals and groups acted as they did, we must see what values and assumptions they held, what they honored, what they sought, and what they feared. By studying a people's religion and

Goals and
Curriculum
Strands

**Goal of
Knowledge
and Cultural
Understanding**

At the core of ethical teaching is respect for each person as a unique individual.

Concern for ethics and human rights is universal.

philosophy as well as their folkways and traditions, we gain an understanding of their ethical and moral commitments. By reading the texts that people revere, we gain important insights into their thinking. The study of religious beliefs and other ideological commitments helps explain both cultural continuity and cultural conflict.

Ethical Literacy

To develop ethical literacy, students must:

Recognize the sanctity of life and the dignity of the individual. At the core of ethical teaching is respect for each person as a unique individual. Governmental policies that disregard the value of human life or that condone inhuman practices are unethical. The curriculum offers many opportunities to explore human rights as an ethical issue.

Understand the ways in which different societies have tried to resolve ethical issues. Students should examine the major religious and philosophical traditions in Western and non-Western societies, particularly in their efforts to establish standards of behavior and values for achieving the good life and the good society.

Understand that the ideas people profess affect their behavior. Students should understand the connection between ideas and actions, between ideology and policy, between policy and practice. Whether they are studying the Holocaust or slavery or some other instance of inhumanity, students should recognize the ethical implications of ideology.

Realize that concern for ethics and human rights is universal and represents the aspirations of men and women in every time and place. Students should be aware of slave revolts in ancient times; of individuals, such as Mohandas K. Gandhi, who led popular movements for freedom; of Bishop Desmond Tutu, Nobel laureate and outspoken opponent of apartheid; of Christians who risked their lives to save Jews during the Holocaust; of dissidents who risked their lives to reveal the gulags in the former U.S.S.R.; and of historic documents such as the United Nations' Universal Declaration of Human Rights.

Cultural Literacy

To develop cultural literacy, students must:

Understand the rich, complex nature of a given culture: its history, geography, politics, literature, art, drama, music, dance, law, religion, philosophy, architecture, technology, science, education, sports, social structure, and economy. Cultural literacy includes but is not limited to knowledge of the humanities. True cultural literacy takes many years to develop, whether one is a student of a foreign country or a student of one's own society. Students should not be under the illusion that they truly know another society as a result of studying it for a few weeks or even for a year. At the very least they should learn how difficult it is to master a culture and should be encouraged to recognize that education is a lifelong process.

Recognize the relationships among the various parts of a nation's cultural life. Mature students should come to appreciate the ways that a nation's literature and arts react to and comment on events in its political and social development and also should study and appreciate the interactions among a nation's governmental system, economic structure, technology, arts, and press. None of the elements of a culture exists in a vacuum, and students will come to an understand the connections as they develop a deeper knowledge of the constituent parts.

Learn about the mythology, legends, values, and beliefs of a people. Ideas are important; to understand a society, students must perceive what its members believe about themselves, what stories and tales explain their origins and common bonds, what religious tenets embody their ethical standards of justice and duty, what heroes capture their imagination, what ideals inspire their sense of purpose, and what visual images portray their idea of themselves as a people.

Recognize that literature and art shape and reflect the inner life of a people. Artists and writers tend to have sensitive antennae. In their work artists and writers record the hopes, fears, aspirations, and anxieties of their society. A culture cannot be fully understood without knowledge of the poems, plays, dance, visual art, and other works that express its spirit.

Take pride in their own cultural heritages and develop a multicultural perspective that respects the dignity and worth of all people. Students should learn from their earliest school years that our nation is composed of people whose backgrounds are rooted in cultures around the world. They should take pride in their own cultural heritages, and should develop a multicultural perspective that respects the human dignity of all people and an understanding of different cultures and ways of life.

Students should develop respect for the human dignity of all people and understanding of different cultures and ways of life.

Goals and
Curriculum
Strands

**Goal of
Knowledge
and Cultural
Understanding**

To understand human
events, students must
first understand the
characteristics of the
places in which those
events occurred.

Geographic Literacy

To develop geographic literacy, students must:

Develop an awareness of place. Geography is
fundamentally concerned with the study of
place. Historical and contemporary events have
occurred in particular places, and generally there
are reasons for those events unfolding as they
did. To understand human events, students
must first understand the characteristics of the places in which those events
occurred. Physical characteristics of a place include its landforms, water bodies,
climate, soils, natural vegetation, and animal life. Human characteristics include
the population; the full array of human activities and settlement patterns on the
land; the ideological, religious, and philosophical beliefs of its people; and their
political and social institutions. In describing a place, students should be able to
identify its physical and human characteristics and to explain how these features
are interrelated to form the unique character of that place. Through this
curriculum students should learn about the earth's continents, the significant
countries and cities, the dominant landscape features of the earth, and the
physical and cultural contexts in which these places exist.

Develop locational skills and understanding. To study geography, students
must be able to use map and globe skills to determine absolute locations in
terms of the map grid; determine directions on the earth's surface; measure
distances between places; and interpret information available through the map's
legend, scale of miles, and symbolic representations.

Students also should be able to judge the significance of the relative
location of a place. They should, for example, learn to judge the importance to
a settlement of location on a natural harbor or in a fertile river valley, close to a
major economic resource, along a major trade route, or in proximity to major
markets. As students mature in their geographic thinking, they should learn to
analyze how the relative location of a place confers important advantages or
disadvantages, consider how these relative advantages or disadvantages can
change over time, and determine how such changes have influenced the course
of human history in that place.

Understand human and environmental interaction. One of the most dynamic
aspects of geographic education is the study of the ways people and environments interact in the human modification of the landscape. From the earliest
grades, students can examine how people in their neighborhood and locality are
"changing the land" by tearing down old structures and building new ones,
converting agricultural lands to urban use, or turning desert lands into agricultural oases. Later, students learn that this process of environmental modification in the development of cities, resort areas, and farmlands has been a

Students should develop
understanding of major
environmental issues and
the consequences of human
decisions that affect the
environment.

dominant theme throughout human history. Geographic systems are in constant flux because of both physical and human influences. Natural resources gain value only through human need, and human need changes over time. Students should develop understanding of the major environmental issues confronting modern societies and of the consequences, intentional and unintentional, of human decisions that affect the environment.

**Goal of
Knowledge
and Cultural
Understanding**

Understand human movement. Humans have been on the move since the beginning of history. Students can observe how early humans migrated from place to place in quest of food, water, and security. Students can analyze how, later in history, great migrations carried people from one continent to another in the search for places of greater opportunity. They should understand major patterns of domestic and international migration, changing environmental preferences and settlement patterns, and the frictions that develop between population groups from broadly distinct cultural regions. Students should also analyze how much of the landscape of cities and countryside is today marked by transportation networks providing for the continual movement of goods, people, ideas, and information throughout a globally interdependent world. For geographers, this theme is vital because movement promotes the diffusion of ideas, technological innovations, and goods and thereby sets change in motion.

Understand world regions and their historical, cultural, economic, and political characteristics. Geographers cannot deal with all the earth at once. For that reason, the concept of region has developed. In this curriculum a local neighborhood may be studied as a region largely composed of Asian or Hispanic immigrants. A Puritan New England colony may be studied as a region largely defined by religious affiliation. Renaissance England or post-World War II America are examples of politically defined regions. The Pacific Basin nations and nations of the North Atlantic Alliance are regions of economic, political, and cultural interaction.

An understanding of the major regions of the Western and non-Western worlds is of major importance if students are to appreciate the growing interdependence and global complexity of their world.

An understanding of the major regions of the Western and non-Western worlds is of major importance if students are to appreciate the growing interdependence and global complexity of their world.

Economic Literacy

To develop economic literacy, students must:

Understand the basic economic problems confronting all societies. Basic to all economic decision making is the problem of scarcity. Scarcity requires that all individuals and societies make choices about how to use their productive resources. Students need to understand this basic problem confronting all societies and to examine

Students must understand the basic economic problems confronting all societies.

Goals and
Curriculum
Strands

Goal of
Knowledge
and Cultural
Understanding

the ways in which economic systems seek to resolve the three basic economic problems of choice (determining what, how, and for whom to produce) created by scarcity.

Understand comparative economic systems. Beginning in the elementary school, students should be introduced to the basic processes through which market economics function and to the growing network of markets and prices that reflect shifting supply and demand conditions in a market economy. In later years students should be able to compare the origins and differentiating characteristics of traditional, command, market, and "mixed" economic systems. Students should understand the mechanisms through which each system functions in regulating the distribution of scarce resources in the production of desired goods and services, and they should analyze their relationships to the social and political systems of the societies in which they function.

Understand the basic economic goals, performance, and problems of our society. Students need to be able to analyze the basic economic goals of their society; that is, freedom of choice, efficiency, equity, full employment, price stability, growth, and security. They need to develop analytical skills to assess economic issues and proposed governmental policies in light of these goals. They also need to know how to explain or describe the performance of the nation's economy. Finally, students need opportunities to examine some of the local, national, and global problems of the nation's mixed economy, including (1) inflationary and deflationary pressures and their effects on workers' real earnings; (2) underemployment and labor; (3) the persistence of poverty in a generally productive economy; (4) the rate of growth and worker production and hence material output; and (5) the successes and failures of governmental programs.

Understand the international economic system. Students need to understand (1) the organization and importance of the international economic system; (2) the distribution of wealth and resources on a global scale; (3) the struggle of the "developing nations" to attain economic independence and a better standard of living for their citizens; (4) the role of the transnational corporation in changing rules of exchange; and (5) the influence of political events on the international economic order.

Sociopolitical Literacy

To develop sociopolitical literacy, students must:

Understand the close relationship between social and political systems. To understand the political system of a society, students must also understand the social system. The two systems are interrelated, with the social values of a society reflected in its political institutions. By the time they reach grade ten, students normally are ready to examine social and political relationships; to analyze how social status, social mobility, political power, and prestige are distributed within a society; and to analyze how these factors affect the opportunities that are available to men and women of all walks of life and of all ethnic and racial backgrounds.

Understand the close relationship between society and the law. To understand a society, one must understand the relationship between the society and its laws. In studying the United States, for example, students should come to understand that important public issues and controversies that are not resolved within the social institutions of the society regularly make their way into the political system and the courts for their ultimate resolution. Students should observe that in recent years every major social issue, whether civil rights, equal educational opportunity, abortion, or criminal justice, has reached the courts. They should come to understand that the interpretations of the Constitution reached by the courts are the result of human decisions, which are influenced by changing perceptions of the fit between constitutional principles and social realities. They also should come to understand how judicial decisions, in turn, influence society's goals and values, its institutions, and the attitudes of individual citizens.

Understand comparative political systems. Students should learn about the differences between democratic and nondemocratic political systems, and they should be able to describe the critical characteristics of each system. In analyzing contemporary and historical societies, students should critically examine such questions as how governments gain power over people and land; to what extent power is allocated among citizens and between citizens and government; how governmental power is limited, maintained, and transferred; what protections exist against the abuse of that power; and what provisions exist for the protection of individual and minority rights and freedoms, an independent judiciary and press, and the processes of constitutional choice and the consent of the governed. Finally, students should consider the significance of all the foregoing on the lives of individual citizens.

**Goal of
Knowledge
and Cultural
Understanding**

Students must understand political and social systems, the relationship between a society and its laws, and the differences between democratic and nondemocratic political systems.

Goal of Democratic Understanding and Civic Values

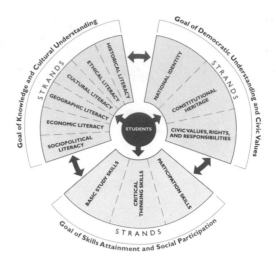

The curricular goal of democratic understanding and civic values is centered on an essential understanding of the nation's identity and constitutional heritage; the civic values that form the foundation of the nation's constitutional order and promote cohesion between all groups in a pluralistic society; and the rights and responsibilities of all citizens.

Understanding our nation's identity, its constitutional heritage, and its civic values prepares our students for their rights and responsibilities in a pluralistic society.

National Identity

To understand this nation's identity, students must:

Recognize that American society is and always has been pluralistic and multicultural, a single nation composed of individuals whose heritages encompass many different national and cultural backgrounds. From the first encounter between indigenous peoples and exploring Europeans, the inhabitants of the North American continent have represented a variety of races, religions, languages, and ethnic and cultural groups. With the passage of time, the United States has grown increasingly diverse in its social and cultural composition. Teachers have an obligation to instill in students a sense of pride in their individual heritages. Students must recognize that whatever our diverse origins may be, we are all Americans.

Students must understand the pluralistic, multicultural nature of American society and the historic struggle to extend constitutional guarantees of equality and freedom to all.

Understand the American creed as an ideology extolling equality and freedom. The American creed is derived from the language and values found in the Declaration of Independence, the Constitution, and the Bill of Rights. Its themes are echoed in patriotic songs such as "America the Beautiful"

Goals and
Curriculum
Strands

Goal of
Democratic
Understanding
and Civic
Values

(" . . . and crown thy good with brotherhood, from sea to shining sea") and "America" (" . . . from every mountainside, let freedom ring"). The creed provides the unifying theme of the memorable discourse of Martin Luther King, Jr., "I Have a Dream": "I have a dream that one day this nation will rise up and live out the true meaning of its creed: *We hold these truths to be self-evident, that all men are created equal.* . . . This will be the day when all of God's children will be able to sing with new meaning 'My Country, 'Tis of Thee, Sweet Land of Liberty. . . .'" Students should learn the radical implications of such phrases as "all men are created equal" and study the historic struggle to extend to all Americans the constitutional guarantees of equality and freedom.

Recognize the status of minorities and women in different times in American history. Students should be aware of the history of prejudice and discrimination against minorities and women as well as efforts to establish equality and freedom. Students should understand how different minorities were treated historically and should see historical events through a variety of perspectives.

Understand the unique experiences of immigrants from Asia, the Pacific Islands, and Latin America. Students should examine the cultural, political, and economic sources of contemporary immigration from these areas to understand the changing demography of California and the United States. Attention should be paid to the contributions of immigrants from Asia, the Pacific islands, and Latin America to life and culture in the United States.

Understand the special role of the United States in world history as a nation of immigrants. The multicultural, multiracial, multiethnic, multireligious character of the United States makes it unusual among the nations of the world. Few, if any, nations can match the United States when compared on a scale of social heterogeneity; few, if any, have opened their doors so wide to immigration and provided such relatively easy access to full citizenship. At the same time students should analyze periodic waves of hostility toward newcomers and recognize that the nation has in different eras restricted immigration on the basis of racial, ethnic, or cultural grounds.

Realize that true patriotism celebrates the moral force of the American idea as a nation that unites as one people the descendants of many cultures, races, religions, and ethnic groups. The American story is unfinished, for it is a story of ideals and aspirations that have not yet been realized. It is a story that is in the making; its main characters are today's students, their parents, and their friends. Unlike other historical events that are wholly in the past, this is a story whose beginning can be traced to the nation's founding and whose outcome rests in the students' hands.

America, as a nation, unites as one people the descendants of many cultures, races, religions, and ethnic groups. The American story is unfinished, and the outcome rests in the students' hands.

**Goal of
Democratic
Understanding
and Civic
Values**

Students must understand
the nation's constitutional
heritage and the principles
of the Constitution that
created our democratic
form of government.

Constitutional Heritage

*To understand the nation's constitutional heritage,
students must:*

Understand the basic principles of democracy.

Students need to understand the central dilemma
that confronts all societies and the basic principles that guide the democratic resolution of that
dilemma: how to endow civil government with
enough power to govern efficiently and yet to limit that power to protect
against the tyranny of government and its infringement on the property and
liberty of individual citizens. Students need to understand how the Founding
Fathers of this nation struggled with these issues and, writing in the context of
the American Enlightenment and their religious traditions, framed a Constitution of principles that created a democratic form of government; instituted the
rule of law over rulers and the ruled alike; and conferred the basic guarantees of
a free society through such fundamental mechanisms as representative government, separation of powers, a system of checks and balances, and limitations on
terms of office.

Students also need to understand the principle that democratic government
exists for the people and that the people rule through the processes of constitutional choice and consent of the governed. At the same time students must
understand the importance of protecting the rights of minorities against the
tyranny of majority rule. They need to develop appreciation for the guarantees
provided in the Bill of Rights and for the importance of a democratic system's
procedural rules that ensure, for example, due process, a free press, periodic
elections, and the peaceable change of government through procedural rules
that guarantee that the majority decides. Students also should understand how
the Constitution has been amended and improved over time.

**Understand the historical origins of basic constitutional concepts such as
representative government, separation of powers, and trial by jury.** Students
need to develop an understanding of the concepts of constitutional government
in their historical context. They should examine key documents, including the
Magna Carta, the English Bill of Rights, the Mayflower Compact, and the
Fundamental Orders of Connecticut, as milestones in the development of
democratic government. They need to study also those ideas of the Enlightenment that influenced the authors of the Constitution, especially the ideas of
John Locke on natural rights and on the social and government contract; of
Charles-Louis Montesquieu on the character of British liberty and the institutional requirements for its attainment; and of Oliver Cromwell's Common-
wealth Tradition. Students should understand that the ideas and writings of the
leading thinkers of the European Enlightenment were widely quoted in the
colonies and that these ideas and writings were discussed by Whigs and Tories

Students need to
understand the principle
that democratic govern-
ment exists for the people
and that the people rule
through the processes of
constitutional choice and
consent of the governed.

Goals and
Curriculum
Strands

**Goal of
Democratic
Understanding
and Civic
Values**

alike. This historical context is important for students to understand because it explains the importance of the Constitution as the most enduring monument of the American Enlightenment.

Civic Values, Rights, and Responsibilities

To understand civic values, rights, and responsibilities, students must:

Understand what is required of citizens in a participatory democracy. Students must develop an understanding of the qualities required of citizens in a participatory democracy. They need to understand, for example, that a democratic society depends on citizens who will vote and participate actively in their local, state, and national governments, take individual responsibility for their own ethical behavior, control inclinations to aggression, and attain a certain level of civility on their own by choosing to live by certain higher rules of ethical conduct. Students need to understand why a democracy needs citizens who value give-and-take on issues, who do not feel it necessary to go to war over every idea, and who seek the middle ground on which consensus and cooperation can flourish.

Students need also to understand that the democratic process ensures its citizens a field of fair play so one can gracefully accept the loss of a debate or an election on the certain knowledge that there is always the chance to compete again. These are essential insights for students to acquire, for they are the basis for peaceful elections in a democracy, for the orderly transfer of power, and for the readiness of winners and losers alike to join ranks behind the candidate elected in a fair contest. Finally, students need to develop a deep and abiding commitment to democratic values in their individual and social behavior.

Understand individual responsibility for the democratic system. Students need to understand the inherent strengths of the democratic system. But they also need to ponder its fragile nature and the processes through which democracies perish: through erosion of democratic protections; through lack of effective leadership or governance; through indifference of citizens to their rights and responsibilities under the Constitution and the Bill of Rights; through lack of will or courage; through selfishness and alienation; and through usurpation of power by tyrants or antidemocratic extremist groups. Students need to develop an appreciation for the informed commitment a democracy requires of its citizens to maintain its basic freedoms. They need to understand that critical thinking and independence of mind are essential characteristics of citizens in a free society and that education develops the critical intelligence necessary for good citizenship. Students need to understand the importance to a democracy of citizens who are willing to vote regularly, participate actively in government, think critically and creatively about issues, confront the unresolved problems of the society, and work through democratic processes toward the fuller realization of its highest ideals in the lives and opportunities of all its citizens.

Goal of Skills Attainment and Social Participation

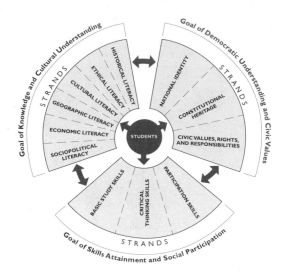

The curricular goal of skills attainment and social participation is pursued by developing students' participation skills, critical thinking skills, and basic study skills.

Skills are attained through practice while students learn the content of the history–social science curriculum.

Participation Skills

While the ability to work with others is an asset in any society, it is a requirement for citizenship in a democracy. Democratic government depends on citizens who are actively involved as well as informed. Civic competence requires the skills that make joint effort and effective cooperation possible. It also requires a willingness to work for the common good. As a major conduit by which the democratic heritage is passed to each new generation, the history–social science curriculum must promote the learning of skills that lead to civic competence.

The history–social science curriculum must promote the learning of skills that lead to civic competence.

To participate effectively in society, students need to:

Develop personal skills. Among the personal skills that students should develop are sensitivity to the needs, problems, and aspirations of others; expression of their personal convictions; recognition of personal biases and prejudices, such as the stereotyping of members of a particular group; understanding of people as

Goals and
Curriculum
Strands

**Goal of Skills
Attainment
and Social
Participation**

individuals rather than as stereotypes; and the adjustment of one's behavior to work effectively with others.

Develop group interaction skills. Among the group interaction skills that students should develop are willingness to listen to the differing views of others; ability to participate in making decisions, setting goals, and planning and taking action in a group setting; leadership skills and the willingness to follow; skills of persuading, compromising, debating, negotiating, and resolving conflicts; and ability to confront controversial issues in ways that work toward reasoned solutions free of aggressions that destroy group relations.

Develop social and political participation skills. Among the social and political participation skills that students should develop are ability to identify issues that require social action; commitment to accept social responsibilities associated with citizenship; willingness to work to influence those in political power to preserve and extend justice, freedom, equity, and human rights; willingness to assume leadership roles in clarifying goals and mobilizing groups for political action; and willingness to accept the consequences of one's own actions.

Critical Thinking Skills

The skills involved in critical thinking enable students to question the validity and meaning of what they read, hear, think, and believe. Critical thinking requires a questioning mind and a skeptical withholding of assent about the truth of a statement until it can be critically evaluated. While such skills are developed through everyday living as well as by schooling, the history–social science classroom is an especially appropriate setting for developing such skills. The ability to think critically about public issues, evaluate candidates for office, and assess decisions of government officials is an essential attribute of good citizenship in a democratic society. Students learn critical thinking skills by confronting issues and writing analytical commentaries. In reading documents and other original materials, students have an opportunity to interpret the writer's language and to extract meaning. When original texts such as the Declaration of Independence, the Constitution, or the Seneca Falls Declaration are read to supplement or replace the textbook, critical discussion and thinking are promoted. Writing about the subject matter of history and social science gives students valuable experience in thinking through their ideas and articulating them.

The following critical thinking skills are to be developed in the context of the history–social science curriculum:

Define and clarify problems. Included in these skills are the ability to identify central issues or problems, to determine which information is relevant, to make

The ability to
think critically about
public issues,
candidates for office,
and governmental
decisions is an essential
attribute of good
citizenship in a
democratic society.

Goals and
Curriculum
Strands

**Goal of Skills
Attainment
and Social
Participation**

distinctions between verifiable and unverifiable information or between essential and incidental information, and to formulate appropriate questions leading to a deeper and clearer understanding of an issue.

Judge information related to a problem. This skill requires ability to distinguish among fact, opinion, and reasoned judgment; to determine whether statements are consistent with one another and with the context from which they are taken; to identify unstated assumptions; and to recognize stereotypes, clichés, bias, propaganda, and semantic slanting.

Solve problems and draw conclusions. Included in these skills are the ability to decide whether the information provided is sufficient in quality and quantity to justify a conclusion; to identify reasonable alternatives for the solution to a problem; to test conclusions or hypotheses; and to predict probable consequences of an event, a series of events, or a policy proposal.

Basic Study Skills

Basic study skills are the skills that students must have in order to acquire knowledge; they are skills that make formal education possible. Most basic skills are not learned primarily through the history–social science curriculum, but some are special to this area of study. The most basic skills of the history–social science fields involve obtaining information and judging its value, reaching reasoned conclusions based on evidence, and developing sound judgment. The skills also include the ability to discuss and debate and the ability to write a well-reasoned and well-organized essay. These skills are outcomes of a well-constructed program, and they take time and practice to develop. Examples of practice include sustained reading and sustained writing.

The most basic skills of history–social science fields involve obtaining information and judging its value, reaching reasoned conclusions based on evidence, and developing sound judgment.

The basic skills of history–social science include the ability to:

1. Acquire information by listening, observing, using community resources, and reading various forms of literature and primary and secondary source materials.
2. Locate, select, and organize information from written sources, such as books, periodicals, government documents, encyclopedias, and bibliographies.
3. Retrieve and analyze information by using computers, microfilm, and other electronic media.
4. Read and interpret maps, globes, models, diagrams, graphs, charts, tables, pictures, and political cartoons.
5. Understand the specialized language used in historical research and social science disciplines.
6. Organize and express ideas clearly in writing and in speaking.

Course Descriptions

Course Descriptions

The course descriptions that follow provide an integrated and sequential development of the goals of this curriculum. Specific learning activities are included in these course descriptions, but they are intended to be illustrative. Imaginative teachers will create their own curricular activities to engage student participation. Specific works of literature are included in these course descriptions, but these too are meant to be illustrative. Annotated bibliographies in the *History–Social Science Course Models, Kindergarten Through Grade Twelve (www.history.ctaponline.org)* will provide a broad range of readings to enrich these studies, including selections for English learners.

Implementation of this integrated and correlated curriculum requires cooperative planning among teachers from different subject areas, as well as school librarians, and should promote team teaching and other collaborative strategies. Teachers should draw on community resources, a wide variety of books, computer software, vidoetapes, and other visual materials. In addition to presenting subjects for class discussion, teachers should provide for students' active learning through experiences such as civic participation, community service, debates, role playing, simulations, mock trials, collaborative and individual projects, preparation of local and oral histories, and mapping activities.

This curriculum attempts to bridge the barriers between the related disciplines and to enable students to see the relationships and connections that exist in real life. The measure of its success will lie not only in test scores but also in the extent to which students develop empathetic insight into the life of other times and places, as well as enlightened understanding of their own time and place. The titles of courses for kindergarten through grade twelve are as follows:

Kindergarten—Learning and Working Now and Long Ago
Grade One—A Child's Place in Time and Space
Grade Two—People Who Make a Difference
Grade Three—Continuity and Change

Grade Four—California: A Changing State
Grade Five—United States History and Geography: Making a New Nation
Grade Six—World History and Geography: Ancient Civilizations
Grade Seven—World History and Geography: Medieval and Early
Modern Times
Grade Eight—United States History and Geography: Growth and Conflict
Grade Nine—Elective Courses in History–Social Science
Grade Ten—World History, Culture, and Geography: The Modern World
Grade Eleven—United States History and Geography: Continuity
and Change in the Twentieth Century
Grade Twelve—Principles of American Democracy (One Semester)
and Economics (One Semester)

The United States and World History Courses

The curriculum departs from current practice by significantly increasing the time allocated to chronological history. The three courses in United States history (grades five, eight, and eleven) and the three courses in world history (grades six, seven, and ten) have the following characteristics:

1. ***Beginning with grade six, each course in this series contributes to students' learning of historical chronology.*** The course in grade six emphasizes the ancient world to A.D. 500. The grade seven course continues world history through medieval and early modern times, A.D. 500–1789. The grade eight course establishes the new American nation in the context of the European Enlightenment, with which the grade seven course just concluded, and emphasizes the years 1783–1914. The grade ten course emphasizes the modern world, 1789 to the present day. The grade eleven course emphasizes United States history in the twentieth century. This interplay between world and United States history helps students recognize the global context in which their nation's history developed and allows teachers to illustrate events that were developing concurrently throughout the world.

2. ***Each course gives major emphasis to a selected historical period that students will study in depth.*** The accompanying chart illustrates the periods to be emphasized in these courses. By limiting the years to be studied in each course, this plan provides the time needed to develop these studies in depth and makes it more likely that students will retain what they have learned. These outcomes cannot be achieved through the superficial treatment that results from rushing across the whole of United States or world history in one survey course.

Chronological Emphases for Courses in World and United States History and Geography

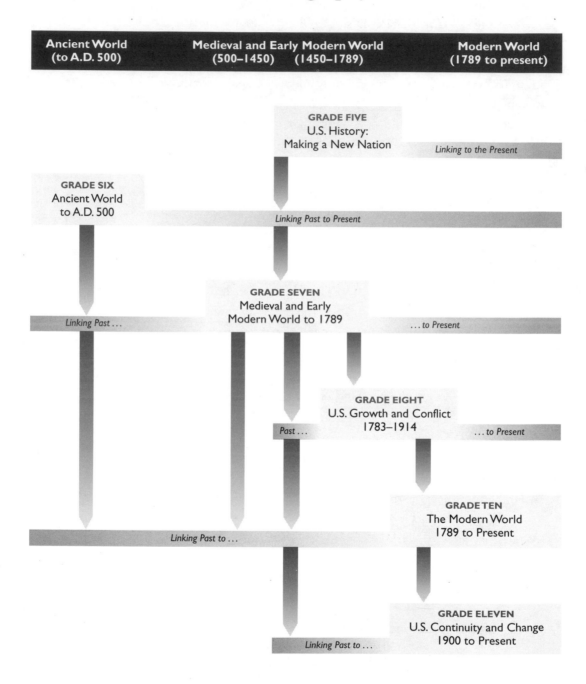

Ancient World (to A.D. 500)	Medieval and Early Modern World (500–1450) (1450–1789)	Modern World (1789 to present)

GRADE FIVE
U.S. History: Making a New Nation

Linking to the Present

GRADE SIX
Ancient World to A.D. 500

Linking Past to Present

GRADE SEVEN
Medieval and Early Modern World to 1789

Linking Past ...   *... to Present*

GRADE EIGHT
U.S. Growth and Conflict 1783–1914

Past ...   *... to Present*

GRADE TEN
The Modern World 1789 to Present

Linking Past to ...

GRADE ELEVEN
U.S. Continuity and Change 1900 to Present

Linking Past to ...

3. *Beginning with grade seven, each course provides for a review of learnings from earlier grades.* Each of these courses begins with one or more review units titled, "Connecting with Past Learnings." The purpose of these units is not to cover everything that was studied in earlier years but to review selectively some essential historical antecedents of the period under study. In all of these reviews, the purpose is not to retread old ground but to develop some deeper understandings that were not possible when students were younger. These review units ensure that learnings of the ancient world will be reinforced in grades seven and ten and that learnings of the medieval and early modern worlds will be reinforced in grades eight, ten, and eleven. Learnings of our nation's seventeenth and eighteenth century beginnings are reinforced in grades eight and eleven.

4. *Each course provides opportunities to link the past with the present.* In the United States history sequence, the courses in grades five and eight both conclude with major units titled, "Linking Past to Present." Each of these units brings the study up to the present day by expanding on the major themes emphasized in the course. In the world history sequence, the courses in grades six and seven give recurrent attention to the contributions of the past to the modern world. In grades ten and eleven, students are brought to the present day through studies of the great changes of the twentieth century that shaped the world in which students live.

The primary curriculum builds on the important learnings young children have already developed during infancy and their early preschool years and then moves outward through geography and back in time through history to link the child with people from the past.

The Primary Curriculum
Kindergarten Through Grade Three

Developmental Considerations

Beginning with kindergarten, the primary curriculum builds on the important learnings young children have already developed during infancy and their early preschool years. By the time they enter kindergarten, some children have developed important space, time, and causal understandings. These understandings can help each child develop a sense of place within his or her world.

To extend these important spatial, temporal, and causal understandings, teachers must recognize the critical role the "home base" plays for the young child. Geographic and historical forays in space and back through time must always be connected with the young child's immediate world and with the fund of meanings the child already has acquired. These primary studies, therefore, begin each year by centering first on the child's immediate present and/or prior knowledge. Studies each year then move spatially outward to develop important linkages with the larger geographic and economic world. Studies each year also reach back in time to link the child with people, ordinary and extraordinary, who came before and whose stories build sensitivity and appreciation for times past and for the long continuity of human experience.

A summary of the course titles for kindergarten and grades one through three, with major subtitles, is as follows:

Kindergarten—Learning and Working Now and Long Ago
- Learning to Work Together
- Working Together: Exploring, Creating, and Communicating
- Reaching Out to Times Past

Grade One—A Child's Place in Time and Space
- Developing Social Skills and Responsibilities
- Expanding Children's Geographic and Economic Worlds
- Developing Awareness of Cultural Diversity, Now and Long Ago

Grade Two—People Who Make a Difference
- People Who Supply Our Needs
- Our Parents, Grandparents, and Ancestors from Long Ago
- People from Many Cultures, Now and Long Ago

Grade Three—Continuity and Change
- Our Local History: Discovering Our Past and Our Traditions
- Our Nation's History: Meeting People, Ordinary and Extraordinary, Through Biography, Story, Folktale, and Legend

Kindergarten—
Learning and Working
Now and Long Ago

In kindergarten, children first begin to understand that school is a place for learning and working. Most children arrive for their first school experience eager to work and learn. Many will be working in groups for the first time. They must learn to share, to take turns, to respect the rights of others, and to take care of themselves and their own possessions. These are learnings that are necessary for good civic behavior in the classroom and in the larger society. Children can also discover how other people have learned and worked together by hearing stories of times past. In kindergarten, children should learn that they make choices and that their choices have consequences for themselves and others.

Learning to Work Together

To help children learn their way as learners, workers, and classroom participants is the purpose of this first study. In their daily life at kindergarten, children are invited to work centers and activities, encouraged to participate, and given guidance in acquiring the complex skills involved in working with others. They must learn to share the attention of the teacher with others and learn to consider the rights of others in the use and care of classroom materials.

Such learnings will be deepened and enriched if teachers use classroom problems that inevitably arise as opportunities for critical thinking and problem solving; for example, problems in sharing scarce resources or space with others or in planning ahead and bringing one's activity to a conclusion to be on time for the next activity. Children need help in analyzing problems such as these; considering why the problem arose; considering other alternatives they might have tried in coping with the problem; developing awareness of how alternative behaviors might bring different results in the ways that others in the group respond to them; and learning to appreciate behaviors and values that are consistent with the democratic ethic. Children must have opportunities to discuss these more desirable behaviors, try them out, and examine how they lead to more harmonious and socially satisfying relationships with others.

To further support these learnings, teachers should introduce stories, fairy tales, and nursery rhymes that incorporate conflict and raise value issues that are both interesting and understandable for young children. A few examples of such stories are "Jack and the Beanstalk," "Goldilocks and the Three Bears," selections from Aesop's Fables, and Virginia Hamilton's *The People Could Fly.* In discussing these stories, children should identify the behavior of characters in the story, observe the effect of this behavior on others, examine why characters

Standard K.1.
Students understand
that being a good
citizen involves acting
in certain ways.

behaved as they did, and consider whether other choices could have changed the results. These discussions are intended to help them acquire those values of deliberation and individual responsibility that are consistent with the democratic ethic.

Working Together: Exploring, Creating, and Communicating

A second major goal of this kindergarten curriculum is to help children build their sense of self and self-worth through extending their understanding of the immediate world and deepening their appreciation of their own ability to explore, create, solve problems, communicate, and assume individual and group responsibilities in classroom activities.

Children should have opportunities, under the teacher's guidance, to explore the school and its environs, a new world for these children, as well as the landscape in the neighborhood, including its topography, streets, transportation systems, structures, and human activities.

Children should have opportunities to use large building blocks, wood, tools, and miniature vehicles as well as a variety of materials from a classroom box filled with imaginative and improvisational objects, clothing, workers' hats, and the like in order to construct real and imagined neighborhood structures. Activities in these centers carried on through group play become important beginnings of map work for young children. Children should be encouraged to build neighborhoods and landscapes and to incorporate such structures as fire stations, airports, houses, banks, hospitals, supermarkets, harbors, and transportation lines. Picture files, stories, and books should be used to deepen children's information about the places they are creating and the work that is carried on in them. In all of these activities, children should understand the importance of literacy as a means of acquiring valuable information and knowledge.

Reaching Out to Times Past

A third goal of this kindergarten curriculum is to help children take their first vicarious steps into times past. Well-selected stories can help children develop a beginning sense of historical empathy. They should consider how it might have been to live in other times and places and how their lives would have been different. They should observe different ways people lived in earlier days; for example, getting water from a well, growing their food, making their clothing, and having fun in ways that are different from those of today. They can compare themselves with children in such stories as *Daniel's Duck,* by Clyde R. Bulla; *Thy Friend, Obadiah* and *The Adventures of Obadiah,* by Brinton Turkle; *Becky and the Bear,* by Dorothy Van Woerkom; and selected chapters from *Little House in the Big Woods,* by Laura I. Wilder. They should recognize that national and state symbols such as the national and state flags, the bald eagle, and the Statue of Liberty were used by people in the past as well as in the present.

Standard K.4.

Students compare and contrast the locations of people, places, and environments and describe their characteristics.

Standard K.3.

Students match simple descriptions of work that people do and the names of related jobs at the school, in the local community, and from historical accounts.

Standard K.6.

Students understand that history relates to events, people, and places of other times.

Standard K.2.

Students recognize national and state symbols and icons such as the national and state flags, the bald eagle, and the Statue of Liberty.

History–Social Science Standards

Kindergarten
Learning and Working Now and Long Ago

K.1 **Students understand that being a good citizen involves acting in certain ways.**

1. Follow rules, such as sharing and taking turns, and know the consequences of breaking them.
2. Learn examples of honesty, courage, determination, individual responsibility, and patriotism in American and world history from stories and folklore.
3. Know beliefs and related behaviors of characters in stories from times past and understand the consequences of the characters' actions.

K.2 **Students recognize national and state symbols and icons such as the national and state flags, the bald eagle, and the Statue of Liberty.**

K.3 **Students match simple descriptions of work that people do and the names of related jobs at the school, in the local community, and from historical accounts.**

K.4 **Students compare and contrast the locations of people, places, and environments and describe their characteristics.**

1. Determine the relative locations of objects using the terms near/far, left/right, and behind/in front.
2. Distinguish between land and water on maps and globes and locate general areas referenced in historical legends and stories.
3. Identify traffic symbols and map symbols (e.g., those for land, water, roads, cities).
4. Construct maps and models of neighborhoods, incorporating such structures as police and fire stations, airports, banks, hospitals, supermarkets, harbors, schools, homes, places of worship, and transportation lines.
5. Demonstrate familiarity with the school's layout, environs, and the jobs people do there.

K.5 **Students put events in temporal order using a calendar, placing days, weeks, and months in proper order.**

K.6 **Students understand that history relates to events, people, and places of other times.**

1. Identify the purposes of, and the people and events honored in, commemorative holidays, including the human struggles that were the basis for the events (e.g., Thanksgiving, Independence Day, Washington's and Lincoln's Birthdays, Martin Luther King Jr. Day, Memorial Day, Labor Day, Columbus Day, Veterans Day).

2. Know the triumphs in American legends and historical accounts through the stories of such people as Pocahontas, George Washington, Booker T. Washington, Daniel Boone, and Benjamin Franklin.

3. Understand how people lived in earlier times and how their lives would be different today (e.g., getting water from a well, growing food, making clothing, having fun, forming organizations, living by rules and laws).

Grade One—
A Child's Place in Time and Space

Children in the first grade are ready to learn more about the world they live in and about their responsibilities to other people. They begin to learn how necessary it is for people and groups to work together and how to resolve problems through cooperation. Children's expanding sense of place and spatial relationships provides readiness for many new geographical learnings. Children also are ready to develop a deeper understanding of cultural diversity and to appreciate the many people from various backgrounds and ways of life that exist in the larger world that they are now beginning to explore. Children begin to develop a sense of an economy in which people work both in and outside the home and exchange goods and services for money.

Developing Social Skills and Responsibilities

Most children in the first grade willingly accept responsibility for classroom chores. With guidance, they should be building the values of responsible classroom participation throughout the school day. Their early learnings of basic civic values can be extended now by emphasizing the values of fair play and good sportsmanship, respect for the rights and opinions of others, and respect for rules by which we all must live.

Again, as in kindergarten, emphasis should be placed on having the children solve the social problems and decision-making dilemmas that naturally arise in the classroom; for example, problems in sharing scarce supplies or in deciding how best to proceed on a group project (such as map making) when a dilemma arises. In using this approach, children will learn that problems are a normal and recurring feature of social life and that the children themselves have the capacity to examine problems.

Beyond the problems that normally occur in classrooms, corridors, and playgrounds, teachers can also introduce value-laden problems for discussion through reading stories and fairy tales that pose dilemmas appropriate for young children. Through listening to these stories and through the discussions and role-playing activities that can follow, children will gain deeper understandings of individual responsibility and social behavior. Throughout these lessons the teacher's purpose should be to help children develop those civic values that are important in a democratic society.

Standard 1.5.

Students describe the human characteristics of familiar places and the varied backgrounds of American citizens and residents in those places.

Standard 1.1.

Students describe the rights and individual responsibilities of citizenship.

Course
Descriptions

Grade One

Standard 1.2.

Students compare and contrast the absolute and relative locations of places and people and describe the physical and/or human characteristics of places.

Chronological and Spatial Thinking 4.

Students use map and globe skills to determine the absolute locations of places and interpret information available through a map's or globe's legend, scale, and symbolic representations.

Expanding Children's Geographic and Economic Worlds

The children's growing sense of place and spatial relationships makes possible important new geographic learnings in grade one. Unless children are new to the area, they probably already have developed a good sense of their neighborhood and the places they regularly go to shop, play, and visit with family and friends. They are now ready to develop a deeper understanding of these places and the interrelationships between these places and the other places, both near and far, that supply their needs.

Regions that are changing provide especially rich opportunities for the geographic and economic education of young children. In these places children can observe firsthand the changes that are occurring in the landscape, such as new shopping malls and freeways, and land-use changes that turn residential neighborhoods into commercial areas and rural areas into urban communities. Children can also analyze why these changes are happening and how these changes are affecting their families and others who live there.

To develop these geographic learnings, children may construct a three-dimensional floor or table map of their immediate geographic region. Such an activity helps develop children's observational skills; teaches the concepts of geographic scale, distance, and relative location; and clarifies for children the spatial relationships among the region's features. Throughout these activities children should consult their textbooks, picture files, and a wide variety of books for information about these workplaces and the work people do in them.

Comparing such a floor or table map to a picture map of this same region will help children make the connections between geographic features in the field, three-dimensional models of this region, and two-dimensional pictures or symbolic maps. Children should observe that the picture-symbol map "tells the same story" as the floor model but does so at a smaller scale. They should also observe that the picture-symbol map can be hung upright without changing the spatial arrangement of these features and without altering their relationships to one another; for example, the supermarket is still north of the post office. Children must have these critical understandings if they are to read and interpret the data that maps represent. These understandings are basic to all subsequent map reading and interpretation skills.

Once children have developed an educated understanding of their neighborhood, they are ready to examine its many geographic and economic connections with the larger world. This study, therefore, progresses to the central post office, through which the letters children mail to relatives and friends are routed for delivery here and abroad; to the trucks and railroad lines that bring products to this neighborhood for eventual sale in its stores; to an industrial region, near or far away, producing one or more needed products, such as bricks and building materials for new home construction or clothing for the stores; and to the airport or regional harbor that links this place with producers, suppliers, and families throughout the world. Children at this age level should understand that the place where they live is interconnected with the wider world.

In these studies the children should be acquiring some basic understanding of economics; for example, of the goods and services that people need and want and of the specialized work that people do to manufacture, transport, and market such goods and services.

At the same time children should be enjoying literature that brings these activities alive and that builds sensitivity toward the many people who work together to get their jobs done. Classic stories such as *Mike Mulligan and His Steam Shovel, Little Toot,* and *The Little Red Lighthouse and the Great Gray Bridge* illustrate working together, teach values, and develop empathy.

Developing Awareness of Cultural Diversity, Now and Long Ago

This unit of study focuses on many people: people from the children's own families and those of their classmates, people from other cultures, people living today, and people from long ago. Through stories of today as well as fairy tales, folktales, and legends that open the richness of the past to young children, this curriculum helps children to discover the many ways in which people, families, and cultural groups are alike as well as those ways in which they differ.

In developing this literature-enriched unit of study, teachers should draw first from the rich fund of literature from those cultures represented among the families in the classroom and school. Then, as time allows, teachers can introduce literature from other cultures for comparison.

Throughout this unit opportunities should be provided for children to discuss and dramatize these stories, discover their moral teachings, and analyze what these stories tell about the culture: its beliefs, customs, ceremonies, traditions, social practices, and the like. In addition, children should read stories about men and women from diverse cultures who are heroes.

Among the literary treasures young children can enjoy are fairy tales by the Brothers Grimm; *Aesop's Fables;* Ethel J. Phelps's *Tatterhood and Other Tales,* a multicultural collection of traditional folktales and stories in which girls are the protagonists; African folktales, including Camille Yarbrough's *Cornrows;* Japanese stories, including Yoshiko Uchida's *Magic Listening Cap* and Taro Yashima's *Umbrella;* Frances Carpenter's *Tales of a Korean Grandmother;* American folktales and hero stories, such as Ezra J. Keats's *John Henry: An American Legend;* selected American Indian tales of California, the Great Plains, and the Southwest; and Leo Politi's stories of Hispanic Los Angeles. By the end of grade one, the children should appreciate the power and pleasure of reading.

Grade One

Standard 1.6.

Students understand basic economic concepts and the role of individual choice in a free-market economy.

Standard 1.3.

Students know and understand the symbols, icons, and traditions of the United States that provide continuity and a sense of community across time.

Standard 1.4.

Students compare and contrast everyday life in different times and places around the world and recognize that some aspects of people, places, and things change over time while others stay the same.

History–Social Science Standards

Grade One
A Child's Place in Time and Space

1.1   **Students describe the rights and individual responsibilities of citizenship.**

1. Understand the rule-making process in a direct democracy (everyone votes on the rules) and in a representative democracy (an elected group of people makes the rules), giving examples of both systems in their classroom, school, and community.

2. Understand the elements of fair play and good sportsmanship, respect for the rights and opinions of others, and respect for rules by which we live, including the meaning of the "Golden Rule."

1.2   **Students compare and contrast the absolute and relative locations of places and people and describe the physical and/or human characteristics of places.**

1. Locate on maps and globes their local community, California, the United States, the seven continents, and the four oceans.

2. Compare the information that can be derived from a three-dimensional model to the information that can be derived from a picture of the same location.

3. Construct a simple map, using cardinal directions and map symbols.

4. Describe how location, weather, and physical environment affect the way people live, including the effects on their food, clothing, shelter, transportation, and recreation.

1.3   **Students know and understand the symbols, icons, and traditions of the United States that provide continuity and a sense of community across time.**

1. Recite the Pledge of Allegiance and sing songs that express American ideals (e.g., "America").

2. Understand the significance of our national holidays and the heroism and achievements of the people associated with them.

3. Identify American symbols, landmarks, and essential documents, such as the flag, bald eagle, Statue of Liberty, U.S. Constitution, and Declaration of Independence, and know the people and events associated with them.

1.4 **Students compare and contrast everyday life in different times and places around the world and recognize that some aspects of people, places, and things change over time while others stay the same.**

1. Examine the structure of schools and communities in the past.
2. Study transportation methods of earlier days.
3. Recognize similarities and differences of earlier generations in such areas as work (inside and outside the home), dress, manners, stories, games, and festivals, drawing from biographies, oral histories, and folklore.

1.5 **Students describe the human characteristics of familiar places and the varied backgrounds of American citizens and residents in those places.**

1. Recognize the ways in which they are all part of the same community, sharing principles, goals, and traditions despite their varied ancestry; the forms of diversity in their school and community; and the benefits and challenges of a diverse population.
2. Understand the ways in which American Indians and immigrants have helped define Californian and American culture.
3. Compare the beliefs, customs, ceremonies, traditions, and social practices of the varied cultures, drawing from folklore.

1.6 **Students understand basic economic concepts and the role of individual choice in a free-market economy.**

1. Understand the concept of exchange and the use of money to purchase goods and services.
2. Identify the specialized work that people do to manufacture, transport, and market goods and services and the contributions of those who work in the home.

Grade Two—
People Who Make a Difference

Children in the second grade are ready to learn about people who make a difference in their own lives and who made a difference in the past. People who make a difference in the child's world are, first, those who care for him or her; second, those who supply the goods and services that are necessary for daily life; and third, those extraordinary men and women who have made a difference in our national life and in the larger world community.

People Who Supply Our Needs

This first study develops children's appreciation of the many people who work to supply their daily needs. Emphasis in this unit is given to those who supply food: people who grow and harvest food crops on wheat and vegetable farms, fruit orchards, or the banana plantations of Central America; dairy workers who supply dairy products; and processors and distributors who move the food from farm to market. In addition, students should consider the interdependence of all these people, consumers and producers, processors and distributors, in bringing these foods to market. Students should develop an understanding of their roles as consumers in a complex economy.

In visits to their local market and to a regional central market, if available, children should observe and identify the great variety of foods that workers in these markets make available to buyers on a daily basis.

Questions of where these foods come from, who produces them, and how they reach these markets give focus to this unit.

To engage children's interest and to help them develop an understanding of the complex interdependence among many workers in the food industry, teachers can guide children in creating three-dimensional maps. Children can observe the many linkages between their homes, the markets that supply their food, the places where people work to produce their food, and the transportation systems that move these products from farm to processor to market.

Picture maps and flowcharts should be introduced to help children analyze the sequences and interrelationships in all these activities. Air photos and regional maps of the immediate and the extended geographic region can be introduced to help children locate the places where these activities occur and observe how farmlands, railroads, highways, and urban markets are distributed in the geographic landscape. In the course of these geographic learnings, children should differentiate between these maps and the globe, understand and

Standard 2.4.

Students understand basic economic concepts and their individual roles in the economy and demonstrate basic economic reasoning skills.

Standard 2.2.

Students demonstrate map skills by describing the absolute and relative locations of people, places, and environments.

use cardinal directions, identify and distinguish between physical geographic features in the natural landscape and on maps, and read and interpret map symbols with the use of a legend.

As part of these studies, children should explore such geographic questions as the following: How does climate affect the crops a farmer can grow? Why are some areas more fertile than others? How do farmers protect their crops against untimely frosts or drought? Why is water such an important resource for farmers? How do irrigation systems work? What can happen to our food supply when any part of the total system breaks down because of a flood or other natural disaster or a strike of transportation workers? What can happen to our food supply if farmlands are overused or rich farmlands are changed or rezoned for urban development?

Throughout this study children should be developing basic economic understandings of human wants and needs, scarcity and choice; the importance of specialization in work today and the economic interdependence that results; the need for exchange in the market system; and the importance of international trade as they learn about bananas from Central America or cocoa products from Ghana.

Comparative studies can be based on episodes drawn from the past—episodes, for example, that introduce young children, through stories, to the domestication of wild grasses by the early peoples of Mesopotamia; the tools and technology people invented long ago to grind their grain and bake their bread; and the important invention of the mill for grinding grain, and, much later, of refrigeration for preserving food. Specific historic dates are meaningless to children of this age, but young children can grasp the drama of humankind's great achievement in taming the wild grasses for a steady food supply and the long history of the use of bread products, along with the inventions that have made the task of producing food easier and more reliable. To place these events in historical sequence, children can differentiate between those that happened long long ago, long ago, and yesterday. Children should explore the benefits of technology in food production.

Other comparative studies can center on the foods indigenous to one or more of the cultures represented in the classroom group; the production of these foods; their use in daily diets, ceremonies, and festivals; and their enjoyment by many families in California today.

Literature should be richly used throughout these studies to bring alive the people who produce and who enjoy the fruits of all these labors. Among the literary selections to be read to children and to be dramatized by them, when appropriate, are the stories of the first Thanksgiving, *The Adventures of Johnny Appleseed,* and a wide selection of folktales, myths, legends, and stories from many cultures, Western and non-Western.

Grade Two

Chronological and Spatial Thinking 5.

Students judge the significance of the relative location of a place (e.g., proximity to a harbor, on trade routes) and analyze how relative advantages or disadvantages can change over time.

Chronological and Spatial Thinking 1.

Students place key events and people of the historical era they are studying in a chronological sequence and within a spatial context; they interpret time lines.

Course
Descriptions

Grade Two

Standard 2.1.

Students differentiate
between things that
happened long ago and
things that happened
yesterday.

**Chronological and
Spatial Thinking 2.**

Students correctly apply
terms related to time,
including *past, present,
future, decade, century,*
and *generation.*

Standard 2.3.

Students explain govern-
mental institutions and
practices in the United
States and other countries.

Standard 2.5.

Students understand the
importance of individual
action and character and
explain how heroes from
long ago and the recent
past have made a
difference in others' lives.

Our Parents, Grandparents, and Ancestors from Long Ago

To understand and appreciate the many ways that parents, grandparents, and ancestors have made a difference is the central purpose of this unit of the second grade curriculum. Another purpose is to help children develop a beginning sense of history through an approach that is understandable and interesting to them.

One way to help children understand how parents and grandparents made a difference is to have them construct a family history of their own family, a relative's or neighbor's family, or a family from books or personal experience. In developing these activities, teachers should be sensitive to family privacy and protect the wishes of children and parents who prefer not to include their families in these activities. Where did the family come from? What was it like to live there? Who was in the family then? Do photos or letters from that time still exist? When did the family come here? How did they make the trip? Were there any adventures? Are there any family legends about the journey?

Through children's dictation, later recorded by the teacher in individual storybooks, children might tell the story of the family's transit and its adventures getting here. The children might be invited to illustrate the family history, either painting or coloring pictures themselves or using photos (if the family agrees) to show how the family has changed over one or more generations.

Class discussions can center on the many places, groups, and nations represented among classmates. A globe and world map can be used to locate places of family origin and to study possible routes followed in getting here. Transportation methods of earlier days should be compared with those a family traveling today might use.

Members of children's families can be invited to tell about the experiences of their families. Readings from literature can be shared to help children acquire deeper insights into the cultures from which the families came; the stories, games, and festivals parents or grandparents might have enjoyed as children; the work that children as well as their families would have been expected to do; their religious practices; and the dress, manners, and morals expected of family members at that time. Comparisons can be drawn with children's lives today to discover how many of these family traditions, practices, and values have carried forward to the present and what kinds of changes have occurred.

People from Many Cultures, Now and Long Ago

In this unit of study, the children will be introduced to the many people, ordinary and extraordinary, who have contributed to their lives and "made a difference." Among the people children should meet are those men and women whose contributions can be appreciated by seven-year-olds and whose achievements have directly or indirectly touched the children's lives or the lives of others like themselves. Included, for example, are scientists who have found a cure for childhood diseases; scientists and inventors, such as George Washington Carver, Marie Curie, Louis Pasteur, Charles Drew, and Thomas Edison; authors, musicians, and artists whose works are great favorites of children and who have brought beauty into the children's lives; athletes, such as Jackie Robinson, who have brought pleasure to sports fans and who have become role models for young people; leaders from all walks of life who have helped to solve community problems, worked for better schools, or improved living conditions and lifelong opportunities for workers, families, women, and children; and children, as well as adults, who have been honored locally for the special courage, responsibility, and concern they have displayed in contributing to the safety, welfare, and happiness of others.

Through reading and listening to biographies, children can learn about the lives of those from many cultures who have made a difference. They should conclude from their studies of this year that people matter: those we know, those who lived long ago, and those who help us even though we do not know their names.

Standard 2.3.

Students explain governmental institutions and practices in the United States and other countries.

History–Social Science Standards

Grade Two
People Who Make a Difference

2.1   Students differentiate between things that happened long ago and things that happened yesterday.

1. Trace the history of a family through the use of primary and secondary sources, including artifacts, photographs, interviews, and documents.
2. Compare and contrast their daily lives with those of their parents, grandparents, and/or guardians.
3. Place important events in their lives in the order in which they occurred (e.g., on a time line or storyboard).

2.2   Students demonstrate map skills by describing the absolute and relative locations of people, places, and environments.

1. Locate on a simple letter-number grid system the specific locations and geographic features in their neighborhood or community (e.g., map of the classroom, the school).
2. Label from memory a simple map of the North American continent, including the countries, oceans, Great Lakes, major rivers, and mountain ranges. Identify the essential map elements: title, legend, directional indicator, scale, and date.
3. Locate on a map where their ancestors live(d), telling when the family moved to the local community and how and why they made the trip.
4. Compare and contrast basic land use in urban, suburban, and rural environments in California.

2.3   Students explain governmental institutions and practices in the United States and other countries.

1. Explain how the United States and other countries make laws, carry out laws, determine whether laws have been violated, and punish wrongdoers.
2. Describe the ways in which groups and nations interact with one another to try to resolve problems in such areas as trade, cultural contacts, treaties, diplomacy, and military force.

2.4   Students understand basic economic concepts and their individual roles in the economy and demonstrate basic economic reasoning skills.

1. Describe food production and consumption long ago and today, including the roles of farmers, processors, distributors, weather, and land and water resources.
2. Understand the role and interdependence of buyers (consumers) and sellers (producers) of goods and services.
3. Understand how limits on resources affect production and consumption (what to produce and what to consume).

2.5   Students understand the importance of individual action and character and explain how heroes from long ago and the recent past have made a difference in others' lives (e.g., from biographies of Abraham Lincoln, Louis Pasteur, Sitting Bull, George Washington Carver, Marie Curie, Albert Einstein, Golda Meir, Jackie Robinson, Sally Ride).

**Chronological and
Spatial Thinking 1.**

Students place key events
and people of the historical
era they are studying in a
chronological sequence and
within a spatial context;
they interpret time lines.

Standard 3.1.

Students describe the
physical and human
geography and use maps,
tables, graphs, photo-
graphs, and charts to
organize information
about people, places,
and environments in
a spatial context.

Grade Three—
Continuity and Change

Although third graders are not ready for a formal
study of history, they can begin to think about
continuity and change in their own locality and
nation. By exploring their locality and locating
some of the features that were built by people
who lived long ago, children can make contact with times past and with the
people whose activities have left their mark on the land.

Through studies of continuity and change in their locality, children can
begin to think about chronological relationships and to analyze how some
things change and others remain the same. To understand changes occurring
today, children should explore the ways in which their locality continues to
evolve. Finally, teachers should introduce children to the great legacy of local,
regional, and national traditions that provide common memories and a shared
sense of peoplehood for all of us.

Our Local History: Discovering Our Past and Our Traditions

Children who have constructed a family history in grade two are now ready
to think about constructing a history of the place where they live today.
Children might recall how the decision of their parents or grandparents to
move to this place made an important difference in their lives. They might
wonder whether the people who came to this place long ago made a difference,
too. Discovering who these people were, when they lived here, and how they
used the land gives children a focus for this first unit.

Because throughout California the geographic setting has had important
effects on where and how localities developed, children should begin their
third-grade studies with the natural landscape. A field trip into the immediate
environment will establish familiarity with the major natural features and
landforms of this region. Field trips are especially important if children have
not had an opportunity before this to explore, observe, and study firsthand
their local environment. Field trips may be augmented by use of videotapes and
photographs of the landscapes. Teachers must evaluate carefully whether the
children have a clear understanding of the mountains, valleys, hills, coastal
areas, oceans, lakes, desert landscapes, and other natural features of the region.
One cannot assume that the children have a knowledge of these features simply
because they live near them. Experience has shown that many children have
never visited these places, even when these places are not far from their homes.

An important activity for children in grade three is to learn the topography
of the local region. In doing the research for this activity, children will develop
an understanding of the physical setting in which their region's history has
unfolded. They will learn to differentiate between major landforms in the

landscape. Once the research is completed, children can consider who the first people were who lived here, how they used the resources of this region, and in what ways they modified the natural environment.

American Indians who lived in the region should be authentically presented, including their tribal identity; their social organization and customs; the location of their villages and why they were located here; the structures they built and the relationship of these structures to the climate in this place; the methods they used to get their food, clothing, tools, and utensils and whether they traded with others for any of these things; and their art and folklore. Museums that specialize in California Indian cultures are a rich source of publications, pictures, and artifacts that can help children appreciate the daily lives and the adaptation of these cultures to the environment of the geographic region.

Children are now ready to consider those who came into this region and the impact each new group had on those who came before. To organize this sequence of events, children should develop a classroom time line by illustrating events and placing those illustrations in sequence with a caption under each. Depending on the local history, this sequence will include the explorers who visited here; the newcomers who settled here; the economy they established; their impact on the American Indians of this region; and their lasting marks on the landscape, including the buildings, streets, political boundaries, names, customs, and traditions that continue today; the people who have continued to come to this region; and the rich legacy of cultural traditions that newcomers brought with them.

Children should observe how their community has changed over time and also why certain features have remained the same. They should compare the kinds of transportation people used long ago, the ways in which people provided water for their growing community and farmlands, the sources of power long ago, and the kinds of work people engaged in years ago. They should discover that the changing history of their locality was, at all stages, closely related to the physical geography of this region: its topography, soil, water, mineral resources, and relative location. Children should analyze how successive groups of settlers made different uses of the land, depending on their skills, technology, and values. Children should observe how each period of settlement in their locality left its mark on the land, and they should analyze how decisions being made today also will leave their effects, good or bad, for those who will come after.

To bring earlier times alive for children, teachers should provide opportunities for them to study historical photos and to observe the changes in the ways families lived, worked, played, dressed, and traveled. Children should have opportunities to role play being an immigrant today and long ago; discover how newcomers, including children, have earned their living, now and long ago; and analyze why such occupations have changed over time. They

Grade Three

Standard 3.2.

Students describe the American Indian nations in their local region long ago and in the recent past.

Standard 3.3.

Students draw from historical and community resources to organize the sequence of local historical events and describe how each period of settlement left its mark on the land.

Standard 3.5.

Students demonstrate basic economic reasoning skills and an understanding of the economy of the local region.

Research, Evidence, and Point of View 1.

Students differentiate between primary and secondary sources.

Course
Descriptions

Grade Three

**Research, Evidence,
and Point of View 2.**

Students pose relevant
questions about events
they encounter in
historical documents,
eyewitness accounts, oral
histories, letters, diaries,
artifacts, photographs,
maps, artworks, and
architecture.

**Chronological and
Spatial Thinking 3.**

Students explain how the
present is connected to the
past, identifying both
similarities and differences
between the two, and how
some things change over
time and some things stay
the same.

Standard 3.4.

Students understand the
role of rules and laws in
our daily lives and the
basic structure of the
U.S. government.

Standard 3.4.6.

Describe the lives of
American heroes who
took risks to secure our
freedoms . . .

should observe how a given place, such as Main Street, looked long ago and how it looks today. Children can compare changes in their community with picture displays provided by the teacher.

The local community newspaper, the historical society, or other community organizations often can provide photos and articles on earlier events in the region—stories and pictures that capture for children a sense of what it was really like the day the town celebrated its new school, turned out for the grand opening of its new railroad station, expanded its harbor, or celebrated a town hero. Children should have opportunities to interview "old-timers" in their community or to invite them to speak to the class to build appreciation of events as seen through the eyes of those who were there. When available, old maps can be a source of wonderful discoveries: where the early rancho that once occupied this land was located; how streets were laid out in an earlier day and how many of them and their names survive today; how boundaries have changed over the years and how settlements have grown; how once-open fields have changed to dense urban development; how a river or coastline has changed in location or size because of a dam constructed upstream, a great earthquake in the past, or breakwaters that have been built to change the action of the sea.

Throughout these studies children should have continuing opportunities to enjoy the literature that brings to life the people of an earlier time. The literary selections, though not specifically written about their community, should illustrate how people lived in the past and convey the way of life of those earlier times.

Finally, in each of these studies, children should be helped to compare the past to changes under way today. Are new developments changing their community? How do people today earn their living or seek recreation? How are people working to protect their region's natural resources? How do people in this community work to influence public policy, elect their city government, and participate in resolving local issues that are important to children and their families, such as the fate of a local park earmarked for commercial use? Children can identify some issues that are important in their immediate community. Informed volunteers in community service or elected officials can be invited to explain why people volunteer and to describe some of the arguments on different sides of an important issue facing the community.

Our Nation's History: Meeting People, Ordinary and Extraordinary, Through Biography, Story, Folktale, and Legend

To understand the common memories that create a sense of community and continuity among people, children should learn about the classic legends, folktales, tall tales, and hero stories of their community and nation. Stories such as Ingri and Edgar D'Aulaire's *Christopher Columbus,* Joan Sandin's *The Long Road to a New Land,* Thomas P. Lewis's *Clipper Ship,* Barbara Brenner's *Wagon Wheels,* Elizabeth Shub's *The White Stallion,* F. N. Monjo's *The Drinking*

Gourd, and Barbara Cohne's *Molly's Pilgrim* help students to appreciate those who dared to move into unknown regions. Children should listen to biographies of the nation's heroes and of those who took the risk of new and controversial ideas and opened new opportunities for many. Such stories convey to the children valuable insights into the history of their nation and its people; they also help children to understand today's great movement of immigrants into California as a part of the continuing history of their nation.

Through stories and the celebration of national holidays, children should learn the meaning of the nation's holidays and the symbols that provide continuity and a sense of community across time; for example, the flag, the eagle, Uncle Sam, and the Statue of Liberty. They should learn the Pledge of Allegiance to the flag and the national songs that express American ideals, such as "America the Beautiful," the "Star Spangled Banner," and "America."

Standard 3.4.3.

Know the histories of important local and national landmarks, symbols, and essential documents that create a sense of community among citizens and exemplify cherished ideals.

History–Social Science Standards

Grade Three
Continuity and Change

3.1 **Students describe the physical and human geography and use maps, tables, graphs, photographs, and charts to organize information about people, places, and environments in a spatial context.**

1. Identify geographical features in their local region (e.g., deserts, mountains, valleys, hills, coastal areas, oceans, lakes).
2. Trace the ways in which people have used the resources of the local region and modified the physical environment (e.g., a dam constructed upstream changed a river or coastline).

3.2 **Students describe the American Indian nations in their local region long ago and in the recent past.**

1. Describe national identities, religious beliefs, customs, and various folklore traditions.
2. Discuss the ways in which physical geography, including climate, influenced how the local Indian nations adapted to their natural environment (e.g., how they obtained food, clothing, tools).
3. Describe the economy and systems of government, particularly those with tribal constitutions, and their relationship to federal and state governments.
4. Discuss the interaction of new settlers with the already established Indians of the region.

3.3 **Students draw from historical and community resources to organize the sequence of local historical events and describe how each period of settlement left its mark on the land.**

1. Research the explorers who visited here, the newcomers who settled here, and the people who continue to come to the region, including their cultural and religious traditions and contributions.
2. Describe the economies established by settlers and their influence on the present-day economy, with emphasis on the importance of private property and entrepreneurship.
3. Trace why their community was established, how individuals and families contributed to its founding and development, and how the community has changed over time, drawing on maps, photographs, oral histories, letters, newspapers, and other primary sources.

3.4 **Students understand the role of rules and laws in our daily lives and the basic structure of the U.S. government.**

1. Determine the reasons for rules, laws, and the U.S. Constitution; the role of citizenship in the promotion of rules and laws; and the consequences for people who violate rules and laws.

2. Discuss the importance of public virtue and the role of citizens, including how to participate in a classroom, in the community, and in civic life.

3. Know the histories of important local and national landmarks, symbols, and essential documents that create a sense of community among citizens and exemplify cherished ideals (e.g., the U.S. flag, the bald eagle, the Statue of Liberty, the U.S. Constitution, the Declaration of Independence, the U.S. Capitol).

4. Understand the three branches of government, with an emphasis on local government.

5. Describe the ways in which California, the other states, and sovereign American Indian tribes contribute to the making of our nation and participate in the federal system of government.

6. Describe the lives of American heroes who took risks to secure our freedoms (e.g., Anne Hutchinson, Benjamin Franklin, Thomas Jefferson, Abraham Lincoln, Frederick Douglass, Harriet Tubman, Martin Luther King, Jr.).

3.5 **Students demonstrate basic economic reasoning skills and an understanding of the economy of the local region.**

1. Describe the ways in which local producers have used and are using natural resources, human resources, and capital resources to produce goods and services in the past and the present.

2. Understand that some goods are made locally, some elsewhere in the United States, and some abroad.

3. Understand that individual economic choices involve trade-offs and the evaluation of benefits and costs.

4. Discuss the relationship of students' "work" in school and their personal human capital.

The Middle Grades Curriculum
Grades Four Through Eight

Developmental Considerations

The intellectual development of a student undergoes important qualitative changes as he or she enters the years of later childhood and early adolescence. Later childhood is a time marked by relative harmony in the inner life of the child. Intellectually, most students enter this period at the level of Piaget's "concrete operations," and they negotiate during these years their transition into the early stages of logical propositional thinking.

Students' thinking during these years becomes increasingly abstract and mutidimensional. They are now able to engage in comparative analyses across multiple sets of data, reason on the basis of differences among the data, and develop and test hypotheses through deductive analysis and the "test of the new case." These are powerful analytical processes that challenge students' interest and attention, but they are skills that must be supported by a wide variety of concrete instructional aids, maps, two- and three-dimensional charts for organizing data, and time lines. With such aids students will be able to make these critical comparisons and draw valid inferences.

Because of these developing capabilities, students throughout grades four through eight can consider a far wider sweep of human affairs. They can reach back in time to study specific people and events that contributed to the evolution of their own society, its values, and its institutions. They can follow with interest the origin and development of major Western and non-Western civilizations. In all these studies, however, teachers must recognize the limitations on what students in grades four through eight can understand. Historical analyses must continue to be grounded in the lives of people and events. Specific periods of history must be given the time required to study each fully and in depth and to learn about the people and events, ordinary and extraordinary, that make these studies exciting. This emphasis on people is especially appropriate in grades four through eight, because these are the years when early adolescents learn about themselves and about people whose experiences and backgrounds are different.

The course titles and major subtitles for grades four through eight are as follows.

Grade Four—California: A Changing State
- The Physical Setting: California and Beyond
- Pre-Columbian Settlements and People

- Exploration and Colonial History
- Missions, Ranchos, and the Mexican War for Independence
- Gold Rush, Statehood, and the Westward Movement
- The Period of Rapid Population Growth, Large-Scale Agriculture, and Linkage to the Rest of the United States
- Modern California: Immigration, Technology, and Cities

Grade Five—United States History and Geography: Making a New Nation

- The Land and People Before Columbus
- Age of Exploration
- Settling the Colonies
  - The Virginia Settlement
  - Life in New England
  - The Middle Colonies
- Settling the Trans-Appalachian West
- The War for Independence
- Life in the Young Republic
- The New Nation's Westward Expansion
- Linking Past to Present: The American People, Then and Now

Grade Six—World History and Geography: Ancient Civilizations

- Early Humankind and the Development of Human Societies
- The Beginnings of Civilization in the Near East and Africa: Mesopotamia, Egypt, and Kush
- The Foundation of Western Ideas: The Ancient Hebrews and Greeks
- West Meets East: The Early Civilizations of India and China
- East Meets West: Rome

Grade Seven—World History and Geography: Medieval and Early Modern Times

- Connecting with Past Learnings: Uncovering the Remote Past
- Connecting with Past Learnings: The Fall of Rome
- Growth of Islam
- African States in the Middle Ages and Early Modern Times
- Civilizations of the Americas
- China
- Japan
- Medieval Societies: Europe and Japan
- Europe During the Renaissance, the Reformation, and the Scientific Revolution
- Early Modern Europe: The Age of Exploration to the Enlightenment
- Linking Past to Present

*Grade Eight—United States History and Geography:
Growth and Conflict*

- Connecting with Past Learnings: Our Colonial Heritage
- Connecting with Past Learnings: A New Nation
- The Constitution of the United States
- Launching the Ship of State
- The Divergent Paths of the American People: 1800–1850
  - The West
  - The Northeast
  - The South
- Toward a More Perfect Union: 1850–1879
- The Rise of Industrial America: 1877–1914
- Linking Past to Present

**Chronological and
Spatial Thinking 3.**

Students explain how the
present is connected to
the past, identifying both
similarities and differences
between the two, and how
some things change over
time and some things stay
the same.

**Historical
Interpretation 1.**

Students summarize the key
events of the era they are
studying and explain the
historical contexts of those
events.

Grade Four—
California: A Changing State

The story of California is an important one for
fourth-grade students to learn. Not only is
California their home; it is a fascinating study
in its own right. The ethnic diversity, the richness
of its culture and multiethnic heritage, the
economic energy of its people, and the variety
of its geographical settings make this state a creative focus of education for
students in the fourth grade.

The story of California begins in pre-Columbian times, in the culture of
the American Indians who lived here before the first Europeans arrived.

The history of California then becomes the story of successive waves of
immigrants from the sixteenth century through modern times and the enduring
marks each left on the character of the state. These immigrants include (1) the
Spanish explorers and the Spanish-Mexican settlers of the Mission and Rancho
period who introduced European plants, agriculture, and a herding economy to
the region; (2) the people from America and around the world who settled here,
established California as a state, and developed its mining, industrial, and
agricultural economy; (3) the Asian and other immigrants of the second half of
the nineteenth century, who provided a new supply of labor for California's
railroads, agriculture, and industry and contributed as entrepreneurs and
innovators, especially in agriculture; (4) the immigrants of the first half of the
twentieth century, including new arrivals from Latin America and Europe; and
(5) the many immigrants arriving today from Latin America, the nations of the
Pacific Basin and Europe, and the continued migration of people from other

parts of the United States. Because of their early arrival in the New World, blacks have been present throughout much of California's history, contributing to the Spanish exploration of California, the Spanish-Mexican settlement of the region, and California's subsequent development throughout the nineteenth and twentieth centuries.

To bring California history and geography to life for students, teachers should emphasize its people in all their ethnic, racial, and cultural diversity. Fourth-grade students should learn about the daily lives, adventures, and accomplishments of these people and the cultural traditions and dynamic energy that have formed the state and shaped its varied landscape.

In grade four emphasis should also be placed on the regional geography of California. Students should analyze how the different regions of the state have developed through the interaction of physical characteristics and cultural forces and how the landscape of California has provided different resources to different people at different times, from the earliest era to the present.

The Physical Setting: California and Beyond

Students should locate California on the map and examine its setting on the western edge of North America, separated from the more densely settled parts of the American heartland by wide desert regions. They should learn to identify the mountain ranges, major coastal bays and natural harbors, and expansive river valleys and delta regions that are a part of the setting that has attracted settlement for tens of thousands of years.

Pre-Columbian Settlements and People

California has long been home to a significant percentage of the American Indian population. Even in pre-Columbian times, approximately 7 to 10 percent of the American Indian population lived along the coast, in the river valleys, and in the desert areas of California. Students should learn about the major language groups of the American Indians and their distribution, social organization, economic activities, legends, and beliefs. Students should become aware of the extent to which early people of California depended on, adapted to, and modified the physical environment by cultivation and the use of sea resources.

Contemporary cities and densely settled areas frequently are located in the same areas as these early American Indian settlements, especially on the coasts where rivers meet the sea. In analyzing how geographical factors have influenced the location of settlements, then and now, students should have an opportunity to observe how the past and the present may be linked by similar dynamics.

Historical Interpretation 2.
Students identify the human and physical characteristics of the places they are studying and explain how those features form the unique character of those places.

Standard 4.1.
Students demonstrate an understanding of the physical and human geographic features that define places and regions in California.

Standard 4.2.
Students describe the social, political, cultural, and economic life and interactions among people of California from the pre-Columbian societies to the Spanish mission and Mexican rancho periods.

Standard 4.2.1.
Discuss the major nations of California Indians, including their geographic distribution, economic activities, legends, and religious beliefs; and describe how they depended on, adapted to, and modified the physical environment by cultivation of land and use of sea resources.

Course
Descriptions

Grade Four

Standard 4.2.3.

Describe the Spanish
exploration and coloniza-
tion of California, including
the relationships among
soldiers, missionaries, and
Indians (e.g., Juan Crespi,
Junipero Serra, and Gaspar
de Portola).

Standard 4.2.5.

Describe the daily lives
of the people, native and
nonnative, who occupied
the presidios, missions,
ranchos, and pueblos.

**Chronological and
Spatial Thinking 5.**

Students judge the
significance of the
relative location of a
place (e.g., proximity to
a harbor, on trade routes)
and analyze how relative
advantages or disadvantages
can change over time.

Standard 4.3.

Students explain the
economic, social, and political
life in California from the
establishment of the Bear
Flag Republic through the
Mexican-American War, the
Gold Rush, and the granting
of statehood.

Exploration and Colonial History

In this unit students will learn about the Spanish exploration of the New World and the colonization of New Spain. Attention should be paid to motives for colonization, especially those that brought Spanish soldiers and missionaries northward from Mexico City to Alta California. The stories of Junipero Serra, Juan Crespi, and Gaspar de Portolá should be told. The presence of black explorers and soldiers in the earliest Spanish expeditions by sea and land and the participation of Spaniards, Mexicans, and blacks in the founding of the Alta California settlements should be noted. In mapping these routes and settlements, students should observe that access to California was difficult because of the physical barriers of mountains, deserts, and ocean currents.

Missions, Ranchos, and the Mexican War for Independence

One reason for the Spanish settling in California was to bring Christianity to the native peoples. Students should understand how the introduction of Christianity affected native cultures. Students should understand the geographical factors involved in locating the missions so that some were close enough to be a long day's walk or horseback ride apart and that they were situated along native pathways near sources of water. Presidios were erected by the colonial governors on sites that could be defended. Cattle ranches and agricultural villages were developed around the missions and presidios. European plants, agriculture, and a herding economy were introduced to the region.

To bring the history of this period to life, teachers should emphasize the daily lives of the people who occupied the ranchos, missions, presidios, haciendas, and pueblos. Reading literature; making field trips to a mission or Early California home; singing songs; and dramatizing a rodeo, fiesta, or trading day when Yankee clipper ships arrived to trade for California hides and tallow will bring this period alive. The Mexican War for Independence should be studied and discussed. What changes did Mexico's independence from Spain bring to Alta California? By analyzing California's geography, students will see how the natural barriers and remoteness of the region influenced settlement patterns during this period.

Gold Rush, Statehood, and the Westward Movement

By developing a time line, students will be able to put into chrono-logical order four events that changed the course of California history: the establishment of the Bear Flag Republic, the Mexican-American War, the Gold Rush, and California's admission to statehood in 1850. These events should be studied, discussed, and analyzed. Students should learn how gold was discovered and how news of the discovery spread throughout the world. Reading about the travels of Jedediah Smith, James Beckwourth, John C.

Fremont, and the Bidwell and Donner parties should help students appreciate the hardships of the overland journey to California. Comparisons should be made with those who took the Panama route and those who came around Cape Horn by ship. The arrivals of Asians, Latin Americans, and Europeans should be noted. To bring this period of life, students should sing the songs and read the literature of the day, including newspapers. They might dramatize a day in the goldfields and compare the life and fortunes of a gold miner with those of traders in the gold towns and merchants in San Francisco.

Students should consider how the Gold Rush changed California by bringing sudden wealth to the state; affecting its population, culture, and politics; and instantly transforming San Francisco from a small village in 1847 to a bustling city in 1849. On the negative side, the Gold Rush robbed many of California's earlier settlers of their land grants and property rights and caused irreparable environmental destruction through the system of hydraulic mining that was introduced in the 1850s. Students should learn about women who helped to build California during these years, such as Bernarda Ruiz and Biddy Mason. Comparisons can be made between governments during the Spanish and Mexican periods and after California became a state. California's state constitution and the government it created should be introduced.

The Period of Rapid Population Growth, Large-Scale Agriculture, and Linkage to the Rest of the United States.

The years following 1850 brought important changes to California. The Pony Express, the Overland Mail Service, and the telegraph service linked California with the East. The completion of the transcontinental railroad in 1869 linked California with the rest of the nation. With the help of topographic maps, students can follow the "sledge and shovel army" of Irish workers who laid the tracks westward across the Great Plains and the legions of Chinese workers who forged eastward from Sacramento through the towering Sierra Nevada mountains, digging tunnels and building bridges with daring skill. Completion of the railroad opened a flourishing trade between the Orient and eastern cities and brought thousands of new settlers to California. Students should analyze the growing hostilities toward the large Chinese labor force in California during the 1870s that led to the Chinese Exclusion Act of 1882.

The invention of the refrigerated railroad car opened eastern markets to California fruit and produce. Students should examine the special significance of water in a state in which agricultural wealth depends on cultivating dry regions with their longer growing seasons and warmer weather. Students should examine the reclamation of California's marshlands west of the Sierra Nevada and the great engineering projects that bring water to the Central Valley and the semiarid south. Students should also examine the continuing conflicts over water rights.

Research, Evidence, and Point of View 3.

Students distinguish fact from fiction by comparing documentary sources on historical figures and events with fictionalized characters and events.

Standard 4.5.

Students understand the structures, functions, and powers of the local, state, and federal governments as described in the U.S. Constitution.

Standard 4.4.

Students explain how California became an agricultural and industrial power, tracing the transformation of the California economy and its political and cultural development since the 1850s.

Standard 4.4.

Students explain how
California became an
agricultural and industrial
power, tracing the
transformation of the
California economy and
its political and cultural
development since
the 1850s.

**Historical
Interpretation 4.**

Students conduct
cost-benefit analyses
of historical and current
events.

Standard 4.5.4.

Explain the structures
and functions of state
governments, including the
roles and responsibilities
of their elected officials.

As California became home to diverse groups of people, its culture reflected a mixture of influences from Central America; South America; eastern, southern, and western Asia; and Europe. Students can compare the many cultural and economic contributions these diverse populations have brought to California and can make the same comparisons for California today.

Modern California: Immigration, Technology, and Cities

Students in grade four should learn about the development of present-day California with its commerce, large-scale commercial agriculture, communications industry, aerospace technology, and important trade links to nations of the Pacific Basin and other parts of the world. Since the beginning of World War II, California has changed from an underdeveloped, resource-producing area to an industrial giant. Students might analyze how California's industrial development was strengthened after the war by the building of an extensive freeway system and water projects, including canals, dams, reservoirs, and power plants, to support the growing population and its need for electrical power. Students should examine the impact of these engineering projects on California's wild rivers and watersheds and the long-term consequences of California's heavy overdraft on its ground water resources. Students should understand the role of labor in industry and agriculture, including how Cesar Chavez, through nonviolent tactics, educated the general public about the working conditions in agriculture and led the movement to improve the lives of farmworkers.

During this time California also developed a public education system, including universities and community colleges, which became a model for the nation. Students should be helped to see how good public education opens new opportunities for immigrant youths as well as native-born residents. They should analyze how California's leadership in computer technology, science, the aerospace industry, agricultural research, economic development, business, and industry depends on strong public education for all.

Students should explore the relationship between California's economic and population growth in the twentieth century and its geographical location and environmental factors. They should look for the linkages between California's location in the Pacific Basin and the sources of recent immigration to the state. They should examine California's growing trade with nations of the Pacific Basin and analyze how California's port cities, economic development, and cultural life benefit from this trade.

This unit will conclude with an examination of some of the unresolved problems facing California today and the efforts of concerned citizens who are seeking to address these issues.

History–Social Science Standards

Grade Four
California: A Changing State

4.1   Students demonstrate an understanding of the physical and human geographic features that define places and regions in California.

1. Explain and use the coordinate grid system of latitude and longitude to determine the absolute locations of places in California and on Earth.

2. Distinguish between the North and South Poles; the equator and the prime meridian; the tropics; and the hemispheres, using coordinates to plot locations.

3. Identify the state capital and describe the various regions of California, including how their characteristics and physical environments (e.g., water, landforms, vegetation, climate) affect human activity.

4. Identify the locations of the Pacific Ocean, rivers, valleys, and mountain passes and explain their effects on the growth of towns.

5. Use maps, charts, and pictures to describe how communities in California vary in land use, vegetation, wildlife, climate, population density, architecture, services, and transportation.

4.2   Students describe the social, political, cultural, and economic life and interactions among people of California from the pre-Columbian societies to the Spanish mission and Mexican rancho periods.

1. Discuss the major nations of California Indians, including their geographic distribution, economic activities, legends, and religious beliefs; and describe how they depended on, adapted to, and modified the physical environment by cultivation of land and use of sea resources.

2. Identify the early land and sea routes to, and European settlements in, California with a focus on the exploration of the North Pacific (e.g., by Captain James Cook, Vitus Bering, Juan Cabrillo), noting especially the importance of mountains, deserts, ocean currents, and wind patterns.

3. Describe the Spanish exploration and colonization of California, including the relationships among soldiers, missionaries, and Indians (e.g., Juan Crespi, Junipero Serra, Gaspar de Portola).

4. Describe the mapping of, geographic basis of, and economic factors in the placement and function of the Spanish missions; and under-

stand how the mission system expanded the influence of Spain and Catholicism throughout New Spain and Latin America.

5. Describe the daily lives of the people, native and nonnative, who occupied the presidios, missions, ranchos, and pueblos.

6. Discuss the role of the Franciscans in changing the economy of California from a hunter-gatherer economy to an agricultural economy.

7. Describe the effects of the Mexican War for Independence on Alta California, including its effects on the territorial boundaries of North America.

8. Discuss the period of Mexican rule in California and its attributes, including land grants, secularization of the missions, and the rise of the rancho economy.

4.3 **Students explain the economic, social, and political life in California from the establishment of the Bear Flag Republic through the Mexican-American War, the Gold Rush, and the granting of statehood.**

1. Identify the locations of Mexican settlements in California and those of other settlements, including Fort Ross and Sutter's Fort.

2. Compare how and why people traveled to California and the routes they traveled (e.g., James Beckwourth, John Bidwell, John C. Fremont, Pio Pico).

3. Analyze the effects of the Gold Rush on settlements, daily life, politics, and the physical environment (e.g., using biographies of John Sutter, Mariano Guadalupe Vallejo, Louise Clapp).

4. Study the lives of women who helped build early California (e.g., Biddy Mason).

5. Discuss how California became a state and how its new government differed from those during the Spanish and Mexican periods.

4.4 **Students explain how California became an agricultural and industrial power, tracing the transformation of the California economy and its political and cultural development since the 1850s.**

1. Understand the story and lasting influence of the Pony Express, Overland Mail Service, Western Union, and the building of the transcontinental railroad, including the contributions of Chinese workers to its construction.

2. Explain how the Gold Rush transformed the economy of California, including the types of products produced and consumed, changes in towns (e.g., Sacramento, San Francisco), and economic conflicts between diverse groups of people.

3. Discuss immigration and migration to California between 1850 and 1900, including the diverse composition of those who came; the countries of origin and their relative locations; and conflicts and accords among the diverse groups (e.g., the 1882 Chinese Exclusion Act).

4. Describe rapid American immigration, internal migration, settlement, and the growth of towns and cities (e.g., Los Angeles).

5. Discuss the effects of the Great Depression, the Dust Bowl, and World War II on California.

6. Describe the development and locations of new industries since the nineteenth century, such as the aerospace industry, electronics industry, large-scale commercial agriculture and irrigation projects, the oil and automobile industries, communications and defense industries, and important trade links with the Pacific Basin.

7. Trace the evolution of California's water system into a network of dams, aqueducts, and reservoirs.

8. Describe the history and development of California's public education system, including universities and community colleges.

9. Analyze the impact of twentieth-century Californians on the nation's artistic and cultural development, including the rise of the entertainment industry (e.g., Louis B. Mayer, Walt Disney, John Steinbeck, Ansel Adams, Dorothea Lange, John Wayne).

4.5   Students understand the structures, functions, and powers of the local, state, and federal governments as described in the U.S. Constitution.

1. Discuss what the U.S. Constitution is and why it is important (i.e., a written document that defines the structure and purpose of the U.S. government and describes the shared powers of federal, state, and local governments).

2. Understand the purpose of the California Constitution, its key principles, and its relationship to the U.S. Constitution.

3. Describe the similarities (e.g., written documents, rule of law, consent of the governed, three separate branches) and differences (e.g., scope of jurisdiction, limits on government powers, use of the military) among federal, state, and local governments.

4. Explain the structures and functions of state governments, including the roles and responsibilities of their elected officials.

5. Describe the components of California's governance structure (e.g., cities and towns, Indian rancherias and reservations, counties, school districts).

**Historical
Interpretation 1.**

Students summarize the
key events of the era they
are studying and explain
the historical contexts
of those events.

**Research, Evidence,
and Point of View 1.**

Students differentiate
between primary and
secondary sources.

Standard 5.1.

Students describe the major
pre-Columbian settlements,
including the cliff dwellers
and pueblo people of the
desert Southwest, the
American Indians of the
Pacific Northwest, the
nomadic nations of the
Great Plains, and the
woodland peoples east
of the Mississippi River.

Standard 5.2.

Students trace the routes
of early explorers and
describe the early
explorations of the
Americas.

Standard 5.4.

Students understand the
political, religious, social, and
economic institutions that
evolved in the colonial era.

Grade Five—
United States History and Geography:
Making a New Nation

This course for grade five presents the story of
the development of the nation, with emphasis on
the period up to 1850. This course focuses on one
of the most remarkable stories in history: the
creation of a new nation, peopled by immigrants from all parts of the globe and
governed by institutions founded on the Judeo-Christian heritage, the ideals of
the Enlightenment, and English traditions of self-government. This experiment
was inspired by the innovative dream of building a new society, a new order for
the ages, in which the promises of the Declaration of Independence would be
realized.

Wherever possible, events should be seen through the eyes of participants
such as explorers, American Indians, colonists, free blacks and slaves, children,
or pioneers. The narrative for the year must reflect the experiences of different
racial, religious, and ethnic groups.

The Land and People Before Columbus

In this unit students examine major pre-Columbian settlements: the cliff
dwellers and pueblo people of the desert Southwest; the American Indians of the
Pacific Northwest; the nomadic tribes of the Great Plains; and the woodland
peoples east of the Mississippi. Students should learn how these people adjusted
to their natural environment; developed an economy and system of government;
and expressed their culture in art, music, and dance. Students should be
introduced to the rich mythology and literature of American Indian cultures.

Age of Exploration

In this unit students will concentrate on European explorers who sought
trade routes, economic gain, adventure, national glory, and "the greater glory
of God." Tracing the routes of these explorers on the globe should encourage
discussion of Europe's innovative use of technological developments that were
invented by other civilizations that made this age of exploration possible: the
compass, the astrolabe, and seaworthy ships. Students might imagine how these
explorers and their crews might have felt when they left charted seas to explore
the unknown. What happened when they encountered indigenous people? How
were they received when they returned home not with exotic spices and silk, but
with native people, animals, plants, and even gold?

Settling the Colonies

A brief survey should be made of French, Portuguese, and Spanish
colonization in the New World. Major emphasis should then be placed on the

English colonies, where the political values and institutions of the new nation were shaped.

The Virginia Settlement. In light of the failure of its predecessors, the settlement of Jamestown was a risky venture. The struggle to survive was lead by Captain John Smith, who refused food to laggards. He directed the digging of wells, the planting of crops, and the construction of shelter. The economy at Jamestown was perilous until John Rolfe introduced West Indian tobacco, which became the foundation of the plantation economy. Students can explore the implications of this event. Why was tobacco grown on large plantations? What type of work force was required? What was an indentured servant? What was the social life of the plantation?

Students will learn of the first Africans who were brought to the colony in 1619. During the seventeenth century some Africans were indentured, some were enslaved, and some were free. Changing economic conditions increasingly caused tobacco planters to turn to slavery as a major source of reliable though costly labor. Map study will clarify the eighteenth-century Atlantic trade that linked Africa, the West Indies, the British colonies, and Europe. Students should use their growing sense of historical empathy to imagine how these young men and women from Africa felt, having been stolen from their families, carried across the ocean in a brutal voyage to a strange land, and then sold into bondage. This is an appropriate time to reflect on the meaning of slavery both as a legal institution and as an extreme violation of human rights. Original documents such as brief excerpts from slave narratives and from southern statutes and laws concerning the treatment of slaves should be used.

In their study of Virginia, students should understand the importance of the House of Burgesses as the first representative assembly in the colonies. Who was allowed to vote? Who was excluded? They also should learn the meaning of the *established church.*

Life in New England. New England provided a dramatic contrast with the southern colonies. This was a region settled by two groups of Puritans who sought a life based on their religious beliefs: the separatist Pilgrims who broke with the Church of England and the Puritans who sought to reform the church from within.

The story of the Pilgrims begins with their flight from England in search of religious freedom, their temporary haven in the Netherlands, and their voyage to the New World aboard the Mayflower. The Pilgrims' religious beliefs and their persecution by the Church of England should be fully discussed. After an arduous trip, they joined in signing the Mayflower Compact, a first step toward self-government. In keeping with the times, women were not asked to sign. Why not? This is an opportunity to discuss what self-government means and to reflect on the importance of the right to vote.

Life in the new land was hard, and at first the Indians aided the settlers. In time the Pilgrim colonies became well established despite bloody conflicts with

Grade Five

**Historical
Interpretation 2.**

Students identify the human and physical characteristics of the places they are studying and explain how those features form the unique character of those places.

Standard 5.4.6.

Describe the introduction of slavery into America, the responses of slave families to their condition, the ongoing struggle between proponents and opponents of slavery, and the gradual institutionalization of slavery in the South.

Research, Evidence, and Point of View 2.

Students pose relevant questions about events they encounter in historical documents, eyewitness accounts, oral histories, letters, diaries, artifacts, photographs, maps, artworks, and architecture.

Standard 5.4.3.

Describe the religious aspects of the earliest colonies (e.g., Puritanism in Massachusetts, Anglicanism in Virginia, Catholicism in Maryland, Quakerism in Pennsylvania).

Standard 5.4.2.

Identify the major individuals
and groups responsible for
the founding of the various
colonies and the reasons for
their founding (e.g., John
Smith, Virginia; Roger
Williams, Rhode Island;
William Penn, Pennsylvania;
Lord Baltimore, Maryland;
William Bradford, Plymouth;
John Winthrop, Massachu-
setts).

Standard 5.3.

Students describe the
cooperation and conflict
that existed among the
American Indians and
between the Indian nations
and the new settlers.

the indigenous people. Students should learn about the political, religious, economic, and social life of the colonies. They should be helped to envision the simple homes and the rigors of each day. They should analyze the work of men, women, and children and see how butter was churned, cloth was dyed, and soap and candles were made; they should see the hornbooks from which children learned their ABCs. By dramatizing a day in a colonial school, students will gain an understanding of the children's lives in this period, the way they learned, and disciplinary practices of that time.

The story of the Puritans is equally important in light of their enduring influence on American literature, education, and attitudes toward life and work. Inspired by their religious zeal, Puritans sought to establish a new Zion, "a city upon a hill," where they might live out their religious ideals. Led by John Winthrop, they founded the city of Boston and within ten years had opened Harvard College and the first common school in Massachusetts. They valued hard work, social obligation, simple living, and self-governing congregations. Their religious views shaped their way of life, their clothing, their laws, their forms of punishment, their education practices, and their institutions of self-government. While they came in pursuit of freedom of religion, however, the Puritans were intolerant of dissent. The stories of Anne Hutchinson and Roger Williams are milestones in the development of religious freedom in Connecticut and Rhode Island.

The Middle Colonies. The colonies of New Amsterdam, New Jersey, Pennsylvania, Maryland, and Delaware provided havens for a wide variety of ethnic, linguistic, and religious groups, including English, Dutch, Swedish, German, Irish, Scottish, Catholic, and Jewish settlers. Special attention should be paid to Pennsylvania, where William Penn founded a Quaker colony that practiced religious freedom and representative government. Industrious farmers, fur traders, skilled craftspersons, merchants, bankers, shipbuilders, and overseas traders made the colony prosperous.

Geographic factors enabled the middle colonies to thrive and contributed to the development of New York and Philadelphia as busy seaports. Excerpts from Benjamin Franklin's *Autobiography,* his annual *Poor Richard's Almanac,* and his story "The Whistle" as well as Margaret Cousins's *Ben Franklin of Old Philadelphia* should give students a sense of these times.

Settling the Trans-Appalachian West

Biographies of Daniel Boone will introduce children to English forays into the French territory west of the Appalachian Mountains and to the French and Indian War, in which Boone served. Students should learn about the importance of the war, in shattering French power in North America. The English attempt to reserve the land west of the Appalachians for the inland Indian nations failed. Students should follow the exploits of pathfinders such as Daniel Boone and read about the settlers who followed his trail over the

Cumberland Gap into Kentucky. They should consider the viewpoint of the American Indians who occupied these same lands and read about the conflicts between the Indians and Kentucky settlers that followed the outbreak of the Revolutionary War. This frontier period is rich in biographies, tall tales, legends, songs, and handicrafts that help to make this period vivid for students.

The War for Independence

Events leading to the Revolutionary War should be presented as a dramatic story. Each effort by the British to impose their will on the colonies resulted in a strong counterreaction and a growing spirit of independence. Students should become familiar with the Stamp Act of 1765 and the outraged colonial reaction to it; the Townshend Acts that again stirred protest and led to the Boston Massacre; and the tax on tea that provoked the Boston Tea Party. Parliament's efforts to repress dissent led to the first Continental Congress of 1774 and the Committees of Correspondence that established communication among the colonies and developed a national consciousness.

Standard 5.5.

Students explain the causes of the American Revolution.

Historical Interpretation 3.

Students identify and interpret the multiple causes and effects of historical events.

In discussing the conflict, students should read excerpts from speeches in the Parliament by William Pitt and Edmund Burke, whose pleas for moderation were ignored. Students should realize that some colonists remained loyal to King George III. Major events in the Revolution should be vividly described, including the battles of Bunker Hill, Lexington, and Concord; the selection of George Washington to command the army; and Patrick Henry's famous appeal to his fellow legislators to support the fight. The role of free blacks in the battles of the American Revolution should be considered. Students should learn about Abigail Adams, Molly Pitcher, Nathan Hale, and Benedict Arnold; and they should understand the significance of the events at Valley Forge, the alliance with France, and the final battle at Yorktown.

Standard 5.6.

Students understand the course and consequences of the American Revolution.

As the war began, young Thomas Jefferson drafted the Declaration of Independence with its idealistic statements that all men are created equal and that governments derive their just power from the consent of the governed. Students should understand the courage required of those who signed this document because they risked their lives and property. Many Americans realized for the first time the contradiction between these ideals and slavery. After the war the northeastern and middle Atlantic states abolished slavery, and the Northwest Ordinance of 1787 banned slavery from the new territories north of the Ohio River. The antislavery movement did not, however, significantly affect the South, where nine out of ten American slaves lived.

To deepen their understanding of this period, students should read biographies of leaders such as George Washington, Thomas Jefferson, and Benjamin Franklin; they should also read Ralph Waldo Emerson's "Concord Hymn," Henry Wadsworth Longfellow's "Paul Revere's Ride," and fine historical fiction such as Esther Forbes's *Johnny Tremain*, Patricia Clapp's *I'm Deborah Sampson: A Soldier in the War of the Revolution*, and James L. Collier's *My Brother Sam Is Dead.*

Research, Evidence, and Point of View 3.

Students distinguish fact from fiction by comparing documentary sources on historical figures and events with fictionalized characters and events.

Course
Descriptions

Grade Five

Standard 5.7.

Students describe the
people and events
associated with the
development of the
U.S. Constitution and
analyze the Constitution's
significance as the foun-
dation of the American
republic.

Standard 5.3.4.

Discuss the role of broken
treaties and massacres and
the factors that led to the
Indians' defeat, including
the resistance of Indian
nations to encroachments
and assimilation (e.g., the
story of the Trail of Tears).

Standard 5.8.

Students trace the
colonization, immigration,
and settlement patterns of
the American people from
1789 to the mid-1800s,
with emphasis on the role
of economic incentives,
effects of the physical and
political geography, and
transportation systems.

Life in the Young Republic

In this unit students examine the daily lives of those who built the young republic under the new Constitution. Between 1789 and 1850, new waves of immigrants arrived from Europe, especially English, Scots-Irish, Irish, and Germans. Traveling by overland wagons, canals, flatboats, and steamboats, these newcomers advanced into the fertile Ohio and Mississippi valleys and through the Cumberland Gap to the South. Students should sing the songs of the boatmen and pioneers and read the tall tales of legendary figures such as Mike Fink and Paul Bunyan. They should read Ingri and Edgar D'Aulaire's *Abraham Lincoln,* which describes his boyhood in Illinois during this period, and books such as Enid Meadowcroft's *By Wagon and Flatboat.* They should learn about the Louisiana Purchase and the expeditions of Lewis and Clark and of John C. Fremont.

Students should learn about the resistance of American Indian tribes to encroachments by settlers and about the government's policy of Indian removal to lands west of the Mississippi. Students can study these events by reading the biographies of leaders such as Chief Tecumseh of the Shawnee, Chief John Ross of the Cherokee tribe, and Chief Osceola of the Seminole tribe, as well as the tragic story of the Cherokees' "Trail of Tears."

The New Nation's Westward Expansion

In this unit students examine the advance of pioneer settlements beyond the Mississippi. The flow of migration westward included grizzled fur traders and mountain men, settlers heading for Texas, Mormon families on their way to the new Zion in Utah, midwestern farmers moving to western Oregon's fertile valleys, and forty-niners bound for the Mother Lode region of California. Not to be forgotten are the whalers, New England sailors engaged in the hide and tallow trade with California, and sea traders in furs (sea otter and seal) who plied their clipper ships around Cape Horn and westward to the Pacific.

This is a period rich with folk songs and sea chanteys, folklore, tall tales, and the journals and diaries that bring this period to life. Students might dramatize the experience of moving west to Oregon by wagon train. Excerpts from Francis Parkman's *The Oregon Trail* and from children's literature will help the children understand how the expeditions were organized, how a trail was scouted, where the trail ran, and what physical dangers the pioneers faced: raging rivers, parched deserts, sandstorms and snowstorms, and lack of water or medicine. Students should understand the resistance of American Indians to encroachments by other people, and internecine Indian conflicts, including the competing claims for control of lands.

Students should compare this trail with the California overland trail, the trail to Santa Fe, and the trail to Texas, comparing each time the purpose of the journey; where the trail ran; the influence of geographic terrain, rivers, vegetation, and climate; and life in the territories at the end of these trails. Students should compare these westward migrations with the continuing northward migrations of Mexican settlers into these great Mexican territories of the West and the South-west. While learning about life on the trail, students should discuss the reactions of the American Indians to the increasing migration and the reasons for their growing concern.

Pioneer women played varied roles in coping with the rigors of daily life on the frontier. Biographies, journals, and diaries disclose the strength and resourcefulness of pioneer women who helped to farm the land and worked as missionaries, teachers, and entrepreneurs. Many slave women gained their freedom in the West. In recognition of the new status that western women achieved, Wyoming in 1869 became the first state to grant suffrage to women.

Maps should be used to explain how and when California, Texas, and other western lands became part of the United States. Settlement was followed by battles for independence. The war with Mexico led to cession of these territories, which then became states. These events provide important opportunities to focus on the Hispanic people of California and the Southwest, on the effects of these events on their lives, and on their distinctive contributions to American culture. Students should also learn how the Oregon boundary conflict was settled by negotiation with England and how that territory became a state.

Linking Past to Present: The American People, Then and Now

In this unit students examine the contributions of the different groups that built the American nation and, in the process, became a new people. Students should understand that we are a people of many races, many religions, and many different national origins and that we live under a common governmental system. While this unit does not include a formal study of the Civil War, students should realize how and when slavery was brought to an end in the United States. They should also learn about the significant contributions that black men and women made to the economic, political, and cultural development of the nation, including its music, literature, art, science, medicine, technology, and scholarship.

Students should learn about the successive waves of new immigration over the years from 1850 until today. Each wave brought new people, new skills, and new cultural contributions to the development of the nation. Immigrants came from Ireland, Germany, Sweden, Norway, Italy, Russia, Poland, Hungary, China, Japan, the Philippines, the West Indies, Mexico, Greece, India, Cuba, and eventually from every direction around the globe. Immigrants farmed the plains, introduced new arts and crafts, built the railroads, developed the great southwestern mines, manned the construction industry and the steel industry, fueled the nation's industrial growth, wrote great literature and music, produced brilliant scientists, created the entertainment industry, and provided

Grade Five

Chronological and Spatial Thinking 5.

Students judge the significance of the relative location of a place (e.g., proximity to a harbor, on trade routes) and analyze how relative advantages or disadvantages can change over time.

Chronological and Spatial Thinking 1.

Students place key events and people of the historical era they are studying in a chronological sequence and within a spatial context; they interpret time lines.

Chronological and Spatial Thinking 3.

Students explain how the present is connected to the past, identifying both similarities and differences between the two, and how some things change over time and some things stay the same.

Standard 5.8.1.

Discuss the waves of immigrants from Europe between 1789 and 1850 and their modes of transportation into the Ohio and Mississippi Valleys and through the Cumberland Gap (e.g., overland wagons, canals, flatboats, steamboats).

**Historical
Interpretation 4.**

Students conduct cost-
benefit analyses of
historical and current
events.

Standard 5.7.5.

Discuss the meaning of the
American creed that calls
on citizens to safeguard
the liberty of individual
Americans within a unified
nation, to respect the rule
of law, and to preserve the
Constitution.

human resources to transform the nation's economic, cultural, and social life. Students should identify the immigrants' countries of origin and locate the regions of the nation where they settled.

To understand the human side of the great drama of migration, students should read literature such as Russell Freedman's *Immigrant Kids,* Marietta Moskin's *Waiting for Mama,* Marilyn Sachs's *Call Me Ruth,* Karen Branson's *Streets of Gold,* Leonard Fisher's *Across the Sea from Galway,* and Charlene Talbot's *An Orphan for Nebraska.* They should see similar dramas re-created in the lives of recent immigrants, including Ann N. Clark's *To Stand Against the Wind,* the story of Vietnamese immigrants to America.

The newcomers often encountered discrimination because of their race, religion, or cultural traditions. They often faced hardships as they learned the new language and adjusted to a new way of life; but even more often they found the opportunity to make a new life in a land where ability and hard work enabled them to get ahead.

To understand the continuing attraction of immigrants to the United States, students should become familiar with the tenets of the American creed by discussing the meaning of key phrases in the Declaration of Independence, the Constitution, and the Bill of Rights. Students should read Emma Lazarus's poem, "The New Colossus," which is attached to the Statue of Liberty, and consider the meaning of symbols such as that statue and the phrase *e pluribus unum.*

After a year of studying American history, students should be able to reflect on the ethical content of the nation's principles and on America's promise to its citizens—the promise of a democratic government in which the rights of the individual are protected by the government, by a free press, and by an informed public. America's ideals are closely related to the nature of American Society. We are strong because we are united in a pluralistic society of many races, cultures, and ethnic groups; we have built a great nation because we have learned to live in peace with each other, respecting each other's right to be different and supporting each other as members of a common community.

Students should understand that the American creed calls on them to safeguard their freedoms and those of their neighbors, to value the nation's diversity, to work for change within the framework of law, and to do their part as citizens in contributing to the welfare of their community. To gain these understandings, students might interview elected public officials, invite volunteers from community organizations to talk about the work they do, and develop projects that can be helpful to others in their school and community. Such projects might include visits to senior citizens' centers and working on school and community beautification projects.

Throughout these activities, students should reflect on the importance of living up to the nation's ideals and of participating in the unfinished struggle to make these principles and ideals a reality for all.

History–Social Science Standards

Grade Five
United States History and Geography:
Making a New Nation

5.1 **Students describe the major pre-Columbian settlements, including the cliff dwellers and pueblo people of the desert Southwest, the American Indians of the Pacific Northwest, the nomadic nations of the Great Plains, and the woodland peoples east of the Mississippi River.**

1. Describe how geography and climate influenced the way various nations lived and adjusted to the natural environment, including locations of villages, the distinct structures that they built, and how they obtained food, clothing, tools, and utensils.
2. Describe their varied customs and folklore traditions.
3. Explain their varied economies and systems of government.

5.2 **Students trace the routes of early explorers and describe the early explorations of the Americas.**

1. Describe the entrepreneurial characteristics of early explorers (e.g., Christopher Columbus, Francisco Vásquez de Coronado) and the technological developments that made sea exploration by latitude and longitude possible (e.g., compass, sextant, astrolabe, seaworthy ships, chronometers, gunpowder).
2. Explain the aims, obstacles, and accomplishments of the explorers, sponsors, and leaders of key European expeditions and the reasons Europeans chose to explore and colonize the world (e.g., the Spanish Reconquista, the Protestant Reformation, the Counter Reformation).
3. Trace the routes of the major land explorers of the United States, the distances traveled by explorers, and the Atlantic trade routes that linked Africa, the West Indies, the British colonies, and Europe.
4. Locate on maps of North and South America land claimed by Spain, France, England, Portugal, the Netherlands, Sweden, and Russia.

5.3 **Students describe the cooperation and conflict that existed among the American Indians and between the Indian nations and the new settlers.**

1. Describe the competition among the English, French, Spanish, Dutch, and Indian nations for control of North America.
2. Describe the cooperation that existed between the colonists and Indians during the 1600s and 1700s (e.g., in agriculture, the fur trade, military alliances, treaties, cultural interchanges).
3. Examine the conflicts before the Revolutionary War (e.g., the Pequot and King Philip's Wars in New England, the Powhatan Wars in Virginia, the French and Indian War).

4. Discuss the role of broken treaties and massacres and the factors that led to the Indians' defeat, including the resistance of Indian nations to encroachments and assimilation (e.g., the story of the Trail of Tears).

5. Describe the internecine Indian conflicts, including the competing claims for control of lands (e.g., actions of the Iroquois, Huron, Lakota [Sioux]).

6. Explain the influence and achievements of significant leaders of the time (e.g., John Marshall, Andrew Jackson, Chief Tecumseh, Chief Logan, Chief John Ross, Sequoyah).

5.4   Students understand the political, religious, social, and economic institutions that evolved in the colonial era.

1. Understand the influence of location and physical setting on the founding of the original 13 colonies, and identify on a map the locations of the colonies and of the American Indian nations already inhabiting these areas.

2. Identify the major individuals and groups responsible for the founding of the various colonies and the reasons for their founding (e.g., John Smith, Virginia; Roger Williams, Rhode Island; William Penn, Pennsylvania; Lord Baltimore, Maryland; William Bradford, Plymouth; John Winthrop, Massachusetts).

3. Describe the religious aspects of the earliest colonies (e.g., Puritanism in Massachusetts, Anglicanism in Virginia, Catholicism in Maryland, Quakerism in Pennsylvania).

4. Identify the significance and leaders of the First Great Awakening, which marked a shift in religious ideas, practices, and allegiances in the colonial period, the growth of religious toleration, and free exercise of religion.

5. Understand how the British colonial period created the basis for the development of political self-government and a free-market economic system and the differences between the British, Spanish, and French colonial systems.

6. Describe the introduction of slavery into America, the responses of slave families to their condition, the ongoing struggle between proponents and opponents of slavery, and the gradual institutionalization of slavery in the South.

7. Explain the early democratic ideas and practices that emerged during the colonial period, including the significance of representative assemblies and town meetings.

5.5   Students explain the causes of the American Revolution.

1. Understand how political, religious, and economic ideas and interests brought about the Revolution (e.g., resistance to imperial policy, the Stamp Act, the Townshend Acts, taxes on tea, Coercive Acts).

2. Know the significance of the first and second Continental Congresses and of the Committees of Correspondence.

3. Understand the people and events associated with the drafting and signing of the Declaration of Independence and the document's significance, including the key political concepts it embodies, the origins of those concepts, and its role in severing ties with Great Britain.

4. Describe the views, lives, and impact of key individuals during this period (e.g., King George III, Patrick Henry, Thomas Jefferson, George Washington, Benjamin Franklin, John Adams).

5.6 Students understand the course and consequences of the American Revolution.

1. Identify and map the major military battles, campaigns, and turning points of the Revolutionary War, the roles of the American and British leaders, and the Indian leaders' alliances on both sides.

2. Describe the contributions of France and other nations and of individuals to the outcome of the Revolution (e.g., Benjamin Franklin's negotiations with the French, the French navy, the Treaty of Paris, The Netherlands, Russia, the Marquis Marie Joseph de Lafayette, Tadeusz Kósciuszko, Baron Friedrich Wilhelm von Steuben).

3. Identify the different roles women played during the Revolution (e.g., Abigail Adams, Martha Washington, Molly Pitcher, Phillis Wheatley, Mercy Otis Warren).

4. Understand the personal impact and economic hardship of the war on families, problems of financing the war, wartime inflation, and laws against hoarding goods and materials and profiteering.

5. Explain how state constitutions that were established after 1776 embodied the ideals of the American Revolution and helped serve as models for the U.S. Constitution.

6. Demonstrate knowledge of the significance of land policies developed under the Continental Congress (e.g., sale of western lands, the Northwest Ordinance of 1787) and those policies' impact on American Indians' land.

7. Understand how the ideals set forth in the Declaration of Independence changed the way people viewed slavery.

5.7 Students describe the people and events associated with the development of the U.S. Constitution and analyze the Constitution's significance as the foundation of the American republic.

1. List the shortcomings of the Articles of Confederation as set forth by their critics.

2. Explain the significance of the new Constitution of 1787, including the struggles over its ratification and the reasons for the addition of the Bill of Rights.

3. Understand the fundamental principles of American constitutional democracy, including how the government derives its power from the people and the primacy of individual liberty.

4. Understand how the Constitution is designed to secure our liberty by both empowering and limiting central government and compare the powers granted to citizens, Congress, the president, and the Supreme Court with those reserved to the states.

5. Discuss the meaning of the American creed that calls on citizens to safeguard the liberty of individual Americans within a unified nation, to respect the rule of law, and to preserve the Constitution.

6. Know the songs that express American ideals (e.g., "America the Beautiful," "The Star Spangled Banner").

5.8 Students trace the colonization, immigration, and settlement patterns of the American people from 1789 to the mid-1800s, with emphasis on the role of economic incentives, effects of the physical and political geography, and transportation systems.

1. Discuss the waves of immigrants from Europe between 1789 and 1850 and their modes of transportation into the Ohio and Mississippi Valleys and through the Cumberland Gap (e.g., overland wagons, canals, flatboats, steamboats).

2. Name the states and territories that existed in 1850 and identify their locations and major geographical features (e.g., mountain ranges, principal rivers, dominant plant regions).

3. Demonstrate knowledge of the explorations of the trans-Mississippi West following the Louisiana Purchase (e.g., Meriwether Lewis and William Clark, Zebulon Pike, John Fremont).

4. Discuss the experiences of settlers on the overland trails to the West (e.g., location of the routes; purpose of the journeys; the influence of the terrain, rivers, vegetation, and climate; life in the territories at the end of these trails).

5. Describe the continued migration of Mexican settlers into Mexican territories of the West and Southwest.

6. Relate how and when California, Texas, Oregon, and other western lands became part of the United States, including the significance of the Texas War for Independence and the Mexican-American War.

5.9 Students know the location of the current 50 states and the names of their capitals.

Course
Descriptions

Kindergarten
Through
Grade Five
Historical
and Social Science
Analysis Skills

Kindergarten Through Grade Five
Historical and Social Sciences Analysis Skills

The intellectual skills noted below are to be learned through, and applied to, the content standards for kindergarten through grade five. They are to be assessed *only in conjunction with* the content standards in kindergarten through grade five.

In addition to the standards for kindergarten through grade five, students demonstrate the following intellectual, reasoning, reflection, and research skills:

Chronological and Spatial Thinking

1. Students place key events and people of the historical era they are studying in a chronological sequence and within a spatial context; they interpret time lines.
2. Students correctly apply terms related to time, including *past, present, future, decade, century,* and *generation.*
3. Students explain how the present is connected to the past, identifying both similarities and differences between the two, and how some things change over time and some things stay the same.
4. Students use map and globe skills to determine the absolute locations of places and interpret information available through a map's or globe's legend, scale, and symbolic representations.
5. Students judge the significance of the relative location of a place (e.g., proximity to a harbor, on trade routes) and analyze how relative advantages or disadvantages can change over time.

Research, Evidence, and Point of View

1. Students differentiate between primary and secondary sources.
2. Students pose relevant questions about events they encounter in historical documents, eyewitness accounts, oral histories, letters, diaries, artifacts, photographs, maps, artworks, and architecture.
3. Students distinguish fact from fiction by comparing documentary sources on historical figures and events with fictionalized characters and events.

Historical Interpretation

1. Students summarize the key events of the era they are studying and explain the historical contexts of those events.
2. Students identify the human and physical characteristics of the places they are studying and explain how those features form the unique character of those places.
3. Students identify and interpret the multiple causes and effects of historical events.
4. Students conduct cost-benefit analyses of historical and current events.

**Historical
Interpretation 1.**

Students explain the central
issues and problems from
the past, placing people and
events in a matrix of time
and place.

**Chronological and
Spatial Thinking 2.**

Students construct various
time lines of key events,
people, and periods of the
historical era they are
studying.

**Historical
Interpretation 5.**

Students recognize that
interpretations of history are
subject to change as new
information is uncovered.

Standard 6.1.

Students describe what is
known through archaeo-
logical studies of the early
physical and cultural
development of humankind
from the Paleolithic era to
the agricultural revolution.

Grade Six—
World History and Geography:
Ancient Civilizations

In the sixth-grade curriculum, students learn
about those people and events that ushered in the
dawn of major Western and non-Western
civilizations. Included are the early societies of the
Near East and Africa, the ancient Hebrew
civilization, Greece, Rome, and the classical civilizations of India and of China.

In studying the ancient world, students should come to appreciate the
special significance of geographic place in the development of the human story.
They should acquire a sense of the everyday life of the people; their problems
and accomplishments; their relationships to the developing social, economic,
and political structures of their society; the tools and technology they
developed; the role of trade, both domestic and international, in their lives; the
art they created; the architecture they lived with; the literature produced by
their finest poets, narrators, and writers; their explanations for natural
phenomena; and the ideas they developed that helped transform their world. In
studying each ancient society, students should examine the role of women and
the presence or absence of slavery.

Among the major figures whom students should come to know are those
who helped to establish these early societies and their codes of ethics and justice
and their rule of law, such as Hammurabi, Abraham, Moses, David, Pericles,
and Asoka; those who extended these early empires and carried their influence
into much of the ancient world, including Alexander the Great, Julius Caesar,
and Augustus Caesar; and those whose ideas and teachings became enduring
influences in Western and non-Western thought, especially Socrates, Jesus, the
Buddha, and Confucius. For all these societies, emphasis should be placed on
those major contributions, achievements, and belief systems that have endured
across the centuries to the present day.

Early Humankind and the Development of Human Societies

This unit should develop the students' awareness of prehistoric peoples'
chronological place on the historical time line. Attention should be given to
paleontological discoveries in East Africa by Donald Johanson, Tim White, and
the Leakey Family (Louis, Mary, and Richard) supporting the belief that
ancestors of present-day humans lived in these regions 4.5 million years ago.
Studies of the Old Stone Age (Paleolithic), Middle Stone Age (Mesolithic), and
New Stone Age (Neolithic) should provide students with an understanding of
the interaction between the environment and the developing lifestyles of
prehistoric peoples as they moved from hunter-gatherers to food producers.

These studies also should focus on early peoples' attempts to explain the universe through cave art and elemental forms of religion; the development of stone tools from simple to complex to metal; and the development of language as a medium for transmitting and accumulating knowledge.

The Beginnings of Civilization in the Near East and Africa: Mesopotamia, Egypt, and Kush

In this unit students learn about the peoples of Mesopotamia, with an emphasis on the Sumerians, their early settlements between the Tigris and Euphrates rivers and the major events marking their sojourn: the spread of their agricultural villages by 4000 B.C. to lower Mesopotamia; their technological and social accomplishments, including invention of the wheel, plow, and irrigation systems; their systems of cuneiform writing, of measurement, and of law; and the developing social, economic, and political systems that these accomplishments made possible.

Moving on to ancient Egypt, the teacher introduces students briefly to the early reign of Khufu and then moves to an emphasis on the New Kingdom in the reigns of Queen Hatshepsut and Ramses II, or "Ramses the Great." During Queen Hatshepsut's reign, Egyptian art and architecture flourished, and trade extended Egyptian influence throughout the Middle East. Ramses II, more typical of the New Kingdom pharaohs, was concerned with warfare and maintaining an Egyptian empire that extended north into the region known as Canaan. Attention should be given to the daily lives of farmers, tradespeople, architects, artists, scribes, women, children, and slaves, as reflected in the detailed images and models from burials. Geographic learnings include the importance of the Nile to Egypt's development and of irrigation practices that are still in use.

This unit concludes with Africa's oldest interior empire, the kingdom of Kush, which conquered Egypt in 728 B.C. and established the twenty-fifth dynasty of pharaohs. Conquered in turn by the Assyrians, the kings of Kush reestablished their capital farther south. Students should be introduced to the culture that developed there, including the development of iron agricultural tools and weapons; an alphabet; and a profitable trade that extended to Arabia, India, sub-Saharan Africa, and possibly China.

The Foundation of Western Ideas: The Ancient Hebrews and Greeks

One of the principal roots of Western civilization can be found in the enduring contributions of the ancient Hebrews to Western ethical and religious thought and literature, most notably by the Old Testament. To understand these traditions, students should read and discuss Biblical literature that is part of the literary heritage and ethical teachings of Western civilization; for

Standard 6.2.

Students analyze the geographic, political, economic, religious, and social structures of the early civilizations of Mesopotamia, Egypt, and Kush.

Standard 6.3.

Students analyze the geographic, political, economic, religious, and social structures of the Ancient Hebrews.

Course
Descriptions

Grade Six

Standard 6.4.

Students analyze the geographic, political, economic, religious, and social structures of the early civilizations of Ancient Greece.

Standard 6.5.

Students analyze the geographic, political, economic, religious, and social structures of the early civilizations of India.

example, stories about the Creation, Noah, the Tower of Babel, Abraham, the Exodus, the Ten Commandments, Ruth and Naomi, David, and Daniel and the Lion's Den; selections from the Psalms and Proverbs; and the Hebrew people's concepts of wisdom, righteousness, law, and justice.

Another principal root of Western civilization is the Creco-Roman civilization. In studying the civilization of the ancient Greeks, students learn of the early democratic forms of government; the dawn of rational thought expressed in Greek philosophy, mathematics, science, and history; and the enduring cultural contributions of Greek art, architecture, drama, and poetry.

In this unit students will learn about the Greek polis (city-state); the rise of Athens; the transition from tyranny and oligarchy to an early form of democracy; the role of slavery, even in democratic Athens; the importance of the great fleet of Athens and its location at the crossroads of the ancient world; the rivalry between Athens and Sparta, culminating in the Peloponnesian War; the Macedonian conquests under Alexander the Great and the emergence and spread of Hellenistic culture throughout the Mediterranean and Middle Eastern worlds; and the fall of Greece to Rome. Attention should be paid to the daily life of women and children in Athens and Sparta, the games and sports of the Olympiad, the education of youths, and the trial of Socrates. Particular emphasis should be placed on reading and discussing the rich mythology and Homeric literature that have deeply influenced Western art, drama, and literature.

West Meets East: The Early Civilizations of India and China

Alexander the Great's conquest of Persia and its territories provides the bridge to a study of the great Eastern civilization of India. Students should understand that the culture Alexander encountered in 327 to 325 B.C. was not the first civilization of this region. Over a thousand years earlier, the Harappan civilization had developed and reached its zenith in the Indus River Valley, having developed complex cities, brick platforms, script, granaries, and craft workshops. After its collapse, succeeding waves of Aryas from the north spread their influence across the Punjab and Ganges plains. This resulted in a composite civilization rich in its aesthetic culture (architecture, sculpture, painting, dance, and music) and in its intellectual traditions (Arabic numbers, the zero, medical tradition, and metallurgy).

Students should be introduced to one of the major religious traditions of India: Buddhism, a great civilizing force that emerged in the sixth century B.C. in the life and moral teachings of "The Buddha" or Siddhartha Gautama. Through the story of the Buddha's life, his Hindu background, and his search for enlightenment, students can be introduced to the Buddha's central beliefs and moral teachings: unselfishness (returning good for evil); compassion for the suffering of others; tolerance and nonviolence; and the prohibition of lying, stealing, killing, finding fault with others, and gossiping. While Buddhism did not survive on Indian soil, Jainism, which introduced the idea *ahimsa*, or nonviolence, has continued to play a role in modern India, especially through Gandhi's idea of nonviolent civil disobedience. Students should also study the development of Hinduism and the role of one of its most revered texts, the *Bhagavad Gita*.

Students also should learn about Asoka, the great philosopher-king who unified almost all of India, renounced violence as a national policy, and established Buddhism as the state religion.

The northward spread of Buddhism in the first century A.D. provides students with a bridge to a study of China during the Qin and Han Dynasties (221 B.C. to A.D. 220). Students should be helped to understand that the roots of this great civilization go far back into ancient times when Shang society (the "molders" of China) first emerged around 1500 B.C. in the Huang-He Valley and established the Chinese language and a highly developed technique of working with bronze.

Standard 6.6.

Students analyze the geographic, political, economic, religious, and social structures of the early civilizations of China.

During succeeding centuries, especially the Zhou Dynasty, China grew by conquering the people on its borders and absorbing the lands of these people as frontier states within Chinese society. By the sixth century B.C., the balance of power between the princes of these newer states and the old imperial centers of central China had broken down, plunging China into political chaos and war. It was during this time, when traditional values were neglected and government was in disarray, that Confucius lived and wrote. He tried to make sense of a troubled world and proposed ways in which individuals and society could achieve goodness. The good person in Confucius's teaching practiced moderation in conduct and emotion, kept one's promises, learned the traditional ways, respected one's elders, improved oneself through education, and avoided people who were not good. Confucius's teaching promoted the dignity and authenticity of humanity. Attention should be paid to the role of women in Confucian society.

Between 221 and 207 B.C. the Qin Dynasty was able to unite China. The longer-lasting Han Dynasty built on the unification, made Confucian teachings official, and placed governmental administration in the hands of the educated civil service. Attention should be paid to the lives of ordinary people and the educated classes during this time of stability and prosperity. Confucian filial piety and family ties strengthened the social structure of Han society. Art, literature, and learning flourished. Agriculture, trade, and manufacturing thrived. Map study should help students analyze the growing trade and cultural interchange among China, India, and Rome at this time. The great caravan, or "Silk Road," that linked China and the Middle East was in operation by the first century B.C. By the second century A.D., the various legs of the sea journey that linked China, Malaya, South India, and Egypt were completed, connecting the Far East with the Mediterranean world and Rome in one great commercial network.

Grade Six

Standard 6.7.

Students analyze the geographic, political, economic, religious, and social structures during the development of Rome.

Chronological and Spatial Thinking 3.

Students use a variety of maps and documents to identify physical and cultural features of neighborhoods, cities, states, and countries and to explain the historical migration of people, expansion and disintegration of empires, and the growth of economic systems.

Historical Interpretation 3.

Students explain the sources of historical continuity and how the combination of ideas and events explains the emergence of new patterns.

East Meets West: Rome

The land and sea routes of the China trade provide students with a bridge for a return to the Mediterranean world and the study of imperial Rome. Students should learn about everyday life in Roman society, including slavery, social conflict, and the rule of Roman law. They should learn about the emergence of the Roman Republic and the spread of the Roman Empire; and about Julius Caesar, his conquests, and his assassination in 44 B.C. They also should learn about the reign of Augustus, the "Pax Romana," and the eventual division of the Roman Empire: Rome in the West and the rising Byzantine Empire in the East.

Students should learn about the rise and spread of Christianity throughout the Mediterranean world and of its origins in the life and teachings of Jesus; Roman efforts to suppress Christianity; the consequences of Constantine's acceptance of Christianity (A.D. 313); and its subsequent establishment by Theodosius I as the official religion of the empire. Through selections from Biblical literature, such as the Sermon on the Mount and the parables of the Good Samaritan, the lost sheep, and the Prodigal Son, the students will learn about those teachings of Jesus that advocate compassion, justice, and love for others.

Finally, students should compare Roman contributions in art, architecture, engineering, political thought, religion, and philosophy with those of the earlier Greeks and consider the influence of both cultures on Western civilization and on our lives today.

Throughout these grade-six studies, students should be engaged in higher levels of critical thinking. They should consider, for example, why these societies developed where they did (the critical geographic relationships between site, resources, and settlement exemplified in the river valley settlements of Mesopotamia, Egypt, India, and China); the roles of technological, agricultural, and economic development and international trade; why societies rose to dominance at particular times in the ancient world (the importance of "relative location" in the case of ancient Greece, for example); and why great civilizations fell, including the collapse of the Indus civilization of India, the decline of Egypt in the years of the later empire, and the fall of Greece to Rome.

Students should examine factors of continuity and change across time in the development of these civilizations, observing how major beliefs, social organization, and technological developments of an earlier era were carried through the centuries and have contributed to our own lives.

Students should engage in comparative analyses across time and across cultures. They should compare, for example, the factors contributing to the evolution of ancient societies across the whole of the ancient world; the evolution of language and its written forms in Mesopotamia, Egypt, and China;

and the origins of major religions and ethical belief systems that unified cultures and defined the good and right way to live. To support their analyses, students should develop mathematically accurate time lines that place events in chronological order and support comparative analyses of events simultaneously occurring in different cultural areas of the world.

Students should be engaged in mapping activities that support their analyses of where these societies first developed, the course of their spatial development over time, and their spatial interactions illustrated in the geographic movement of ideas, religious beliefs, economic trade, and military expansion throughout the ancient world.

To make these studies relevant for today, students should develop appreciation of the continuity of human experience, the great debt we owe to those who came before us and established the foundations on which modern civilizations rest, and the responsibilities we owe to those who will come after us.

Grade Six

Research, Evidence, and Point of View 1.

Students frame questions that can be answered by historical study and research.

Chronological and Spatial Thinking 1.

Students explain how major events are related to one another in time.

History–Social Science Standards

Grade Six
World History and Geography:
Ancient Civilizations

6.1   Students describe what is known through archaeological studies of the early physical and cultural development of humankind from the Paleolithic era to the agricultural revolution.

1. Describe the hunter-gatherer societies, including the development of tools and the use of fire.
2. Identify the locations of human communities that populated the major regions of the world and describe how humans adapted to a variety of environments.
3. Discuss the climatic changes and human modifications of the physical environment that gave rise to the domestication of plants and animals and new sources of clothing and shelter.

6.2   Students analyze the geographic, political, economic, religious, and social structures of the early civilizations of Mesopotamia, Egypt, and Kush.

1. Locate and describe the major river systems and discuss the physical settings that supported permanent settlement and early civilizations.
2. Trace the development of agricultural techniques that permitted the production of economic surplus and the emergence of cities as centers of culture and power.
3. Understand the relationship between religion and the social and political order in Mesopotamia and Egypt.
4. Know the significance of Hammurabi's Code.
5. Discuss the main features of Egyptian art and architecture.
6. Describe the role of Egyptian trade in the eastern Mediterranean and Nile valley.
7. Understand the significance of Queen Hatshepsut and Ramses the Great.
8. Identify the location of the Kush civilization and describe its political, commercial, and cultural relations with Egypt.
9. Trace the evolution of language and its written forms.

6.3   Students analyze the geographic, political, economic, religious, and social structures of the Ancient Hebrews.

1. Describe the origins and significance of Judaism as the first monotheistic religion based on the concept of one God who sets down moral laws for humanity.

2. Identify the sources of the ethical teachings and central beliefs of Judaism (the Hebrew Bible, the Commentaries): belief in God, observance of law, practice of the concepts of righteousness and justice, and importance of study; and describe how the ideas of the Hebrew traditions are reflected in the moral and ethical traditions of Western civilization.

3. Explain the significance of Abraham, Moses, Naomi, Ruth, David, and Yohanan ben Zaccai in the development of the Jewish religion.

4. Discuss the locations of the settlements and movements of Hebrew peoples, including the Exodus and their movement to and from Egypt, and outline the significance of the Exodus to the Jewish and other people.

5. Discuss how Judaism survived and developed despite the continuing dispersion of much of the Jewish population from Jerusalem and the rest of Israel after the destruction of the second Temple in A.D. 70.

6.4   Students analyze the geographic, political, economic, religious, and social structures of the early civilizations of Ancient Greece.

1. Discuss the connections between geography and the development of city-states in the region of the Aegean Sea, including patterns of trade and commerce among Greek city-states and within the wider Mediterranean region.

2. Trace the transition from tyranny and oligarchy to early democratic forms of government and back to dictatorship in ancient Greece, including the significance of the invention of the idea of citizenship (e.g., from *Pericles' Funeral Oration*).

3. State the key differences between Athenian, or direct, democracy and representative democracy.

4. Explain the significance of Greek mythology to the everyday life of people in the region and how Greek literature continues to permeate our literature and language today, drawing from Greek mythology and epics, such as Homer's *Iliad* and *Odyssey*, and from *Aesop's Fables*.

5. Outline the founding, expansion, and political organization of the Persian Empire.

6. Compare and contrast life in Athens and Sparta, with emphasis on their roles in the Persian and Peloponnesian Wars.

7. Trace the rise of Alexander the Great and the spread of Greek culture eastward and into Egypt.

8. Describe the enduring contributions of important Greek figures in the arts and sciences (e.g., Hypatia, Socrates, Plato, Aristotle, Euclid, Thucydides).

6.5   **Students analyze the geographic, political, economic, religious, and social structures of the early civilizations of India.**

1. Locate and describe the major river system and discuss the physical setting that supported the rise of this civilization.

2. Discuss the significance of the Aryan invasions.

3. Explain the major beliefs and practices of Brahmanism in India and how they evolved into early Hinduism.

4. Outline the social structure of the caste system.

5. Know the life and moral teachings of the Buddha and how Buddhism spread in India, Ceylon, and Central Asia.

6. Describe the growth of the Maurya empire and the political and moral achievements of the emperor Asoka.

7. Discuss important aesthetic and intellectual traditions (e.g., Sanskrit literature, including the *Bhagavad Gita;* medicine; metallurgy; and mathematics, including Hindu-Arabic numerals and the zero).

6.6   **Students analyze the geographic, political, economic, religious, and social structures of the early civilizations of China.**

1. Locate and describe the origins of Chinese civilization in the Huang-He Valley during the Shang Dynasty.

2. Explain the geographic features of China that made governance and the spread of ideas and goods difficult and served to isolate the country from the rest of the world.

3. Know about the life of Confucius and the fundamental teachings of Confucianism and Daoism.

4. Identify the political and cultural problems prevalent in the time of Confucius and how he sought to solve them.

5. List the policies and achievements of the emperor Shi Huangdi in unifying northern China under the Qin Dynasty.

6. Detail the political contributions of the Han Dynasty to the development of the imperial bureaucratic state and the expansion of the empire.

7. Cite the significance of the trans-Eurasian "silk roads" in the period of the Han Dynasty and Roman Empire and their locations.

8. Describe the diffusion of Buddhism northward to China during the Han Dynasty.

6.7 **Students analyze the geographic, political, economic, religious, and social structures during the development of Rome.**

1. Identify the location and describe the rise of the Roman Republic, including the importance of such mythical and historical figures as Aeneas, Romulus and Remus, Cincinnatus, Julius Caesar, and Cicero.

2. Describe the government of the Roman Republic and its significance (e.g., written constitution and tripartite government, checks and balances, civic duty).

3. Identify the location of and the political and geographic reasons for the growth of Roman territories and expansion of the empire, including how the empire fostered economic growth through the use of currency and trade routes.

4. Discuss the influence of Julius Caesar and Augustus in Rome's transition from republic to empire.

5. Trace the migration of Jews around the Mediterranean region and the effects of their conflict with the Romans, including the Romans' restrictions on their right to live in Jerusalem.

6. Note the origins of Christianity in the Jewish Messianic prophecies, the life and teachings of Jesus of Nazareth as described in the New Testament, and the contribution of St. Paul the Apostle to the definition and spread of Christian beliefs (e.g., belief in the Trinity, resurrection, salvation).

7. Describe the circumstances that led to the spread of Christianity in Europe and other Roman territories.

8. Discuss the legacies of Roman art and architecture, technology and science, literature, language, and law.

Course
Descriptions

Grade Seven

Grade Seven—
World History and Geography:
Medieval and Early Modern Times

The study of world history and geography continues this year with an examination of social, cultural, and technological change during the period A.D. 500–1789. A review unit on the ancient world begins with a study of the ways archaeologists and historians uncover the past. Then, with the fall of Rome, this study moves to Islam, a rising force in the medieval world; follows the spread of Islam through Africa; crosses the Atlantic to observe the rise of the Mayan, Incan, and Aztec civilizations; moves westward to compare the civilizations of China and Japan during the Middle Ages; returns to a comparative study of Europe during the High Middle Ages; and concludes with the turbulent age of the Renaissance, Reformation, and Scientific Revolution that ushered in the Enlightenment and the modern world.

The sequence of these units is both *historical,* advancing across the years A.D. 500–1789, and *geographic,* advancing across the major continents of the earth. The units are focused on the great civilizations that were developing concurrently over these years. By developing world maps and time lines, students can locate these cultures in time and in place, compare events that were developing concurrently in the world, and observe the transmission of ideas, beliefs, scientific developments, and economic trade throughout this important period of history.

Connecting with Past Learnings: Uncovering the Remote Past

In the first review unit of this course, the students address this question: How do we know about the past? They will see that archaeologists develop their theories by looking for clues in the legends, artifacts, and fossils left behind by ancient peoples. For more recent periods, historians use written records as well as material culture to find out what happened in the past. Through examples, students will observe that historians and archaeologists work as detectives by formulating appropriate questions and drawing conclusions from available evidence to try to reconstruct past societies and cultures; their social structure and family life; their political and economic systems; and their language, art, architecture, beliefs, and values. Students will also learn that new discoveries by archaeologists and historians change our view of the past. The process of reconstructing the past requires knowledge, an open mind, and critical thinking.

Historical
Interpretation 2.

Students understand and distinguish cause, effect, sequence, and correlation in historical events, including the long- and short-term causal relations.

Historical
Interpretation 5.

Students recognize that interpretations of history are subject to change as new information is uncovered.

Connecting with Past Learnings: The Fall of Rome

This second unit builds on the sixth-grade study of Roman civilization. Students should develop a map of the Roman Empire at its height, review briefly the reign of Augustus, and consider the reasons for Rome's fall to invading Germanic tribes with attention to the role of Clovis, a Christian Frank.

To help students relate this remote historical period to the present, teachers should emphasize the lasting contributions of Roman civilization, especially in the areas of law, language, technology, and the transmission of the Christian religion to the West. By learning that the law codes of most Latin countries are still based on Roman law, students will appreciate the continuing importance of Roman law and justice. Critical thinking skills can be developed by students as they compare citizens' civic duties as taught by Roman Stoic philosophers with citizens' civic responsibilities in America today. Such skills also can be developed by comparing modern-day public works, architecture, and technology with those of the Roman Empire.

Growth of Islam

In this unit students examine the rise of Islam as a religion and as a civilization. Attention should be given to the historic events of A.D. 636–651 when Arab armies reunited the ancient Middle East. Students should analyze the geographic and economic significance of the trade routes between Asia and Europe that were used by Arab merchants. They should consider the importance of a common literary language (Arabic) and religion (Islamic) in unifying the many ethnic groups of this region. The religious ideas of Mohammed, the founder of Islam, should be discussed both for their ethical teachings and as a way of life. Mohammed should be seen as a major historical figure who helped establish the Islamic way of life, its code of ethics and justice, and its rule of law. Students should examine the position of Christians and Jews in the Islamic world who, as "People of the Book," were allowed to practice their religious beliefs. Contributions of Islamic scholars, including mathematicians, scientists, geographers, astronomers, and physicians from many ethnic groups, should be emphasized and their relationship to Greek thought acknowledged. Scholars at Baghdad and Córdoba, the two great centers of Muslim learning, helped to preserve much of the learning of the ancient world; and, by the end of the ninth century, they added important new discoveries of their own in mathematics, medicine, geography, history, and science. Attention should be paid to the flowering of Jewish civilization in Córdoba, where poets, philosophers, and scholars established a vibrant culture.

In time the influence of Greek rationalism waned, and religious mysticism came to dominate orthodox Islamic thought. In this intellectual climate, poetry and literature flourished. Students can be introduced to these achievements through selections from *The Thousand and One Nights* (Arabic) and the poetry of Omar Khayyam, a Sufi mystic (Persian).

Grade Seven

Standard 7.1.

Students analyze the causes and effects of the vast expansion and ultimate disintegration of the Roman Empire.

Standard 7.2.

Students analyze the geographic, political, economic, religious, and social structures of the civilizations of Islam in the Middle Ages.

Islam spread to the area known today as Turkey, where, in the fourteenth century, the Ottoman Turks began gradually to absorb other Turkish tribes and to establish control over most of Asia Minor. In 1453 they captured Constantinople, the seat of the Byzantine Empire, and expanded into Christian Europe until nearly 1700. In studying the social structure of the Ottoman Empire, students should give attention to the role of women; the privileges of its conquered peoples; slavery; the political system; and the legal code. Analysis should be made of the geographic conditions that facilitated the expansion of Islam through the Middle East, through North and sub-Saharan Africa, to Spain, and east through Persia to India and Indonesia, with influences that persist in these regions to the present day.

African States in the Middle Ages and Early Modern Times

This unit begins with a geographic survey of sub-Saharan Africa and the landforms, climate, vegetation, rivers, and resources associated with its major geographic regions.

Standard 7.4.

Students analyze the geographic, political, economic, religious, and social structures of sub-Saharan civilizations of Ghana and Mali in Medieval Africa.

Students should analyze the importance of an iron technology and of geographic location and trade in the development of the sub-Saharan empires of Ghana and Mali. Both became states of great wealth—Ghana, by controlling the trade in gold from the south; and Mali, by controlling both the southern trade in gold and the northern trade in salt. Students should also understand that slavery existed in these kingdoms and was part of the western African economy at the time. Both kingdoms exercised commercial, cultural, and political power over a large part of Africa.

The Muslim conquest of Ghana ended in destruction of the kingdom (1076). Mali's rulers, on the other hand, converted to Islam. Under Islamic rule, the nation achieved recognition as a major power. Its leading city, Timbuktu, with its university became known throughout the Muslim world as a center of learning, a tradition that lasted through Mali's conquest by Songhay in the fourteenth century and Songhay's fall two centuries later to Moroccan invaders.

Civilizations of the Americas

Standard 7.7.

Students compare and contrast the geographic, political, economic, religious, and social structures of the Meso-American and Andean civilizations.

In this unit students are introduced to three great civilizations of Middle and South America: the Mayans, Aztecs, and Incas. By developing maps and time lines, students should be able to place these cultures in geographic and historical perspectives. With the development of maize agriculture around 2000 B.C., foundations were laid for cultural advances in these regions. Mayan civilization achieved its Classic Age about the time the Greco-Roman civilization collapsed. The great cultural advance that began in Peru around 1000 B.C. culminated in the Imperial Incan civilization of the fourteenth century A.D. The Aztec civilization, which incorporated the achievements of its conquered neighbors, reached its height by the sixteenth century A.D.

The accomplishments of these civilizations should be explored: the Mayans for their noble architecture, calendar, pictographic writing, and astronomy; the Incas for their excellence in engineering and administration; and the Aztecs for their massive temple architecture and Aztec calendar. Historical and archaeological records should help students understand the daily lives and beliefs of these people.

China

In this unit students examine Chinese culture and society during the Middle Ages, a period that saw the remarkable development in China of great cities; construction of large seagoing vessels; and great technological progress, including the invention of the compass, gunpowder, and printing. Important economic changes during the T'ang Dynasty (A.D. 618–906) and Song Dynasty (A.D. 960–1279) established a "modern" form of Chinese society that lasted well into the twentieth century. Students should analyze the economic foundations of this society in the conversion of the jungle regions of the Yangtze Valley into productive rice paddies. Elaborate irrigation systems and canals supported the production and distribution of vast quantities of rice to the imperial centers of the north. The wealth that resulted supported, in turn, a money economy, a merchant class engaged in extensive private trading, and the growth of China's provincial cities.

Standard 7.3.

Students analyze the geographic, political, economic, religious, and social structures of the civilizations of China in the Middle Ages.

During the Mongol Ascendancy (1264–1368), a flourishing sea trade developed between China, India, and the coast of Southeast Asia. Foreign merchants such as Marco Polo were given special privileges and high office. The Ming Dynasty undertook between 1405 and 1423 a series of great maritime expeditions that eclipsed in scale the European exploits of a century later. Abruptly, in 1433, the Emperor suspended these enterprises, however, and forbade even the construction of seagoing vessels. Students should examine how the Chinese ideal of a unified state under one leader, with a strong bureaucracy controlling the machinery of government, restrained progress. Unable to control the growth of its maritime commerce, the bureaucracy chose instead to withdraw from it.

Students should analyze how Confucian thought supported these actions and returned China to its traditional values. The merchant class was subordinated as a necessary evil of society, and little priority was placed on Chinese trade and manufacturing, which, in A.D. 1000, had been the most advanced in the world. The Chinese invention of printing fostered scholarly study and spread traditional ideas more widely throughout society. The outlook of the Chinese scholarly class came to dominate Chinese thought and government well into the twentieth century. Students should critically analyze the different ways in which Chinese inventions—gunpowder, the compass, and printing—affected China and the West.

Historical Interpretation 6.

Students interpret basic indicators of economic performance and conduct cost-benefit analyses of economic and political issues.

Course
Descriptions

Grade Seven

Standard 7.5.

Students analyze the
geographic, political,
economic, religious, and
social structures of the
civilizations of Medieval
Japan.

Standard 7.6.

Students analyze the
geographic, political,
economic, religious, and
social structures of
the civilizations of
Medieval Europe.

**Research, Evidence,
and Point of View 4.**

Students assess the
credibility of primary and
secondary sources and
draw sound conclusions
from them.

Japan

Students will focus next on Japan during the time of Prince Shotoku's regency (A.D. 592–632). Students should observe Japan's close geographic proximity to the more ancient civilization of China and analyze how that led to the borrowing of ideas, institutions, and technology. At the same time they should consider how its insular location facilitated Japan's political independence, allowing it to borrow selectively and to fashion a culture uniquely its own.

With the establishment of direct relations between the Chinese and Japanese courts in A.D. 607, Japanese artists, craftspersons, scribes, interpreters, and diplomatic dignitaries made frequent visits to China. Members of Japan's upper classes studied Chinese language, literature, philosophy, art, science, and government. Buddhism was introduced and blended with Japan's traditional Shinto religion, "the way of the gods."

Students might compare Chinese poetry and painting appreciated in Japanese imperial courts with the distinctive Japanese style of painting that developed in the ninth century and with Noh drama, a unique Japanese art form. Between the ninth and eleventh centuries, Japanese literature entered a golden age and included the works of several gifted women authors, among them Murasaki Shikibu, whose *Tale of Genji* ranks among the classics of world literature.

Medieval Societies: Europe and Japan

In this unit students will encounter Europe during the High Middle Ages. This study will focus on the economic and political structure of feudal society; daily life and the role of women in medieval times; the growth of towns, trade, and technology; and the development of universities. Special attention should be paid to Christianity in the Middle Ages because the Church, more powerful than any feudal state, influenced every aspect of medieval life in Europe. The story of St. Francis of Assisi should be told, both for his embodiment of the Christian ideal and for the accessibility to students of his gentle beliefs. Attention also should be given to the Crusades, with these European undertakings viewed from both the Christian and Muslim vantage points. What were the Crusades? Why did they begin? What were their results?

To understand what was distinctive about European culture during this period, students should compare Western Europe with Japan during the High Middle Ages. They will see that the two cultures had aspects in common: a feudal, lord-vassal system, with military leaders (shogun), great lords (daimyo), and knights (samurai). Both feudal societies emphasized personal loyalty to the lord, military skills, a strict code of honor, self-discipline, and fearlessness in battle. Students will also see striking differences in cultural values, religious beliefs, and social customs, including differences in women's roles. Japanese Haiku poetry and European epic poetry, such as *Beowulf,* provide an interesting contrast. By seeing that some cultural traditions have survived since the Middle Ages, including the importance that Japanese place on family loyalty and ceremonial rituals, students should better understand the meaning of historical continuity. They also should appreciate the significance of change by seeing how much both cultures have been transformed by forces of modernization while retaining aspects of their cultural heritage.

Another aspect of medieval societies that students should understand was the continuing persecution of the Jewish minority; the massacre of Jews by the Crusaders; and the expulsion of Jews from England in 1290, from France in 1306 and 1394, and from many German cities during the time of the Black Death. Students should learn of the conflicts between Christians and Muslims in Spain, beginning in 1085, and the plight of the Jews caught between the warring faiths. Examination of the Spanish and Portuguese inquisitions, during which people were tortured and burned at the stake, should demonstrate the lengths to which religious authorities went to force conversions and to destroy as heretics those who continued in their Judaic faith. The expulsion of the Jews and Muslims from Spain in 1492 should be noted.

Europe During the Renaissance, the Reformation, and the Scientific Revolution

This unit focuses on an unusually rich and important period whose effects continue to influence politics, religion, culture, and the arts of the present day.

A remarkable burst of creativity that began in the fourteenth century in northern Italy and spread through Europe produced the artistic and literary advances of the Renaissance. Classical literature was rediscovered, and humanistic studies flourished. Particular attention should be paid to Florence, Italy, as a major center of commerce, creativity, and artistic genius. Students should be introduced to the writings of Shakespeare, Cervantes, and Machiavelli and to the art of Michelangelo, da Vinci, Botticelli, Raphael, Titian, Van Eyck, and Dürer. Examination of masterpieces such as Michelangelo's *Moses* and Dürer's *The Four Horsemen of the Apocalypse* will demonstrate the powerful vision of these artists as well as the power of art to communicate ideas. Students should analyze how Renaissance painting differed from that of the Middle Ages, even though both reflected many of the same religious themes and symbolisms. They should observe how Renaissance art reflected the advances of that age in science, mathematics, engineering techniques, and understanding of human anatomy.

Students should closely examine the Protestant Reformation and become familiar with the religious beliefs of Martin Luther and John Calvin as well as the history of the English Bible. To understand why Luther's 95 theses, nailed to the Wittenberg church door, had such historic results, students should consider the growing religious, political, and economic resistance to the supremacy of the Renaissance popes. Through vivid narrative, attention should

Standard 7.8.

Students analyze the origins, accomplishments, and geographic diffusion of the Renaissance.

Standard 7.9.

Students analyze the historical developments of the Reformation.

Standard 7.10.

Students analyze the
historical developments of
the Scientific Revolution
and its lasting effect on
religious, political, and
cultural institutions.

Standard 7.11.

Students analyze political
and economic change in
the sixteenth, seventeenth,
and eighteenth centuries
(the Age of Exploration,
the Enlightenment, and the
Age of Reason).

be given to the dramatic series of events leading to Luther's excommunication,
the peasants' revolt, the spread of the Reformation throughout northern Europe
and England, the Catholic response in the Counter-Reformation, the revival of
the Inquisition, and the bloody religious conflicts that followed. Most of
Germanic Europe became Protestant, while most of Latin Europe remained
loyal to Rome. Throughout Europe, the secular power of kings and local rulers
grew at the expense of church authority and led to the age of kings. Students
should learn the meaning of the divine right of kings, particularly in relation to
the French monarchy.

The beginnings of modern science can be found in these same tumultuous
years of the sixteenth and early seventeenth centuries. Students should draw on
their science courses to examine the significance of the methods of scientific
observation, mathematical proof, and experimental science developed by such
giants of this age as Galileo, Johannes Kepler, Francis Bacon, and Sir Isaac
Newton. Students should consider the significance of the inventions of this
age—the telescope, microscope, thermometer, barometer, and printing press—
and observe how all these developments spurred European leadership in
commerce and helped to usher in the age of exploration and the
Enlightenment.

Early Modern Europe: The Age of Exploration to the Enlightenment

This unit begins with the age of exploration, with special attention given to
Spanish and Portuguese explorations in the New World. Mapping activities will
clarify the routes and empires established in these voyages of exploration and
conquest. A brief review of the great heights attained by the Aztec and Incan
civilizations should help students place in perspective the plunder and
destruction of native cultures that followed the Spanish conquest of these lands.
The role of disease in aiding the Spanish conquest and the long-term effects on
native populations should also be examined. The drama of the Spanish galleons
and maritime rivalries between Spain and England culminated in the English
defeat of the Spanish Armada in 1588; the consequences of that event should
be analyzed.

Northern European seaports thrived as enterprising merchants expanded
international commerce. In the 1600s Holland and England welcomed the
return of the Jews, who brought their highly developed culture and commercial
experience. By focusing on the origins of modern capitalism and the development of a market economy in seventeenth-century Europe, students should
deepen their understanding of economics, recognizing the components of a
market system and developing an understanding of the forces of supply and
demand.

This unit concludes with a study of the Enlightenment and its impact on
the future of Western political thought, including the political ideas and
institutions of the United States. The Enlightenment provoked a clash of ideas

between reason and authority, between the natural rights of human beings and the divine right of kings, and between experimentalism in science and dogmatic belief. Students will learn about the major figures of the Enlightenment and their influence on the ways Europeans viewed government and society. They also will see how the principles implicit in the Magna Carta were embodied in the English Bill of Rights, the French Declaration of the Rights of Man and of the Citizen, and the American Declaration of Independence.

Linking Past to Present

This study will conclude with an examination of the political and economic forces let loose in the Western world by the rise of capitalism and the Enlightenment and the impact of the ideas of this period on Western society in the future, especially on the young American republic that the students will be studying in grade eight. To carry this theme into modern times, students will consider the ways in which these ideas continue to influence our nation and the world today; for example, the importance of rationalism in science and technology; the effort to solve problems rationally in local, state, national, and international arenas; and the ideal of human rights, a vital issue today throughout the world.

**Historical
Interpretation 3.**
Students explain the sources of historical continuity and how the combination of ideas and events explains the emergence of new patterns.

History–Social Science Standards

Grade Seven
World History and Geography:
Medieval and Early Modern Times

7.1 **Students analyze the causes and effects of the vast expansion and ultimate disintegration of the Roman Empire.**

1. Study the early strengths and lasting contributions of Rome (e.g., significance of Roman citizenship; rights under Roman law; Roman art, architecture, engineering, and philosophy; preservation and transmission of Christianity) and its ultimate internal weaknesses (e.g., rise of autonomous military powers within the empire, undermining of citizenship by the growth of corruption and slavery, lack of education, and distribution of news).

2. Discuss the geographic borders of the empire at its height and the factors that threatened its territorial cohesion.

3. Describe the establishment by Constantine of the new capital in Constantinople and the development of the Byzantine Empire, with an emphasis on the consequences of the development of two distinct European civilizations, Eastern Orthodox and Roman Catholic, and their two distinct views on church-state relations.

7.2 **Students analyze the geographic, political, economic, religious, and social structures of the civilizations of Islam in the Middle Ages.**

1. Identify the physical features and describe the climate of the Arabian peninsula, its relationship to surrounding bodies of land and water, and nomadic and sedentary ways of life.

2. Trace the origins of Islam and the life and teachings of Muhammad, including Islamic teachings on the connection with Judaism and Christianity.

3. Explain the significance of the Qur'an and the Sunnah as the primary sources of Islamic beliefs, practice, and law, and their influence in Muslims' daily life.

4. Discuss the expansion of Muslim rule through military conquests and treaties, emphasizing the cultural blending within Muslim civilization and the spread and acceptance of Islam and the Arabic language.

5. Describe the growth of cities and the establishment of trade routes among Asia, Africa, and Europe, the products and inventions that traveled along these routes (e.g., spices, textiles, paper, steel, new crops), and the role of merchants in Arab society.

6. Understand the intellectual exchanges among Muslim scholars of Eurasia and Africa and the contributions Muslim scholars made to later civilizations in the areas of science, geography, mathematics, philosophy, medicine, art, and literature.

7.3   Students analyze the geographic, political, economic, religious, and social structures of the civilizations of China in the Middle Ages.

1. Describe the reunification of China under the Tang Dynasty and reasons for the spread of Buddhism in Tang China, Korea, and Japan.
2. Describe agricultural, technological, and commercial developments during the Tang and Song periods.
3. Analyze the influences of Confucianism and changes in Confucian thought during the Song and Mongol periods.
4. Understand the importance of both overland trade and maritime expeditions between China and other civilizations in the Mongol Ascendancy and Ming Dynasty.
5. Trace the historic influence of such discoveries as tea, the manufacture of paper, wood-block printing, the compass, and gunpowder.
6. Describe the development of the imperial state and the scholar-official class.

7.4   Students analyze the geographic, political, economic, religious, and social structures of the sub-Saharan civilizations of Ghana and Mali in Medieval Africa.

1. Study the Niger River and the relationship of vegetation zones of forest, savannah, and desert to trade in gold, salt, food, and slaves; and the growth of the Ghana and Mali empires.
2. Analyze the importance of family, labor specialization, and regional commerce in the development of states and cities in West Africa.
3. Describe the role of the trans-Saharan caravan trade in the changing religious and cultural characteristics of West Africa and the influence of Islamic beliefs, ethics, and law.
4. Trace the growth of the Arabic language in government, trade, and Islamic scholarship in West Africa.
5. Describe the importance of written and oral traditions in the transmission of African history and culture.

7.5   Students analyze the geographic, political, economic, religious, and social structures of the civilizations of Medieval Japan.

1. Describe the significance of Japan's proximity to China and Korea and the intellectual, linguistic, religious, and philosophical influence of those countries on Japan.

2. Discuss the reign of Prince Shotoku of Japan and the characteristics of Japanese society and family life during his reign.

3. Describe the values, social customs, and traditions prescribed by the lord-vassal system consisting of *shogun, daimyo,* and *samurai* and the lasting influence of the warrior code throughout the twentieth century.

4. Trace the development of distinctive forms of Japanese Buddhism.

5. Study the ninth and tenth centuries' golden age of literature, art, and drama and its lasting effects on culture today, including Murasaki Shikibu's *Tale of Genji.*

6. Analyze the rise of a military society in the late twelfth century and the role of the samurai in that society.

7.6   Students analyze the geographic, political, economic, religious, and social structures of the civilizations of Medieval Europe.

1. Study the geography of Europe and the Eurasian land mass, including their location, topography, waterways, vegetation, and climate and their relationship to ways of life in Medieval Europe.

2. Describe the spread of Christianity north of the Alps and the roles played by the early church and by monasteries in its diffusion after the fall of the western half of the Roman Empire.

3. Understand the development of feudalism, its role in the medieval European economy, the way in which it was influenced by physical geography (the role of the manor and the growth of towns), and how feudal relationships provided the foundation of political order.

4. Demonstrate an understanding of the conflict and cooperation between the Papacy and European monarchs (e.g., Charlemagne, Gregory VII, Emperor Henry IV).

5. Know the significance of developments in medieval English legal and constitutional practices and their importance in the rise of modern democratic thought and representative institutions (e.g., Magna Carta, parliament, development of habeas corpus, an independent judiciary in England).

6. Discuss the causes and course of the religious Crusades and their effects on the Christian, Muslim, and Jewish populations in Europe, with emphasis on the increasing contact by Europeans with cultures of the Eastern Mediterranean world.

7. Map the spread of the bubonic plague from Central Asia to China, the Middle East, and Europe and describe its impact on global population.

8. Understand the importance of the Catholic church as a political, intellectual, and aesthetic institution (e.g., founding of universities, political and spiritual roles of the clergy, creation of monastic and mendicant religious orders, preservation of the Latin language and

religious texts, St. Thomas Aquinas's synthesis of classical philosophy with Christian theology, and the concept of "natural law").

9. Know the history of the decline of Muslim rule in the Iberian Peninsula that culminated in the Reconquista and the rise of Spanish and Portuguese kingdoms.

7.7   **Students compare and contrast the geographic, political, economic, religious, and social structures of the Meso-American and Andean civilizations.**

1. Study the locations, landforms, and climates of Mexico, Central America, and South America and their effects on Mayan, Aztec, and Incan economies, trade, and development of urban societies.

2. Study the roles of people in each society, including class structures, family life, warfare, religious beliefs and practices, and slavery.

3. Explain how and where each empire arose and how the Aztec and Incan empires were defeated by the Spanish.

4. Describe the artistic and oral traditions and architecture in the three civilizations.

5. Describe the Meso-American achievements in astronomy and mathematics, including the development of the calendar and the Meso-American knowledge of seasonal changes to the civilizations' agricultural systems.

7.8   **Students analyze the origins, accomplishments, and geographic diffusion of the Renaissance.**

1. Describe the way in which the revival of classical learning and the arts fostered a new interest in humanism (i.e., a balance between intellect and religious faith).

2. Explain the importance of Florence in the early stages of the Renaissance and the growth of independent trading cities (e.g., Venice), with emphasis on the cities' importance in the spread of Renaissance ideas.

3. Understand the effects of the reopening of the ancient "Silk Road" between Europe and China, including Marco Polo's travels and the location of his routes.

4. Describe the growth and effects of new ways of disseminating information (e.g., the ability to manufacture paper, translation of the Bible into the vernacular, printing).

5. Detail advances made in literature, the arts, science, mathematics, cartography, engineering, and the understanding of human anatomy and astronomy (e.g., by Dante Alighieri, Leonardo da Vinci, Michelangelo di Buonarroti Simoni, Johann Gutenberg, William Shakespeare).

7.9   Students analyze the historical developments of the Reformation.

1. List the causes for the internal turmoil in and weakening of the Catholic church (e.g., tax policies, selling of indulgences).

2. Describe the theological, political, and economic ideas of the major figures during the Reformation (e.g., Desiderius Erasmus, Martin Luther, John Calvin, William Tyndale).

3. Explain Protestants' new practices of church self-government and the influence of those practices on the development of democratic practices and ideas of federalism.

4. Identify and locate the European regions that remained Catholic and those that became Protestant and explain how the division affected the distribution of religions in the New World.

5. Analyze how the Counter Reformation revitalized the Catholic church and the forces that fostered the movement (e.g., St. Ignatius of Loyola and the Jesuits, the Council of Trent).

6. Understand the institution and impact of missionaries on Christianity and the diffusion of Christianity from Europe to other parts of the world in the medieval and early modern periods; locate missions on a world map.

7. Describe the Golden Age of cooperation between Jews and Muslims in medieval Spain that promoted creativity in art, literature, and science, including how that cooperation was terminated by the religious persecution of individuals and groups (e.g., the Spanish Inquisition and the expulsion of Jews and Muslims from Spain in 1492).

7.10   Students analyze the historical developments of the Scientific Revolution and its lasting effect on religious, political, and cultural institutions.

1. Discuss the roots of the Scientific Revolution (e.g., Greek rationalism; Jewish, Christian, and Muslim science; Renaissance humanism; new knowledge from global exploration).

2. Understand the significance of the new scientific theories (e.g., those of Copernicus, Galileo, Kepler, Newton) and the significance of new inventions (e.g., the telescope, microscope, thermometer, barometer).

3. Understand the scientific method advanced by Bacon and Descartes, the influence of new scientific rationalism on the growth of democratic ideas, and the coexistence of science with traditional religious beliefs.

7.11 **Students analyze political and economic change in the sixteenth, seventeenth, and eighteenth centuries (the Age of Exploration, the Enlightenment, and the Age of Reason).**

1. Know the great voyages of discovery, the locations of the routes, and the influence of cartography in the development of a new European worldview.

2. Discuss the exchanges of plants, animals, technology, culture, and ideas among Europe, Africa, Asia, and the Americas in the fifteenth and sixteenth centuries and the major economic and social effects on each continent.

3. Examine the origins of modern capitalism; the influence of mercantilism and cottage industry; the elements and importance of a market economy in seventeenth-century Europe; the changing international trading and marketing patterns, including their locations on a world map; and the influence of explorers and map makers.

4. Explain how the main ideas of the Enlightenment can be traced back to such movements as the Renaissance, the Reformation, and the Scientific Revolution and to the Greeks, Romans, and Christianity.

5. Describe how democratic thought and institutions were influenced by Enlightenment thinkers (e.g., John Locke, Charles-Louis Montesquieu, American founders).

6. Discuss how the principles in the Magna Carta were embodied in such documents as the English Bill of Rights and the American Declaration of Independence.

Grade Eight— United States History and Geography: Growth and Conflict

The eighth-grade course of study begins with an intensive review of the major ideas, issues, and events preceding the founding of the nation. Students will concentrate on the critical events of the period—from the framing of the Constitution to World War I.

Connecting with Past Learnings: Our Colonial Heritage

This year's study of American history begins with a selective review of significant developments of the colonial era with emphasis on the development of democratic institutions founded in Judeo-Christian religious thinking, in Enlightenment philosophy, and in English parliamentary traditions; the development of an economy based on agriculture, commerce, and handicraft manufacturing; and the emergence of major regional differences in the colonies.

Connecting with Past Learnings: A New Nation

This unit begins with an in-depth examination of the major events and ideas leading to the American War for Independence. Readings from the Declaration of Independence should be used to discuss these questions: What are "natural rights" and "natural law"? What did Jefferson mean when he wrote that "all men are created equal" and "endowed by their Creator with certain unalienable rights"? What were the "Laws of Nature" and "Nature's God" to which Jefferson appealed?

Close attention should be paid to the moral and political ideas of the Great Awakening and its effect on the development of revolutionary fervor. By reading excerpts from original documents such as sermons of the Great Awakening and Thomas Paine's *Common Sense,* students should be able to understand the revolutionary and moral thinking of the times. Students should become familiar with the debates between Whigs and Tories, the major turning points in the War for Independence, and the contributions of George Washington, Thomas Jefferson, Benjamin Franklin, and other leaders of the new nation. Students should understand the significance that the American Revolution had for other nations, especially France.

The Constitution of the United States

In this unit students concentrate on the shaping of the Constitution and the nature of the government that it created. Students should review the major ideas of the Enlightenment and the origins of self-government in the Magna

Standard 8.1.

Students understand the major events preceding the founding of the nation and relate their significance to the development of American constitutional democracy.

Standard 8.1.

Students understand the major events preceding the founding of the nation and relate their significance to the development of American constitutional democracy.

Research, Evidence, and Point of View 1.

Students frame questions that can be answered by historical study and research.

Standard 8.2.

Students analyze the political principles underlying the U.S. Constitution and compare the enumerated and implied powers of the federal government.

Carta, the English Bill of Rights of 1689, the Mayflower Compact, the Virginia House of Burgesses, and the New England town meeting. This background will help students appreciate the framers' efforts to create a government that was neither too strong (because it might turn into despotism) nor too weak (as the Articles of Confederation proved to be).

Excerpts from the document written at the Constitutional Convention in Philadelphia should be read, discussed, and analyzed. Students should consider the issues that divided the Founding Fathers and examine the compromises they adopted. Although the Constitution never explicitly mentions slavery, several compromises preserved the institution; namely, the three-fifths rule of representation, the slave importation clause, and the fugitive slave clause. Why were these provisions so important to southern delegates? Why were these contradictions with the nation's ideals adopted? What were their long-term costs to black men and women and to the nation? To analyze these issues, students must recognize that the American Revolution had transformed slavery from a national to a sectional institution and that nine out of ten American slaves lived in the South. Students should discuss the status of women as reflected in the Constitution of 1787. They should recognize as well the great achievements of the Constitution: (1) it created a democratic form of government based on the consent of the governed—a rarity in history; and (2) it established a government that has survived more than 200 years by a delicate balancing of power and interests and by providing a process of amendment to adapt the Constitution to the needs of a changing society.

Launching the Ship of State

In this unit students consider the enormous tasks that faced the new nation and its leaders through this difficult period; for example, Washington, Jefferson, Madison, Hamilton, and the Adamses. The new nation had to demonstrate that its government would work, and in 1812 it had to fight a war to prove its sovereignty. Students should discuss the belief of the nation's founders that the survival of a democratic society depends on an educated people. Students should analyze the connection between education and democracy symbolized in the Northwest Ordinance and in Jefferson' dictum, "If a nation expects to be ignorant and free, in a state of civilization, it expects what never was and never will be." Attention should be paid to the types of education received in church schools, dame schools, and at home.

Students also should examine the daily life of ordinary people in the new nation, including farmers, merchants, and traders; women; blacks, both slave and free; and American Indians. Reading excerpts from works by James Fenimore Cooper and Washington Irving will help bring this period alive.

Grade Eight

Research, Evidence, and Point of View 5.

Students detect the different historical points of view on historical events and determine the context in which the historical statements were made (the questions asked, sources used, author's perspectives).

Standard 8.3.

Students understand the foundation of the American political system and the ways in which citizens participate in it.

Standard 8.4.

Students analyze the aspirations and ideals of the people of the new nation.

Standard 8.5.

Students analyze U.S. foreign policy in the early Republic.

Standard 8.8.

Students analyze
the divergent paths
of the American people
in the West from 1800
to the mid-1800s and
the challenges they faced.

The Divergent Paths of the American People: 1800–1850

This unit follows the nation's regional development in the West, Northeast, and South. Throughout this study students should be encouraged to view historical events empathetically as though they were there, working in places such as mines, cotton fields, and mills.

The West. The West should be studied for its deep influence on the politics, economy, mores, and culture of the nation. It opened domestic markets for seaboard merchants; it offered new frontiers for immigrants and discontented Easterners; and it provided a folklore of individualism and rugged frontier life that has become a significant aspect of our national self-image.

The election of Andrew Jackson in 1828 reflected the steady expansion of male suffrage, symbolized the shift of political power to the West, and opened a new era of political democracy in the United States. President Jackson was both a remarkable man and a symbol of his age. Jacksonian Democracy should be analyzed in terms of its supporters—farmers with small holdings, artisans, laborers, and middle-class businessmen. The democratizing effect of frontier life on the relations between men and women should be noted. Original documents will show the varied roles played by frontier women such as California's Annie Bidwell, who promoted women's rights and worked for social change.

In studying Jackson's presidency, students should debate his spoils system, veto of the National Bank, policy of Indian removal, and opposition to the Supreme Court. Alexis de Tocqueville's nine-month visit to the United States at this time, during which he sought to identify the general principles of democracy in America, can provide students an opportunity to compare his description of national character in the 1830s with American life today.

The story of the acquisition, exploration, and settlement of the trans-Mississippi West, from the Louisiana Purchase in 1803 to the admission of California as a state in 1850, should be reviewed. This was a period marked by a strong spirit of nationalism and "manifest destiny." To deepen their understanding of the changing geography and settlement of this immense land, students might read from the journals of the Lewis and Clark Expedition to the Northwest; map the explorations of trailblazers such as Zebulon Pike; discuss the searing accounts of the removal of Indians and the Cherokees' "Trail of Tears"; and interpret maps and documents relating to the long sea voyages and overland treks that opened the West. Attention should be given to the role of the great rivers and the struggles over water rights in the development of the West. Students should study the northward movement of settlers from Mexico into the great Southwest, with emphasis on the location of Mexican settlements, their cultural traditions, their attitudes toward slavery, their land-grant system, and the economy they established in these regions. Students need this background before they can analyze the events that followed the arrival of westward-moving settlers from the East into these Mexican territories. Special attention should be given to the Mexican-American War, its territorial settlements, and its aftermath in the lives of the Mexican families who first lived in the region.

The Northeast. The industrial revolution in the Northeast had important repercussions throughout the nation. Inventions between 1790 and 1850 transformed manufacturing, transportation, mining, communications, and agriculture and profoundly affected how people lived and worked. Skilled craftspersons were replaced by mechanized production in shops, mills, and factories, so well depicted by Charles Dickens in his *American Notes* and in the letters written by young women who left home to work in the mills of Lowell, Massachusetts. Immigrants flocked to the cities. Periods of boom and bust created both progress and poverty.

An age of reform began that made life more bearable for the less fortunate and expanded opportunities for many. Students should imagine what life was like for young people in the 1830s in order to appreciate Horace Mann's crusade for free public education for all. Students should read excerpts from original documents explaining the social and civic purposes of public education. Typical schoolbooks of the period should be used with attention to their elocution exercises, moral lessons, and orations (for example, *The Columbian Orator*). Role playing should enable students to imagine life in a mill or factory and a day in a Lancastrian school. Students should review the legal and economic status of women and learn about the major impetus given to the women's rights movement by leaders such as Susan B. Anthony and Elizabeth Cady Stanton. They should read and discuss the Seneca Falls Declaration of Sentiment and compare it with the Declaration of Independence. Efforts by educators such as Emma Willard and Mary Lyon to establish schools and colleges for women should be noted. Major campaigns to reform mental institutions and prisons should be explained by vividly portraying the conditions that evoked them. Students also should become familiar with the work of Dorothea Dix and the significance of Charles Finney as the leader of the second Great Awakening, inspiring religious zeal, moral commitment, and support for the abolitionist movement. Students should examine the relationship of these events to contemporary issues.

The South. During these years, the South diverged dramatically from the Northeast and the West. Its aristocratic tradition and plantation economy depended on a system of slave labor to harvest such cash crops as cotton, rice, sugarcane, and tobacco. Black slavery, the "peculiar institution" of the South, had marked effects on the region's political, social, economic, and cultural development. Increasingly at odds with the rest of the nation, the South was unable to share in the egalitarian surge of the Jacksonian era or in the reform campaigns of the 1840s. Its system of public education lagged far behind the rest of the nation.

Grade Eight

Standard 8.6.

Students analyze the divergent paths of the American people from 1800 to the mid-1800s and the challenges they faced, with emphasis on the Northeast.

Standard 8.6.3.

List the reasons for the wave of immigration from Northern Europe to the United States and describe the growth in the number, size, and spatial arrangements of cities (e.g., Irish immigrants and the Great Irish Famine).

Standard 8.7.

Students analyze the divergent paths of the American people in the South from 1800 to the mid-1800s and the challenges they faced.

Course
Descriptions

Grade Eight

The institution of slavery in the South should be studied in its historical context. Students should review their seventh-grade studies of West African civilizations before the coming of the Europeans and compare the American system of chattel slavery, which considered people as property, with slavery in other societies. Attention should be paid to the daily lives of slaves on the plantations, the inhuman practices of slave auctions, the illiteracy enforced on slaves by law, and the many laws that suppressed the efforts of slaves to win their freedom. Students should observe how these laws became increasingly severe following the 1831 slave revolts in South Carolina and Virginia. Particular attention should be paid to the more than 100,000 free blacks in the South and the laws that curbed their freedom and economic opportunity. Students should also compare the situations of free blacks in the South and in the North and note that freedom from slavery did not necessarily lead to acceptance and equality.

The dramatic story of the abolitionist movement, led by people such as Theodore Weld and William Lloyd Garrison, should be told. Attention should be given to what blacks did themselves in working for their own freedom: their organizations, which mobilized legal action; their petitions to Congress for redress of the fugitive slave laws and for emancipation of the slaves; the activities of leading black abolitionists such as Frederick Douglass, Charles Remond, and Sojourner Truth; and the direct actions of free blacks such as Harriet Tubman and Robert Purvis in the underground movement to assist slaves to escape.

Excerpts from Frederick Douglass's *What the Black Man Wants,* David Walker's *Appeal,* Harriet Beecher Stowe's *Uncle Tom's Cabin,* and Fanny Kemble's *Description of Life on a Southern Plantation,* as well as excerpts from slave narratives and abolitionist tracts of this period, will bring these people and events alive for students.

Research, Evidence, and Point of View 4.

Students assess the credibility of primary and secondary sources and draw sound conclusions from them.

Standard 8.9.

Students analyze the early and steady attempts to abolish slavery and to realize the ideals of the Declaration of Independence.

Toward a More Perfect Union: 1850–1879

In this unit students concentrate on the causes and consequences of the Civil War. They should discover how the issue of slavery eventually became too divisive to ignore or tolerate. They should understand the significance of such events as the Wilmot Proviso, the Compromise of 1850, the Kansas-Nebraska Act, the Ostend Manifesto, the Dred Scott case, and the Lincoln-Douglas debates. Students should understand the basic challenge to the Constitution and the Union posed by the secession of the southern states and the doctrine of nullification. The war itself should be studied closely, both the critical battlefield campaigns and the human meaning of the war in the lives of soldiers, free blacks, slaves, women, and others. Special attention should be paid to Abraham Lincoln's presidency, including his Gettysburg Address, the Emancipation Proclamation, and his inaugural addresses.

The Civil War should be treated as a watershed in American history. It resolved a challenge to the very existence of the nation, demolished (and mythologized) the antebellum way of life in the South, and created the prototype of modern warfare. To understand the ordeal of Reconstruction, students should consider the economic and social changes that came with the end of slavery and how blacks attained political freedom and exercised power within a few years after the war. They should learn of the postwar struggle for control of the South and of the impeachment of President Andrew Johnson. A federal civil rights bill granting full equality to black Americans was followed by adoption of the thirteenth, fourteenth, and fifteenth amendments. Black citizens, newly organized as Republicans, influenced the direction of southern politics and elected 22 members of Congress. Students should examine the Reconstruction governments in the South; observe the reaction of Southerners toward northern "carpetbaggers" and to the Freedman's Bureau, which sent northern teachers to educate the ex-slaves; and consider the consequences of the 1872 Amnesty Act and the fateful election of 1876, followed by the prompt withdrawal of federal troops from the South.

Grade Eight

Standard 8.10.

Students analyze the multiple causes, key events, and complex consequences of the Civil War.

Students should analyze how events during and after Reconstruction raised and then dashed the hopes of black Americans for full equality. They should understand how the thirteenth, fourteenth, and fifteenth amendments to the Constitution were undermined by the courts and political interests. They should learn how slavery was replaced by black peonage, segregation, Jim Crow laws, and other legal restrictions on the rights of blacks, capped by the Supreme Court's *Plessy* v. *Ferguson* decision in 1896 ("separate but equal"). Racism prevailed, enforced by lynch mobs, the Ku Klux Klan, and popular sentiment. Students also should understand the connection between these amendments and the civil rights movement of the 1960s. Although undermined by the courts a century ago, these amendments became the basis for all civil rights progress in the twentieth century.

Standard 8.11.

Students analyze the character and lasting consequences of Reconstruction.

Historical Interpretation 4.

Students recognize the role of chance, oversight, and error in history.

The Rise of Industrial America: 1877–1914

The period from the end of Reconstruction to World War I transformed the nation. This complex period was marked by the settling of the trans-Mississippi West, the expansion and concentration of basic industries, the establishment of national transportation networks, a human tidal wave of immigration from southern and eastern Europe, growth in the number and size of cities, accumulation of great fortunes by a small number of entrepreneurs, the rise of organized labor, and increased American involvement in foreign affairs. The building of the transcontinental railroad, the destruction of the buffalo, the Indian wars, and the removal of American Indians to reservations are events to be studied and analyzed. Reading Chief Joseph's words of surrender to U.S. Army troops in 1877 will help students grasp the heroism

Standard 8.12.

Students analyze the transformation of the American economy and the changing social and political conditions in the United States in response to the Industrial Revolution.

Course
Descriptions

Grade Eight

**Historical
Interpretation 6.**

Students interpret basic
indicators of economic
performance and conduct
cost-benefit analyses of
economic and political
issues.

and human tragedy that accompanied the conquest of this last frontier. By
1914 the frontier was closed, and the forty-eighth state had entered the Union.

Progress was spurred by new technology in the farming, manufacturing,
engineering, and producing of consumer goods. Mass production, the
department store, suspension bridges, the telegraph, the discovery of electricity,
high-rise buildings, and the streetcar seemed to confirm the idea of unending
progress, only occasionally slowed by temporary periods of financial distress.
Yet, beneath the surface of the "Gilded Age," there was a dark side, seen in the
activities of corrupt political bosses; in the ruthless practices of businesses; in
the depths of poverty and unemployment experienced in the teeming cities; in
the grinding labor of women and children in sweatshops, mills, and factories; in
the prejudice displayed against blacks, Hispanics, Catholics, Jews, Asians, and
other newcomers; and in the violence associated with labor unrest.

Attention should be given to the developing West and Southwest during
these years. The great mines and large-scale commercial farming of this region
provided essential resources for the industrial development of the nation.
Families from Mexico increasingly provided the labor force that developed this
region. Students should understand the social, economic, and political
handicaps encountered by these immigrants. Yet, Mexican-American
communities survived and even thrived, strengthened by their rich cultural
traditions and community life.

Students should examine the importance of social Darwinism as a
justification for child labor, unregulated working conditions, and laissez-faire
policies toward big business. They should consider the political programs and
activities of Populists, Progressives, settlement house workers, muckrakers, and
other reformers. They should follow the rise of the labor movement and
understand the changing role of government in ameliorating social and
economic conditions.

The consolidation of public education in the United States and the
dramatic growth of public high school enrollments should be noted. By
discussing what a typical day was like for their counterparts during these years
and reading stories and poems from the *McGuffey Readers,* which were used by
more than half the school-age population in the late nineteenth century,
students gain a sense of what these schools were like.

This period also was notable for the extension of the United States beyond
its borders. Students can trace the major trends in our foreign policy, from
George Washington's Farewell Address to the Monroe Doctrine, from our
involvement in the Spanish-American War to interventionist policies of
Theodore Roosevelt and Woodrow Wilson, culminating in our entry into
World War I. By discussing and debating the issues, students should be able
to formulate appropriate questions about the American role in these wars.

Literature should deepen students' understanding of the life of this period, including the immigrant experience, portrayed in Willa Cather's *My Antonia* and O. E. Rolvaag's *Giants in the Earth;* life in the slums, portrayed in Jacob Riis's books; and Mark Twain's *Huckleberry Finn,* unsurpassed as a sardonic commentary on the times.

Linking Past to Present

In this last unit students should examine the transformation of social conditions in the United States from 1914 to the present. They should assess major changes in the social and economic status of blacks, immigrants, women, religious minorities, children, and workers. Students should analyze the economic handicaps on the life chances of a person without an education then and now. They should understand how economic changes have eliminated certain kinds of jobs and created others. They should have a sense of the economic growth in twentieth-century America that has drawn most people into the middle class while leaving a significant minority behind.

To understand the changes that have occurred in social conditions over time, students should analyze the role of the Constitution as a mechanism to guarantee the rights of individuals and to ban discrimination. Teachers should encourage discussion of the citizen's ethical obligation to oppose discrimination against individuals and groups and the converse obligation to work toward a society in which all people enjoy equal rights and a good life. In this unit students should ask themselves: How have things changed over time? Why did these changes occur? They should discuss how citizens in a democracy can influence events and, through participation, apply ethical standards to public life.

Course
Descriptions

Grade Eight

Research, Evidence, and Point of View 3.

Students distinguish . . . verifiable from unverifiable information in historical narratives and stories.

Chronological and Spatial Thinking 1.

Students explain how major events are related to one another in time.

Historical Interpretation 3.

Students explain the sources of historical continuity and how the combination of ideas and events explains the emergence of new patterns.

History–Social Science Standards

Grade Eight
United States History and Geography:
Growth and Conflict

8.1 **Students understand the major events preceding the founding of the nation and relate their significance to the development of American constitutional democracy.**

1. Describe the relationship between the moral and political ideas of the Great Awakening and the development of revolutionary fervor.

2. Analyze the philosophy of government expressed in the Declaration of Independence, with an emphasis on government as a means of securing individual rights (e.g., key phrases such as "all men are created equal, that they are endowed by their Creator with certain unalienable Rights").

3. Analyze how the American Revolution affected other nations, especially France.

4. Describe the nation's blend of civic republicanism, classical liberal principles, and English parliamentary traditions.

8.2 **Students analyze the political principles underlying the U.S. Constitution and compare the enumerated and implied powers of the federal government.**

1. Discuss the significance of the Magna Carta, the English Bill of Rights, and the Mayflower Compact.

2. Analyze the Articles of Confederation and the Constitution and the success of each in implementing the ideals of the Declaration of Independence.

3. Evaluate the major debates that occurred during the development of the Constitution and their ultimate resolutions in such areas as shared power among institutions, divided state-federal power, slavery, the rights of individuals and states (later addressed by the addition of the Bill of Rights), and the status of American Indian nations under the commerce clause.

4. Describe the political philosophy underpinning the Constitution as specified in the *Federalist Papers* (authored by James Madison, Alexander Hamilton, and John Jay) and the role of such leaders as Madison, George Washington, Roger Sherman, Gouverneur Morris, and James Wilson in the writing and ratification of the Constitution.

5. Understand the significance of Jefferson's Statute for Religious Freedom as a forerunner of the First Amendment and the origins,

purpose, and differing views of the founding fathers on the issue of the separation of church and state.

6. Enumerate the powers of government set forth in the Constitution and the fundamental liberties ensured by the Bill of Rights.

7. Describe the principles of federalism, dual sovereignty, separation of powers, checks and balances, the nature and purpose of majority rule, and the ways in which the American idea of constitutionalism preserves individual rights.

8.3   Students understand the foundation of the American political system and the ways in which citizens participate in it.

1. Analyze the principles and concepts codified in state constitutions between 1777 and 1781 that created the context out of which American political institutions and ideas developed.

2. Explain how the ordinances of 1785 and 1787 privatized national resources and transferred federally owned lands into private holdings, townships, and states.

3. Enumerate the advantages of a common market among the states as foreseen in and protected by the Constitution's clauses on interstate commerce, common coinage, and full-faith and credit.

4. Understand how the conflicts between Thomas Jefferson and Alexander Hamilton resulted in the emergence of two political parties (e.g., view of foreign policy, Alien and Sedition Acts, economic policy, National Bank, funding and assumption of the revolutionary debt).

5. Know the significance of domestic resistance movements and ways in which the central government responded to such movements (e.g., Shays' Rebellion, the Whiskey Rebellion).

6. Describe the basic law-making process and how the Constitution provides numerous opportunities for citizens to participate in the political process and to monitor and influence government (e.g., function of elections, political parties, interest groups).

7. Understand the functions and responsibilities of a free press.

8.4   Students analyze the aspirations and ideals of the people of the new nation.

1. Describe the country's physical landscapes, political divisions, and territorial expansion during the terms of the first four presidents.

2. Explain the policy significance of famous speeches (e.g., Washington's Farewell Address, Jefferson's 1801 Inaugural Address, John Q. Adams's Fourth of July 1821 Address).

3. Analyze the rise of capitalism and the economic problems and conflicts that accompanied it (e.g., Jackson's opposition to the

National Bank; early decisions of the U.S. Supreme Court that reinforced the sanctity of contracts and a capitalist economic system of law).

4. Discuss daily life, including traditions in art, music, and literature, of early national America (e.g., through writings by Washington Irving, James Fenimore Cooper).

8.5   Students analyze U.S. foreign policy in the early Republic.

1. Understand the political and economic causes and consequences of the War of 1812 and know the major battles, leaders, and events that led to a final peace.

2. Know the changing boundaries of the United States and describe the relationships the country had with its neighbors (current Mexico and Canada) and Europe, including the influence of the Monroe Doctrine, and how those relationships influenced westward expansion and the Mexican-American War.

3. Outline the major treaties with American Indian nations during the administrations of the first four presidents and the varying outcomes of those treaties.

8.6   Students analyze the divergent paths of the American people from 1800 to the mid-1800s and the challenges they faced, with emphasis on the Northeast.

1. Discuss the influence of industrialization and technological developments on the region, including human modification of the landscape and how physical geography shaped human actions (e.g., growth of cities, deforestation, farming, mineral extraction).

2. Outline the physical obstacles to and the economic and political factors involved in building a network of roads, canals, and railroads (e.g., Henry Clay's American System).

3. List the reasons for the wave of immigration from Northern Europe to the United States and describe the growth in the number, size, and spatial arrangements of cities (e.g., Irish immigrants and the Great Irish Famine).

4. Study the lives of black Americans who gained freedom in the North and founded schools and churches to advance their rights and communities.

5. Trace the development of the American education system from its earliest roots, including the roles of religious and private schools and Horace Mann's campaign for free public education and its assimilating role in American culture.

6. Examine the women's suffrage movement (e.g., biographies, writings, and speeches of Elizabeth Cady Stanton, Margaret Fuller, Lucretia Mott, Susan B. Anthony).

7. Identify common themes in American art as well as transcendentalism and individualism (e.g., writings about and by Ralph Waldo Emerson, Henry David Thoreau, Herman Melville, Louisa May Alcott, Nathaniel Hawthorne, Henry Wadsworth Longfellow).

8.7 **Students analyze the divergent paths of the American people in the South from 1800 to the mid-1800s and the challenges they faced.**

1. Describe the development of the agrarian economy in the South, identify the locations of the cotton-producing states, and discuss the significance of cotton and the cotton gin.

2. Trace the origins and development of slavery; its effects on black Americans and on the region's political, social, religious, economic, and cultural development; and identify the strategies that were tried to both overturn and preserve it (e.g., through the writings and historical documents on Nat Turner, Denmark Vesey).

3. Examine the characteristics of white Southern society and how the physical environment influenced events and conditions prior to the Civil War.

4. Compare the lives of and opportunities for free blacks in the North with those of free blacks in the South.

8.8 **Students analyze the divergent paths of the American people in the West from 1800 to the mid-1800s and the challenges they faced.**

1. Discuss the election of Andrew Jackson as president in 1828, the importance of Jacksonian democracy, and his actions as president (e.g., the spoils system, veto of the National Bank, policy of Indian removal, opposition to the Supreme Court).

2. Describe the purpose, challenges, and economic incentives associated with westward expansion, including the concept of Manifest Destiny (e.g., the Lewis and Clark expedition, accounts of the removal of Indians, the Cherokees' "Trail of Tears," settlement of the Great Plains) and the territorial acquisitions that spanned numerous decades.

3. Describe the role of pioneer women and the new status that western women achieved (e.g., Laura Ingalls Wilder, Annie Bidwell; slave women gaining freedom in the West; Wyoming granting suffrage to women in 1869).

4. Examine the importance of the great rivers and the struggle over water rights.

5. Discuss Mexican settlements and their locations, cultural traditions, attitudes toward slavery, land-grant system, and economies.

6. Describe the Texas War for Independence and the Mexican-American War, including territorial settlements, the aftermath of the wars, and the effects the wars had on the lives of Americans, including Mexican Americans today.

8.9 **Students analyze the early and steady attempts to abolish slavery and to realize the ideals of the Declaration of Independence.**

1. Describe the leaders of the movement (e.g., John Quincy Adams and his proposed constitutional amendment, John Brown and the armed resistance, Harriet Tubman and the Underground Railroad, Benjamin Franklin, Theodore Weld, William Lloyd Garrison, Frederick Douglass).

2. Discuss the abolition of slavery in early state constitutions.

3. Describe the significance of the Northwest Ordinance in education and in the banning of slavery in new states north of the Ohio River.

4. Discuss the importance of the slavery issue as raised by the annexation of Texas and California's admission to the union as a free state under the Compromise of 1850.

5. Analyze the significance of the States' Rights Doctrine, the Missouri Compromise (1820), the Wilmot Proviso (1846), the Compromise of 1850, Henry Clay's role in the Missouri Compromise and the Compromise of 1850, the Kansas-Nebraska Act (1854), the *Dred Scott* v. *Sandford* decision (1857), and the Lincoln-Douglas debates (1858).

6. Describe the lives of free blacks and the laws that limited their freedom and economic opportunities.

8.10 **Students analyze the multiple causes, key events, and complex consequences of the Civil War.**

1. Compare the conflicting interpretations of state and federal authority as emphasized in the speeches and writings of statesmen such as Daniel Webster and John C. Calhoun.

2. Trace the boundaries constituting the North and the South, the geographical differences between the two regions, and the differences between agrarians and industrialists.

3. Identify the constitutional issues posed by the doctrine of nullification and secession and the earliest origins of that doctrine.

4. Discuss Abraham Lincoln's presidency and his significant writings and speeches and their relationship to the Declaration of Independence, such as his "House Divided" speech (1858), Gettysburg

Address (1863), Emancipation Proclamation (1863), and inaugural
addresses (1861 and 1865).

5. Study the views and lives of leaders (e.g., Ulysses S. Grant, Jefferson
   Davis, Robert E. Lee) and soldiers on both sides of the war, including
   those of black soldiers and regiments.

6. Describe critical developments and events in the war, including the
   major battles, geographical advantages and obstacles, technological
   advances, and General Lee's surrender at Appomattox.

7. Explain how the war affected combatants, civilians, the physical
   environment, and future warfare.

**8.11 Students analyze the character and lasting consequences of
Reconstruction.**

1. List the original aims of Reconstruction and describe its effects on the
   political and social structures of different regions.

2. Identify the push-pull factors in the movement of former slaves to the
   cities in the North and to the West and their differing experiences in
   those regions (e.g., the experiences of Buffalo Soldiers).

3. Understand the effects of the Freedmen's Bureau and the restrictions
   placed on the rights and opportunities of freedmen, including racial
   segregation and "Jim Crow" laws.

4. Trace the rise of the Ku Klux Klan and describe the Klan's effects.

5. Understand the Thirteenth, Fourteenth, and Fifteenth Amendments
   to the Constitution and analyze their connection to Reconstruction.

**8.12 Students analyze the transformation of the American economy
and the changing social and political conditions in the United States
in response to the Industrial Revolution.**

1. Trace patterns of agricultural and industrial development as they
   relate to climate, use of natural resources, markets, and trade and
   locate such development on a map.

2. Identify the reasons for the development of federal Indian policy and
   the wars with American Indians and their relationship to agricultural
   development and industrialization.

3. Explain how states and the federal government encouraged business
   expansion through tariffs, banking, land grants, and subsidies.

4. Discuss entrepreneurs, industrialists, and bankers in politics, commerce, and industry (e.g., Andrew Carnegie, John D. Rockefeller,
   Leland Stanford).

5. Examine the location and effects of urbanization, renewed immigration, and industrialization (e.g., the effects on social fabric of cities,
   wealth and economic opportunity, the conservation movement).

6. Discuss child labor, working conditions, and laissez-faire policies toward big business and examine the labor movement, including its leaders (e.g., Samuel Gompers), its demand for collective bargaining, and its strikes and protests over labor conditions.

7. Identify the new sources of large-scale immigration and the contributions of immigrants to the building of cities and the economy; explain the ways in which new social and economic patterns encouraged assimilation of newcomers into the mainstream amidst growing cultural diversity; and discuss the new wave of nativism.

8. Identify the characteristics and impact of Grangerism and Populism.

9. Name the significant inventors and their inventions and identify how they improved the quality of life (e.g., Thomas Edison, Alexander Graham Bell, Orville and Wilbur Wright).

Course
Descriptions

Grades Six
Through Eight
Historical
and Social Sciences
Analysis Skills

Grades Six Through Eight
Historical and Social Sciences Analysis Skills

The intellectual skills noted below are to be learned through, and applied to, the content standards for grades six through eight. They are to be assessed *only in conjunction with* the content standards in grades six through eight.

In addition to the standards for grades six through eight, students demonstrate the following intellectual reasoning, reflection, and research skills:

Chronological and Spatial Thinking

1. Students explain how major events are related to one another in time.
2. Students construct various time lines of key events, people, and periods of the historical era they are studying.
3. Students use a variety of maps and documents to identify physical and cultural features of neighborhoods, cities, states, and countries and to explain the historical migration of people, expansion and disintegration of empires, and the growth of economic systems.

Research, Evidence, and Point of View

1. Students frame questions that can be answered by historical study and research.
2. Students distinguish fact from opinion in historical narratives and stories.
3. Students distinguish relevant from irrelevant information, essential from incidental information, and verifiable from unverifiable information in historical narratives and stories.
4. Students assess the credibility of primary and secondary sources and draw sound conclusions from them.
5. Students detect the different historical points of view on historical events and determine the context in which the historical statements were made (the questions asked, sources used, author's perspectives).

Historical Interpretation

1. Students explain the central issues and problems from the past, placing people and events in a matrix of time and place.
2. Students understand and distinguish cause, effect, sequence, and correlation in historical events, including the long- and short-term causal relations.
3. Students explain the sources of historical continuity and how the combination of ideas and events explains the emergence of new patterns.
4. Students recognize the role of chance, oversight, and error in history.
5. Students recognize that interpretations of history are subject to change as new information is uncovered.
6. Students interpret basic indicators of economic performance and conduct cost-benefit analyses of economic and political issues.

The Secondary Curriculum
Grades Nine Through Twelve

Developmental Considerations

The years of early adolescence have been termed a watershed in the development of students' political and historical thought.[1] Students who at age twelve are only beginning to be able to entertain abstract historical or political ideas or reasoning processes will normally, by age sixteen, have the capacity to engage in analytical thought that is "recognizably adult." This change does not emerge full-blown nor, once under development, is it consistently displayed. High school teachers, just as those in junior high schools, must recognize the continuing need of many students for concrete illustrations and instructional approaches if they are to understand and relate to these political and historical studies. However, the secondary school curriculum must provide learning opportunities that challenge students' growing abstract analytical thinking capabilities if high school students are to be helped to develop these skills.

These more abstract reasoning skills emerge with the adolescent's development of formal thought. Formal thought allows students to develop abstract understanding of historical causality—the often complex patterns of relationships between historical events, their multiple antecedents, and their consequences considered over time. Formal thought also allows students to grasp the workings of political and social systems as *systems* and to engage in higher levels of policy analysis and decision making. In addition, formal thought permits students to deepen and extend their understanding of the more demanding civic learnings: understanding, for example, political conflict in a free society and its resolution under law; understanding the fundamental substantive and procedural values guaranteed by the Constitution; and understanding the close and reciprocating relationships between society and the law within a nation whose Constitution is a charter of principles, not a Napoleonic code.

In this curriculum these advanced historical, political, and civic learnings and advanced critical thinking skills are developed in grades nine through twelve. The course titles for grades nine through twelve with major subtitles are as follows:

Grade Nine—Elective Courses in History–Social Science
- Our State in the Twentieth and Twenty-First Centuries
- Physical Geography

---

[1]Daniel Keating, "Adolescent Thinking," in *At the Threshold: The Developing Adolescent,* S. Feldman and G. Elliot, editors, Cambridge, Mass.: Harvard University Press, 1990, pp. 54–89, and Joseph Adelson, "The Political Imagination of the Young Adolescent," *Daedalus,* Vol. 100 (Fall 1971), pp. 1013–50.

- World Regional Geography
- The Humanities
- Comparative World Religions
- Area Studies: Cultures
- Anthropology
- Psychology
- Sociology
- Women in Our History
- Ethnic Studies
- Law-Related Education

Grade Ten—World History, Culture, and Geography: The Modern World

- Unresolved Problems of the Modern World
- Connecting with Past Learnings: The Rise of Democratic Ideas
- The Industrial Revolution
- The Rise of Imperialism and Colonialism: A Case Study of India
- World War I and Its Consequences
- Totalitarianism in the Modern World: Nazi Germany and Stalinist Russia
- World War II: Its Causes and Consequences
- Nationalism in the Contemporary World
  - The Soviet Union and China
  - The Middle East: Israel and Syria
  - Sub-Saharan Africa: Ghana and South Africa
  - Latin America: Mexico and Brazil

Grade Eleven—United States History and Geography: Continuity and Change in the Twentieth and Twenty-First Centuries

- Connecting with Past Learnings: The Nation's Beginnings
- Connecting with Past Learnings: The United States to 1900
- The Progressive Era
- The Jazz Age
- The Great Depression
- World War II
- The Cold War
- Hemispheric Relationships in the Postwar Era
- The Civil Rights Movement in the Postwar Era
- American Society in the Postwar Era
- The United States in Recent Times

Grade Twelve—Principles of American Democracy (One Semester)

- The Constitution and the Bill of Rights
- The Courts and the Governmental Process
- Our Government Today: The Legislative and Executive Branches

- Federalism: State and Local Government
- Comparative Governments, with Emphasis on Communism in the World Today
- Contemporary Issues in the World Today

Grade Twelve—Economics (One Semester)

- Fundamental Economic Concepts
- Comparative Economic Systems
- Microeconomics
- Macroeconomics
- International Economic Concepts

Grade Nine— Elective Courses in History–Social Science

The ninth-grade history–social science curriculum consists of two semesters of elective courses. These courses might consist of two separate topics of one semester each or a two-semester study of a single topic. These courses should build on the knowledge and experience that students have gained in kindergarten through grade eight. They also should contribute substantially to students' preparation for the three *subsequent* years of history–social science education that are mandated in *Education Code* Section 51225.3.

Courses offered should be planned carefully by the district and school and should be consistent with the curricular goals presented in this framework. Placement of students in elective courses should reflect thoughtful counseling at the local school level and should consider the particular needs or interests of the student and the length of time the student has been in the United States. Courses that are not considered appropriate as a history–social science elective include freshman orientation studies, computer literacy, driver training, student government or leadership, drug abuse education, career planning, family life education, and courses that reflect state requirements. Such offerings are more appropriate for other departments. The following courses meet the intent and philosophy of this framework:

Our State in the Twentieth and Twenty-First Centuries

This course, which can be presented in one or two semesters, provides students with the opportunity to study contemporary California, its history and geography, its multicultural heritage, its government and economy, the major issues facing the state, and the ways in which students can become active participants in its future.

Opportunities should be included for students to become familiar with the local community through field studies, special community projects, interviews, and other participation activities. In addition, teachers are encouraged to use the community as a major resource for speakers. In drawing on evidence from the present as well as the past, students should learn that individual citizens can influence public policy through participation and can make a difference in the economic, political, and social development of their state.

In studying California's government, students should learn the organization and function of local, county, and state political systems and their relation to the federal government. The role of public education should be included. Study of the legal system should include the procedures of our court system and the basic legal issues relevant to criminal, civil, and juvenile justice. The role and activities of law enforcement should be examined within this context.

Case studies provide students with opportunities to apply and refine critical thinking skills associated with problem solving and civic participation. These studies should focus on contemporary California issues and controversies in such fields as:

- The conflict between increased economic growth and environmental priorities
- The increasing diversity within every aspect of the state: economic, social, cultural, and political
- The types of job opportunities available and the education needed to be employed successfully

By studying contemporary issues, students learn that various forces have brought California to its present position of influence in the United States, the Pacific Basin, and the rest of the world.

Physical Geography

This one-semester course develops the basic themes of physical geography, including a systematic discussion of the physical landscape through geomorphology and topography; the patterns and processes of climate and weather; and water resources through hydrology. These studies equip students with an understanding of the constraints and possibilities that the physical environment places on human development. In addition to these systematic themes, attention is given to the nature of natural resources and their relation to physical geography. Finally, a component of the course is given to place-name geography so that students develop a good sense of where major physical features of the earth are located.

World Regional Geography

One of the realities of the contemporary world is the increasing influence of other nations in the daily life of the American citizen. This course in World

Regional Geography is designed to provide understanding of the distribution and characteristics of the world's major cultures and of the dynamics of human migration and cultural diffusion.

A unit on "The Earth and Its Peoples" introduces basic physical geography and map-reading skills. In the remainder of the course, students consider the regional mosaic of the world through a series of studies moving from Western Europe to the Soviet Union and Eastern Europe, the Middle East, and North Africa. They then study sub-Saharan Africa, Asia, the Pacific Basin, and Latin America. For each of these regions, selected nations are studied in depth.

The final unit focuses on Canada and the United States, with emphasis on cultural and political comparisons between these nations and on their economic relationships today. Attention is given to the traditional and contemporary roles foreign nations play in the growth of American culture.

The Humanities

This course focuses on this question: What does it mean to be human? The purpose of this course is to stretch students' imagination, enrich their experience, and increase their distinctively human potential.[2]

Traditionally, humanities studies have emphasized written works, enriched by the arts of painting, sculpture, architecture, music, drama, and dance. In studying the humanities today, students look not only at books and works of art, but also at buildings, rituals, social groups, and political institutions as examples of the creative power of the human mind and spirit. Recently expanded fields of study have included linguistics, archaeology, architecture, law, the history of religions, and the humanistic approach to science and technology.

In designing a humanities course, teachers should draw on the specific records and artifacts of particular people; the things they make, say, or sing; and the expressive forms and objects they create. Classical texts of Western and non-Western cultures should be used. Selections from the arts should be included because they constitute major forms of expression and offer students modes of learning no other discipline provides. Oral cultural forms, film, television, computer-generated designs, and new technology used in the study of cultural artifacts can be introduced. Students' writing should serve as an expressive response to the works of others as well as a major way of forming one's own ideas. The role of racial and ethnic groups within American society and their contributions to our common civilization can be studied in the quest to determine how we came to be what we are today.

Through these varied approaches to the study of the humanities, the teacher fosters critical analysis and understanding, sympathetic insight, perception of the motivation and intentions of others, the ability to distinguish

---

[2]*Humanities in American Life.* Berkeley: University of California Press, 1980, p. 29.

between different values, and the power of the imagination and all the senses to respond intuitively and creatively to the many possibilities of human expression.

Survey of World Religions

In this course students consider the principal religions of the world that are active today, influencing the lives of millions and impressing their image on the contemporary world. Students deal with basic questions: What does humankind believe and what does it worship? In what ways? With what understandings of the ethical life? And with what influence on contemporary times and cultures? In this course students are introduced to:

- Judaism's basis in ethical monotheism; its historic belief in the covenant between God and the Jewish people; the Torah as the source of Judaism's beliefs, rituals, and laws; and the Torah's ethical injunction, "Do justice, love mercy, and walk humbly with thy God"
- Christianity's continuity with Judaism; its belief that Jesus of Nazareth fulfilled Old Testament expectations of the Messiah; and its faith that in His Crucifixion and Resurrection, Jesus Christ reconciled the world to God so that, through forgiveness of sin, the eternal life of God could now flow into the lives of human beings
- Islam's continuity with Judaism and Christianity in its proclamation of belief in one God; its belief that God's will has been given final expression in the Koran in words revealed to the last and the greatest of the prophets, Mohammed; and its observances of the "Five Pillars of Islam"
- Buddhism's origins in the Buddha or Enlightened One; its path of enlightenment through meditation; its ethical mandate to inflict no suffering; and its acceptance of the transmigration of the soul, of Karma, and of Nirvana, the ultimate state of all being
- Hinduism's belief in monism, the oneness of all gods and all living things in the Divine One, Brahma; in pure and unchanging spirit behind the impermanence of the material world; in the peace found only in union with the eternal spirit of Brahma; and in reincarnation, Karma, and Hindu ethics

Beyond these central beliefs, students also develop understandings of the following:

- The explanations given by different religions for the origin of humankind
- The present-day numbers, influence, and geographic distribution of followers of each faith
- The differences between the original tenets of these religions; their historical development; and the major variations in beliefs, sects, or interpretations presently associated with each

Area Studies: Cultures

A course in area studies focuses on an investigation of one or more cultures within a geographic region of the world today; for example, culture studies of the Middle East, Latin America, or Southeast Asia. This study might also compare characteristics of the culture(s) studied with those of similar and diverse cultures.

In the study of a culture, attention should be given to its geographic setting; the population, including traditional and modern family and social life; the status and roles of women and minority groups; and processes of cultural change and exchange. Topics of study should include the philosophies, religions, ideologies, ethics, and values of the culture; its language; its law and education; its literature; its science, mathematics, and medicine; its technology; and its arts, both performing and applied. Attention should be given to the culture's historical, economic, and political developments, including nation building, across time.

Cultures selected for emphasis could include one that is introduced in the curriculum for kindergarten through grade twelve and presented here to deepen and expand students' knowledge. Cultures also can be chosen to enrich students' understanding of cultural diversity and to provide balance in the representation of ethnic groups and societies around the world.

Anthropology

In this introduction to anthropology, students learn about human beings and their cultures. The two major divisions of anthropology, physical and cultural, are studied.

In physical anthropology students consider the biological characteristics of human beings, their adaptation to their environment, and development in the context of various forms of animal life. In cultural anthropology students learn about the culture of a specific people, past and present, as well as those components of culture universally found among human societies. These components include technology or tools and the ability to use them: language; institutions or organized long-lasting ways of doing things; and belief systems. The course includes a study of the evolution of cultures, the organization of societies, and the processes and consequences of cultural change. By studying a variety of cultures, students should increase their understanding of their own culture and appreciation of humankind's universal qualities.

Psychology

In this course students are introduced to psychology, with a focus on the scientific study of human development, learning, motivation, and personality. Students should develop some basic concepts of psychology and a historical perspective on psychology as the study of individual behavior. They should read about the contributions of one or more major scholars in the field; for example, Sigmund Freud, Abraham Maslow, Ivan Pavlov, Carl Rogers, and B. F. Skinner. Students should have opportunities to explore implications for everyday life of a scientific perspective on human behavior, and they should learn about the various careers associated with this field of study.

Sociology

In this course students are introduced to sociological concepts, theories, and procedures. Students should learn how sociologists analyze the basic structures and functions of societies and of groups within societies, discover how these societies became organized, identify the conditions under which they become disorganized, and predict the conditions for their reorganization.

The topics studied include the family as the basic unit of society; the structure of groups; group phenomena; the role of the individual in groups; society and communication; personality and the socialization process; social relations and culture; demography and human ecology; social processes; and social control. Sociologists use the scientific method and social research to understand social behavior. Those interested in solving social problems also use these means of investigation together with the application of group processes. Typical study units for this course would include such social issues as crime, poverty, and the problem of discrimination toward the aged and minorities.

Women in Our History

In this course students study the history of American women, their roles in historical events, and the effects of historical events on women. This history of American women should demonstrate dramatic change as well as continuity. Women have influenced, as well as have been influenced by, improved access to education, changes in medicine and health, expanded economic opportunities, and areas of legal, political, and social equality.

The complexities of women's changing roles can be studied by using the following outline:

- Women as immigrants and as settlers, 1600–1900 (social change, status, and role)
- Women in the formation of the nation, 1776–1865 (political status, intellectual leadership, and social conscience), including women's roles in the abolitionist movement and the 1848 Women's Rights Convention
- Women's work and the response to industrialization, 1865–1900 (capital formation, economic exploitation, specialization, and role modification)
- The awakening women's movement in America, 1900–1940 (political justice, social justice, and role of ethnicity), including women in the Progressive movement, women's suffrage movement, and changing social roles

- The American feminist revolution, 1940 to the present (economic equality, legal equality, and role modification), including the effects of World War II, the creation of the Women's Movement, the Equal Rights Amendment, the issues of fair pay and equity, and changing roles and responsibilities in the family
- Creative endeavors, past and present

Ethnic Studies

In this course students focus on an in-depth study of ethnic groups, including their history, culture, contributions, and current status in the United States. They learn about the characteristics of America's ethnic groups and the similarities and differences of these groups in both their past and present experiences.

Students should understand the national origins of American ethnic groups. They should study the social, economic, and political forces that caused people to come to America. They should gain insights into the barriers that various ethnic groups have had to overcome in the past and present. They should learn about the opportunities these groups encountered and the contributions made by each to American society. Biographies of individual women and men should be read and analyzed. The experiences of ethnic groups should be examined within their historical context to help students recognize how these events were influenced by the social, economic, and political conditions of the time.

As a result of these studies, students should gain a deeper understanding of American society and its diverse ethnic composition and develop acceptance and respect for cultural diversity in our pluralistic society.

Law-Related Education

In this course students should gain a practical understanding of the law and the legal system that have been developed under the United States Constitution and Bill of Rights. They should become aware of current issues and controversies relating to law and the legal system and be encouraged to participate as citizens in the legal system. Students should be given opportunities to consider their attitudes toward the roles that lawyers, law enforcement officers, and others in the legal system play in our society. In addition, students should be exposed to the many vocational opportunities that exist within the legal system.

The course includes a study of concepts underlying the law as well as an introduction to the origin and development of our legal system, including civil and criminal law. In a unit on civic rights and responsibilities, students should learn about the rights guaranteed by the first, fourth, fifth, sixth, eighth, and fourteenth amendments. In a unit on education law, students should study the growing role of the courts in influencing school policy and practice. Mock trials and other simulated legal procedures together with the use of resource experts should help students understand this area.

Grade Ten— World History, Culture, and Geography: The Modern World

In this course students examine major turning points in the shaping of the modern world, from the late eighteenth century to the present. The year begins with an introduction to current world issues and then continues with a focus on the expansion of the West and the growing interdependence of people and cultures throughout the world.

Unresolved Problems of the Modern World

This course begins with a study of major problems in the world today. Examples include government-produced famine in parts of Africa; political instability, poverty, and crushing national debt in Latin America; war and terrorism; the global consequences of destruction of natural resources; economic and cultural dislocations caused by technological change; the proliferation of nuclear weapons; and the struggle to defend human rights and democratic freedoms against governments that respect neither. Each problem will be examined to illustrate the relationships between current issues and their historical, geographic, political, economic, and cultural contexts. Wherever possible, students should be made aware of those organizations that work to alleviate severe problems of poverty, disease, famine, and catastrophe. By discussing specific needs and the various means of sending aid, students can develop a positive response to many world problems and can feel their involvement will make a difference. Students should be encouraged to work on behalf of organizations appropriate to their interests and the point of view of their families.

Connecting with Past Learnings: The Rise of Democratic Ideas

Following an introduction to current world problems, this course will move to a review of the rise of democratic ideas. Students need to know the source of the ideas by which we judge ourselves as a political system and a society. Close attention will be paid to the evolution of democratic principles.

Students should review the moral and ethical principles of Judaism and Christianity that have profoundly influenced Western democratic thought, including belief in the dignity and equality of all; the search for social systems that ensure the freedom to make individual moral choice; and the duty of each to work for morally just communities.

Students should examine the significance of the Greek philosophers' belief in reason and natural law in relation to democratic ideas. Students should read

Chronological and Spatial Thinking 1.

Students compare the present with the past, evaluating the consequences of past events and decisions and determining the lessons that were learned.

Chronological and Spatial Thinking 3.

Students use a variety of maps and documents to interpret human movement, including major patterns of domestic and international migration, changing environmental preferences and settlement patterns, the frictions that develop between population groups, and the diffusion of ideas, technological innovations, and goods.

Standard 10.1.

Students relate the moral and ethical principles in ancient Greek and Roman philosophy, in Judaism, and in Christianity to the development of Western political thought.

Course
Descriptions

Grade Ten

Standard 10.2.

Students compare and
contrast the Glorious
Revolution of England, the
American Revolution, and
the French Revolution and
their enduring effects
worldwide on the political
expectations for self-
government and individual
liberty.

Standard 10.3.

Students analyze the effects
of the Industrial Revolution
in England, France,
Germany, Japan, and the
United States.

Standard 10.4.

Students analyze patterns
of global change in the era
of New Imperialism in at
least two of the following
regions or countries:
Africa, Southeast Asia,
China, India, Latin America,
and the Philippines.

selections from Plato's *Republic,* Aristotle's *Politics,* and books concerning political life in the city-state of Athens. The teacher should review significant democratic developments in England, particularly the Magna Carta, common law, the Parliament, and the English Bill of Rights of 1689.

Students should review the significant ideas of the Enlightenment thinkers, such as Locke and Rousseau, and their effect on democratic revolutions in England, the United States, France, and Latin America. These revolutions were mileposts in the development of political systems committed to a democratic form of government. The philosophy of natural rights and natural law on which the democratic revolutions were based should be fully discussed and analyzed, with particular attention to the language of the American Declaration of Independence.

Finally, the United States Constitution should be assessed as the summation of this evolving tradition of democratic ideals. Students should understand that political ideals such as equality, justice under law, and freedom, which we now take for granted, were achieved at a high price, remain vulnerable in the West, and are still not practiced in many parts of the world. Although democratic ideals first emerged in the West, almost every nation pays them at least rhetorical homage. In the present world even tyrants feel it necessary to clothe their regimes in the language of democratic ideas. The broad contemporary appeal of these ideas can be found by examining the United Nations' Universal Declaration of Human Rights.

The Industrial Revolution

In the next period of concentrated study, students focus on the Industrial Revolution, beginning in eighteenth-century England, and the major changes that the mechanization of production wrought in England's economy, politics, society, culture, and physical environment. Students should examine critical responses to the Industrial Revolution, such as the development of labor unions, the emergence of socialist thought, the Romantic impulse in art and literature (for example, the poetry of William Blake and William Wordsworth and the criticism of John Ruskin and William Morris), and the social criticism of Charles Dickens (for example, *Hard Times*). They also should be aware of successful social reforms, such as the abolition of slavery and reform of the "poor laws." It should be noted that the Industrial Revolution occurred somewhat later, though not with precisely the same consequences, in France, Germany, Japan, and Russia.

The Rise of Imperialism and Colonialism: A Case Study of India

In this unit students examine the worldwide imperial expansion that was fueled by the industrial nations' demand for natural resources and markets and by their nationalist aspirations. By studying maps, students will become aware of the colonial possessions of such nations as France, Germany, Italy, Japan, the Netherlands, and the United States.

Study of colonialism in India should begin with a review of Indian history preceding British rule as well as a consideration of the factors that opened India to colonial domination. Throughout the historical study of the Raj (British rule), students should view British imperialism both from the perspective of the peoples of India and of the colonial rulers. To understand the cultural conflicts between rulers and ruled, students should examine the principal beliefs of Hinduism, including the caste system, that have shaped the traditional, agrarian society of India for more than 5,000 years. The imagery of the *Ramayana*, both in art and the oral tradition, expresses the continuity and unity of traditional Indian society.

Students should discuss the differing beliefs and values of Hindu and Muslim cultures in India and the British contention that their presence prevented religious conflict. The study should conclude with a brief review of the historical aftermath of colonialism in India up to the present time, including the national movement; religious divisions; the important roles of Mohandas K. Gandhi, Jawaharlal Nehru, and Louis Mountbatten in preparing India for self-government; and the creation of the two states of Pakistan and India.

World War I and Its Consequences

The growth of nationalism, imperialism, and militarism provides the backdrop for consideration of World War I, which permanently changed the map of Europe and deeply affected the rest of the world. Students should understand the political conditions that led to the outbreak of the war in Europe. Caused in large measure by nationalism, the war stimulated even greater nationalist impulses by dissolving old empires, unleashing irredentist movements, and promoting the spirit of self-determination. Within the context of human rights and genocide, students should learn of the Ottoman government's planned mass deportation and systematic annihilation of the Armenian population in 1915. Students should also examine the reactions of other governments, including that of the United States, and world opinion during and after the Armenian genocide. They should examine the effects of the genocide on the remaining Armenian people, who were deprived of their historic homeland, and the ways in which it became a prototype of subsequent genocides.

Through novels, poems, posters, and videotapes, students should gain an understanding of prewar European culture; of the meaning of total war (targeting civilian populations); of malicious wartime propaganda and false reports of German atrocities; of the opposition to the war in the United States; and of the disillusion that followed the war, including the sense of a world lost, despair over the destruction of a generation of young men, and loss of idealism when the world turned out not to be "safe for democracy" after all. In studying the significant consequences of the war, students should understand the importance of Woodrow Wilson's abortive campaign for the League of Nations;

Standard 10.5.

Students analyze the causes and course of the First World War.

Standard 10.5.5.

Discuss human rights violations and genocide, including the Ottoman government's actions against Armenian citizens.

Course Descriptions

Grade Ten

Standard 10.6.

Students analyze the effects of the First World War.

Standard 10.7.

Students analyze the rise of totalitarian governments after World War I.

Historical Interpretation 1.

Students show the connections, causal and otherwise, between particular historical events and larger social, economic, and political trends and developments.

Standard 10.8.5.

Analyze the Nazi policy of pursuing racial purity, especially against the European Jews; its transformation into the Final Solution; and the Holocaust that resulted in the murder of six million Jewish civilians.

Historical Interpretation 4.

Students understand the meaning, implication, and impact of historical events and recognize that events could have taken other directions.

the rise of isolationism in the United States; the punitive terms of the peace imposed on Germany; the Russian Revolution and the national revolutions that resulted in the establishment of independent democratic republics such as Estonia, Latvia, Lithuania, Poland, and Ukraine; the Balfour Declaration (significant in the eventual creation of Israel); the role of women in the war efforts and the effect women's involvement had on social attitudes; the cultural changes after the war (for example, the "lost generation" of Ernest Hemingway, Gertrude Stein, F. Scott Fitzgerald, and others); the impact of Freudian psychology; and the changes wrought by new technology, such as the automobile, radio, and telephone.

Totalitarianism in the Modern World

The aftermath of World War I planted the seeds for another world conflict a generation later. The study of Nazi Germany and Stalinist Russia will illustrate the methods used by a totalitarian state to extinguish political freedom and to amass total control of a society and its politics within a single party and under a single leader. Special attention should be devoted to the destruction of human rights by these two dictatorships. The Holocaust and the famine in Ukraine should receive close attention. This unit offers rich opportunities for analyzing relationships among history, political ideology, governmental structure, economics, cultural traditions, and geography and observing the ways that art and literature can reflect and comment on social conditions.

Nazi Germany

The rise of Hitler should be examined in relation to Germany's postwar economic crisis; the collapse of the Weimar Republic; and Hitler's successful appeal to racism and what the historian Fritz Stern called "the politics of cultural despair." German art, music, and literature (for example, George Grosz and Bertolt Brecht) will deepen students' understanding of this era.

Hitler's policy of pursuing racial purity and its transformation into the Final Solution and the Holocaust should receive close attention. To place Hitler's claim to Aryan superiority in perspective, students should examine the highly developed Jewish culture of central Europe that produced a great number of artists such as Marc Chagall, Gustav Mahler, Arnold Schoenberg, and Franz Kafka; scientists such as Albert Einstein and Sigmund Freud; and scholars such as Edmund Husserl and Rudolph Lipschitz.

Study of the Holocaust should focus students' attention on the Nazi party's racist ideology, the suppression of rights and freedoms, and the Final Solution— a systematic policy of extermination of all Jews and other "non-Aryan" peoples. The Holocaust's horror is underscored by the number of people killed, including 6 million Jews, as well as the Nazis' ruthless utilization of bureaucratic social organization and modern technology to gather, classify, and eradicate their victims. Genocides, such as that perpetrated on the Armenians, already had demonstrated the human capacity for mass murder. The Nazis perfected the social organization of human evil and provided an efficient and frightening model for future despots such as Pol Pot in Cambodia. Students should learn about *Krystallnacht;* about death camps; and about the Nazi persecution of Gypsies, homosexuals, and others who failed to meet the Aryan ideal. They should analyze the failure of Western governments to offer refuge to those fleeing nazism. They should discuss abortive revolts such as that which occurred in the Warsaw Ghetto, and they should discuss the moral courage of Christians such as Dietrich Bonhoeffer and Raoul Wallenberg, who risked their lives to save Jews.

Numerous videotapes and books (for example, *The Diary of Anne Frank* and Elie Wiesel's *Night*) are available to demonstrate the gruesome reality of the Final Solution. The purpose is not to shock but to engage students in thinking about why one of the world's most civilized nations participated in the systematic murder of millions of innocent people, mainly because of their religious identity.

Stalinist Russia

The Stalin era should be set in the historical context of the czarist regimes with their secret police, censorship, and imprisonment of dissidents. Within this context, students should learn of the many abortive efforts at reform and revolution, the massive underdevelopment of the nation, and the Russian Revolution. Students should examine the Bolshevik overthrow of the Kerensky government and understand the difference between the Bolsheviks and the Mensheviks. They should recognize the roles of Lenin, Trotsky, and Stalin; and they should analyze the meaning of communist ideology.

Students should perceive the connection between economic policies, political policies, the absence of a free press, and systematic violations of human rights, including the crushing of workers' strikes. With this background they should examine the forced collectivization of agriculture; the murder of millions of kulaks; the government-created famine in Ukraine that led to the starvation of millions of people; the political purges of party leaders, artists, engineers, and intellectuals; and the show trials of the 1930s.

By analyzing examples of socialist realist art and reading Yevgeny Zamyatin's *We,* the first antiutopian novel, and Arthur Koestler's classic *Darkness at Noon,* students will acquire deeper insights into this period.

As a result of these in-depth studies of Nazi Germany and Stalinist Russia, students should understand the nature of totalitarian rule and recognize the danger of concentrating unlimited power in the hands of the central government. They should develop understanding of the importance of a free press, the right to criticize the government without fear of reprisal, an independent judiciary, opposition political parties, free trade unions, and other

Standard 10.7.2
Trace Stalin's rise to power in the Soviet Union and the connection between economic policies, political policies, the absence of a free press, and systematic violations of human rights (e.g., the Terror Famine in Ukraine).

Historical Research, Evidence, and Point of View 4.

Students construct and test hypotheses; collect, evaluate, and employ information from multiple primary and secondary sources; and apply it in oral and written presentations.

Standard 10.8.

Students analyze the causes
and consequences of
World War II.

Standard 10.9.

Students analyze
the international developments in the post–World
War II world.

safeguards of individual rights. This is an appropriate point at which to reflect on the role of the individual when confronted with governmental actions such as the Final Solution and other violations of human rights.

World War II: Its Causes and Consequences

The study of nazism and Stalinism leads directly to an analysis of World War II and its causes and consequences. Students should realize which major nations formed the Allied and the Axis Powers. They should understand the significance of the Nazi-Soviet Nonaggression Pact and its effects in partitioning Poland and bringing Latvia, Lithuania, and Estonia under Soviet control. They should examine the German offensive, the battle of Britain, the major turning points of the war (for example, Stalingrad and the Normandy invasion), and the effects of the Yalta Conference.

Attention should be given to the war in the Pacific, including Japan's prewar expansion in east and southeast Asia, its attack on Pearl Harbor, and the struggle for the Pacific. In discussing President Truman's decision to use the atomic bomb against Japan, students could read John Hersey's *Hiroshima,* contemporary newspaper accounts, and the autobiographical statements of those involved.

Particular attention should be paid to the consequences of World War II, which continue to have so much importance in shaping the contemporary world. Students should discuss the importance of the Marshall Plan and the Truman Doctrine (targeted to Greece and Turkey), which established the pattern for the postwar American policy of supplying economic and military aid to prevent the spread of communism and to assist the economic development of our allies. American assistance to Japan and Germany contributed to their phenomenal postwar reconstruction and their emergence as major world economic powers.

A study of Poland should provide understanding of the consequences of World War II for the nations of Eastern Europe. In addition to the more than three million Polish Jews slaughtered, approximately one-half million other Poles were systematically executed, including Poland's political and military leaders, church leaders who spoke out against nazism, and educators. Then, in agreements reached in the Tehran, Yalta, and Potsdam conferences, Western leaders abandoned the Polish government-in-exile and acquiesced to Stalin's demands for Poland. Mass arrests of noncommunist leaders, expropriation of private land, and nationalization of industry followed. Despite decades of strikes, protests, and the organization of industrial workers in the Solidarity movement, the Soviet-dominated regime retained its power. Students should analyze how a nondemocratic government retains power without the consent of the governed and the institutions it destroys to maintain its control (for example, free elections, competing political parties, freedom of speech and religion, a free press, free trade unions, and an independent judiciary).

Other important postwar developments to be studied include the establishment of the state of Israel; the population movement within and immigration to Europe; the changing roles of women in industrialized countries; the creation of the United Nations; the Warsaw Pact, SEATO, and NATO; the Cold War; the Korean War; the Hungarian Revolution; and the Vietnam War and its aftermath, particularly the genocide committed in Cambodia by the Pol Pot regime.

Nationalism in the Contemporary World

The last major topic in this course is the study of nationalism in the contemporary world, illustrated by brief analyses of four pairs of nations connected either by political ideology (the former Soviet Union and China) or by regional location (Israel and Syria, Ghana and South Africa, and Mexico and Brazil). In the development of these case studies, particular attention should be paid to the connections among political systems, economic development, and individual rights. By analyzing the problems that these studies illustrate, students should be able to understand major national and international dilemmas occurring today.

Standard 10.10.

Students analyze instances of nation-building in the contemporary world in at least two of the following regions or countries: the Middle East, Africa, Mexico and other parts of Latin America, and China.

The Former Soviet Union and China. A comparative study of the former Soviet Union and China offers students an instructive comparison of two societies that became world powers because of their size, military might, natural resources, and economic potential. Both were created in the twentieth century as a result of communist revolutions. Both were underdeveloped countries whose leaders imposed collectivist means to modernize the economy and the society. In comparing these two nations, students must understand the conditions that preceded the revolution, their revolutionary leaders (Lenin, Stalin, and Mao), the nature of communist ideology, and the human consequences of both revolutions: the millions of "class enemies" and political dissidents who were murdered during and after the revolutions, the stifling of religious freedom, the conformity imposed on artists and intellectuals, the economic disruptions caused by forced collectivization, and the establishment of party elites exerting absolute control over the government and media.

In this unit students have an opportunity to discuss differences among revolutions. What is a revolution? Why are some revolutions, such as the French Revolution and communist revolutions, followed by political purges and mass killings? Why are others, such as the American Revolution, followed by the establishment of democratic institutions and mechanisms for orderly change?

Geopolitical analyses (such as the drive for warm water ports and agricultural resources) should be introduced in considering Soviet hegemony in Eastern Europe (for example, Poland, Hungary, Czechoslovakia, Yugoslavia, and the Baltic States) and Chinese aspirations in Asia. Students should read excerpts from Nikita Khrushchev's speech of 1956 denouncing the crimes of

Chronological and
Spatial Thinking 2.

Students analyze how change happens at different rates at different times; understand that some aspects can change while others remain the same; and understand that change is complicated and affects not only technology and politics but also values and beliefs.

Joseph Stalin, Aleksandr Solzhenitsyn's *The Gulag Archipelago,* and memoirs describing the Chinese Cultural Revolution. Examination of current problems should demonstrate the ways in which today's leaders are attempting to modify their political and economic structures by incorporating elements of a free market economy.

The Middle East: Israel and Syria. Since World War II, the Middle East has been a political hotbed unsettled by the passions of nationalism and religion. This region has been in almost continual ferment not only because of wars between Israel and the Arab nations but also because of tensions between Arab nations and among different Islamic groups, including the differences between Sunni and Shiite Muslims. The fragile political affairs of the area are further aggravated by its strategic importance as a supplier of oil to the industrialized world, the unresolved problems of the displaced Palestinian refugees, the recurrent use of terrorism among adversaries, the disruptions associated with the interaction of traditional cultures and the forces of modernization, and the importance of this region as a focus of East-West rivalries. Careful study of political and resource maps should help students understand the relative location and the geopolitical, cultural, military, and economic significance of such key states as Saudi Arabia, Turkey, Syria, Lebanon, Jordan, Israel, Kuwait, Iraq, and Iran. Students can more deeply analyze the problems of this vital region by an examination of two strategically important states, Israel and Syria.

A review of the history of Israel should include the importance of the land in Jewish religious history and should trace the history of Zionism, with special reference to the Holocaust as a factor in the creation of Israel in 1948. Attention should be paid to its democratic parliamentary government, free press, and independent judiciary. Students should understand challenges such as accommodating the demands of orthodox religious groups, the internal debate over the West Bank, the issue of Palestinian statehood, the conflict between Jews and Arabs within Israel, an economy overburdened by military expenditures, and Israel's existence in a hostile region.

Students should trace Syria's long history and examine its present status as a strategically important Arab nation. Syria should be seen within the context of a region that has sought Pan Arab unity while working to overcome problems of illiteracy, shortage of health services, ethnic rivalries, and religious tensions. Attention should be paid to the form of government in Syria, the status of minorities, government control of the media, and Syria's regional and military importance in the world today.

Students should be aware of the peace process in the Middle East and the role of the United States, including the Camp David Accords in 1978, the Treaty of Peace between Israel and Jordan in 1994, and the Israeli-Palestinian Interim Agreement.

Sub-Saharan Africa: Ghana and South Africa. In this unit on sub-Saharan Africa in the twentieth century, students should examine the west coast nation of Ghana and the nation of South Africa. Both nations should be studied in their historic and geographic contexts and in their international relationships within today's increasingly complex and interdependent world.

As they begin their study of Ghana, students should review briefly the once-great kingdoms of Ghana and Mali, which were studied in grade seven. They should learn that between the seventeenth and nineteenth centuries more than ten million Africans were enslaved and transported to the Western Hemisphere; about 400,000 of these were brought to British North America. Students should recognize that the African slave trade existed centuries before the first European contacts; however, the acute labor shortage in the New World created a vast new market for slave labor and systematically depleted Africa of successive generations of young men and women. This social, cultural, and economic disruption of West Africa was further aggravated in the late nineteenth century by the introduction of European colonization and economic exploitation of the region. Students should analyze the effects of centuries of exploitation of African states that have only recently achieved their independence from colonial rule.

A case study of Ghana today should provide students a graphic example of the political and economic problems of one African nation, a former British colony and the first to gain its independence. This nation, rich in gold resources and once the world's largest cocoa producer, is working to overcome the economic collapse engendered during its 26 years under socialism.

In South Africa the large settlement of Europeans has complicated human and cultural relations, with results culminating in political and racial crises. Students should observe how the government of South Africa developed out of European colonial roots and how its system of apartheid denied legal equality and political participation to the black majority up to 1994. The political tensions in South Africa should be analyzed for their effects throughout the entire region. Students can engage in activities such as debating the future of South Africa from the perspectives of a former leader of the white minority government, an elected black national leader, and a spokesperson for the white liberals in South Africa. Reading excerpts from Mark Mathabane's auto-biography, *Kaffir Boy,* will give students insight into growing up as a black under apartheid. Students will also learn the promise as well as the problems facing postapartheid South Africa by reading Nelson Mandela's inaugural address.

Latin America: Mexico and Brazil. In this unit students examine two developing Latin American nations, Mexico and Brazil. This unit begins with a geographic overview of Central and South America, including the region's political divisions, natural features, resources, and population patterns. The unit continues with a case study of present-day Mexico, a nation greatly shaped by its great social revolution of 1910-20 and the political and social system that emerged from it. Among Mexico's strengths have been its sense of national identity, political stability, and successful economic development until the

1970s. Mexico has a dominant party system and social disparities, and experienced economic difficulties in the last part of the twentieth century. Students should consider Mexico's experience in an international context, emphasizing its ties to other Latin American nations as well as its complex relationship with the United States, especially in light of the North American Free Trade Agreement.

In the unit on Brazil, students should examine the cultural diversity of the nation, including its immigrant population from many nations; and the economic contrasts between its highly industrialized southern cities, its agricultural and mineral wealth, and its sporadically settled interior regions. Students can compare the burgeoning growth of Brazil's major cities with that of Mexico City and analyze the social, economic, and political problems that are created as the rural poor continue to move to these cities.

Attention should be given to resettlement programs of the vast interior of Brazil, including the Amazon. Students should analyze the massive destruction of the tropical rain forests as settlers speculate in ranching and agriculture; the long-term costs to the earth's biosphere as these irreplaceable forests are systematically destroyed; the countless species of wildlife and vegetation lost; and the future of this region as grasses lose their nutritional value in the areas of shallow soil and speculative ranches are abandoned.

In all of these studies, students should develop an understanding of the historic as well as the contemporary geographic, social, political, and economic contexts in which these problems have arisen and which must be taken into account if each nation's contemporary problems and national aspirations are to be understood. It is especially important at this grade level that students be presented with differing perspectives on these issues and events in order to develop the critical thinking skills of an informed citizen in the contemporary world.

Standard 10.11.

Students analyze the integration of countries into the world economy and the information, technological, and communications revolutions (e.g., television, satellites, computers).

History–Social Science Standards

Grade Ten
World History, Culture, and Geography: The Modern World

10.1 **Students relate the moral and ethical principles in ancient Greek and Roman philosophy, in Judaism, and in Christianity to the development of Western political thought.**

1. Analyze the similarities and differences in Judeo-Christian and Greco-Roman views of law, reason and faith, and duties of the individual.

2. Trace the development of the Western political ideas of the rule of law and illegitimacy of tyranny, using selections from Plato's Republic and Aristotle's Politics.

3. Consider the influence of the U.S. Constitution on political systems in the contemporary world.

10.2 **Students compare and contrast the Glorious Revolution of England, the American Revolution, and the French Revolution and their enduring effects worldwide on the political expectations for self-government and individual liberty.**

1. Compare the major ideas of philosophers and their effects on the democratic revolutions in England, the United States, France, and Latin America (e.g., John Locke, Charles-Louis Montesquieu, Jean-Jacques Rousseau, Simón Bolívar, Thomas Jefferson, James Madison).

2. List the principles of the Magna Carta, the English Bill of Rights (1689), the American Declaration of Independence (1776), the French Declaration of the Rights of Man and the Citizen (1789), and the U.S. Bill of Rights (1791).

3. Understand the unique character of the American Revolution, its spread to other parts of the world, and its continuing significance to other nations.

4. Explain how the ideology of the French Revolution led France to develop from constitutional monarchy to democratic despotism to the Napoleonic empire.

5. Discuss how nationalism spread across Europe with Napoleon but was repressed for a generation under the Congress of Vienna and Concert of Europe until the Revolutions of 1848.

10.3 Students analyze the effects of the Industrial Revolution in England, France, Germany, Japan, and the United States.

1. Analyze why England was the first country to industrialize.

2. Examine how scientific and technological changes and new forms of energy brought about massive social, economic, and cultural change (e.g., the inventions and discoveries of James Watt, Eli Whitney, Henry Bessemer, Louis Pasteur, Thomas Edison).

3. Describe the growth of population, rural to urban migration, and growth of cities associated with the Industrial Revolution.

4. Trace the evolution of work and labor, including the demise of the slave trade and the effects of immigration, mining and manufacturing, division of labor, and the union movement.

5. Understand the connections among natural resources, entrepreneurship, labor, and capital in an industrial economy.

6. Analyze the emergence of capitalism as a dominant economic pattern and the responses to it, including Utopianism, Social Democracy, Socialism, and Communism.

7. Describe the emergence of Romanticism in art and literature (e.g., the poetry of William Blake and William Wordsworth), social criticism (e.g., the novels of Charles Dickens), and the move away from Classicism in Europe.

10.4 Students analyze patterns of global change in the era of New Imperialism in at least two of the following regions or countries: Africa, Southeast Asia, China, India, Latin America, and the Philippines.

1. Describe the rise of industrial economies and their link to imperialism and colonialism (e.g., the role played by national security and strategic advantage; moral issues raised by the search for national hegemony, Social Darwinism, and the missionary impulse; material issues such as land, resources, and technology).

2. Discuss the locations of the colonial rule of such nations as England, France, Germany, Italy, Japan, the Netherlands, Russia, Spain, Portugal, and the United States.

3. Explain imperialism from the perspective of the colonizers and the colonized and the varied immediate and long-term responses by the people under colonial rule.

4. Describe the independence struggles of the colonized regions of the world, including the roles of leaders, such as Sun Yat-sen in China, and the roles of ideology and religion.

10.5   Students analyze the causes and course of the First World War.

1. Analyze the arguments for entering into war presented by leaders from all sides of the Great War and the role of political and economic rivalries, ethnic and ideological conflicts, domestic discontent and disorder, and propaganda and nationalism in mobilizing the civilian population in support of "total war."

2. Examine the principal theaters of battle, major turning points, and the importance of geographic factors in military decisions and outcomes (e.g., topography, waterways, distance, climate).

3. Explain how the Russian Revolution and the entry of the United States affected the course and outcome of the war.

4. Understand the nature of the war and its human costs (military and civilian) on all sides of the conflict, including how colonial peoples contributed to the war effort.

5. Discuss human rights violations and genocide, including the Ottoman government's actions against Armenian citizens.

10.6   Students analyze the effects of the First World War.

1. Analyze the aims and negotiating roles of world leaders, the terms and influence of the Treaty of Versailles and Woodrow Wilson's Fourteen Points, and the causes and effects of the United States's rejection of the League of Nations on world politics.

2. Describe the effects of the war and resulting peace treaties on population movement, the international economy, and shifts in the geographic and political borders of Europe and the Middle East.

3. Understand the widespread disillusionment with prewar institutions, authorities, and values that resulted in a void that was later filled by totalitarians.

4. Discuss the influence of World War I on literature, art, and intellectual life in the West (e.g., Pablo Picasso, the "lost generation" of Gertrude Stein, Ernest Hemingway).

10.7   Students analyze the rise of totalitarian governments after World War I.

1. Understand the causes and consequences of the Russian Revolution, including Lenin's use of totalitarian means to seize and maintain control (e.g., the Gulag).

2. Trace Stalin's rise to power in the Soviet Union and the connection between economic policies, political policies, the absence of a free press, and systematic violations of human rights (e.g., the Terror Famine in Ukraine).

3. Analyze the rise, aggression, and human costs of totalitarian regimes (Fascist and Communist) in Germany, Italy, and the Soviet Union, noting especially their common and dissimilar traits.

10.8 Students analyze the causes and consequences of World War II.

1. Compare the German, Italian, and Japanese drives for empire in the 1930s, including the 1937 Rape of Nanking, other atrocities in China, and the Stalin-Hitler Pact of 1939.

2. Understand the role of appeasement, nonintervention (isolationism), and the domestic distractions in Europe and the United States prior to the outbreak of World War II.

3. Identify and locate the Allied and Axis powers on a map and discuss the major turning points of the war, the principal theaters of conflict, key strategic decisions, and the resulting war conferences and political resolutions, with emphasis on the importance of geographic factors.

4. Describe the political, diplomatic, and military leaders during the war (e.g., Winston Churchill, Franklin Delano Roosevelt, Emperor Hirohito, Adolf Hitler, Benito Mussolini, Joseph Stalin, Douglas MacArthur, Dwight Eisenhower).

5. Analyze the Nazi policy of pursuing racial purity, especially against the European Jews; its transformation into the Final Solution; and the Holocaust that resulted in the murder of six million Jewish civilians.

6. Discuss the human costs of the war, with particular attention to the civilian and military losses in Russia, Germany, Britain, the United States, China, and Japan.

10.9 Students analyze the international developments in the post–World War II world.

1. Compare the economic and military power shifts caused by the war, including the Yalta Pact, the development of nuclear weapons, Soviet control over Eastern European nations, and the economic recoveries of Germany and Japan.

2. Analyze the causes of the Cold War, with the free world on one side and Soviet client states on the other, including competition for influence in such places as Egypt, the Congo, Vietnam, and Chile.

3. Understand the importance of the Truman Doctrine and the Marshall Plan, which established the pattern for America's postwar policy of supplying economic and military aid to prevent the spread of Communism and the resulting economic and political competition in arenas such as Southeast Asia (i.e., the Korean War, Vietnam War), Cuba, and Africa.

4. Analyze the Chinese Civil War, the rise of Mao Zedong, and the subsequent political and economic upheavals in China (e.g., the Great Leap Forward, the Cultural Revolution, and the Tiananmen Square uprising).

5. Describe the uprisings in Poland (1956), Hungary (1956), and Czechoslovakia (1968) and those countries' resurgence in the 1970s and 1980s as people in Soviet satellites sought freedom from Soviet control.

6. Understand how the forces of nationalism developed in the Middle East, how the Holocaust affected world opinion regarding the need for a Jewish state, and the significance and effects of the location and establishment of Israel on world affairs.

7. Analyze the reasons for the collapse of the Soviet Union, including the weakness of the command economy, burdens of military commitments, and growing resistance to Soviet rule by dissidents in satellite states and the non-Russian Soviet republics.

8. Discuss the establishment and work of the United Nations and the purposes and functions of the Warsaw Pact, SEATO, NATO, and the Organization of American States.

10.10 Students analyze instances of nation-building in the contemporary world in at least two of the following regions or countries: the Middle East, Africa, Mexico and other parts of Latin America, and China.

1. Understand the challenges in the regions, including their geopolitical, cultural, military, and economic significance and the international relationships in which they are involved.

2. Describe the recent history of the regions, including political divisions and systems, key leaders, religious issues, natural features, resources, and population patterns.

3. Discuss the important trends in the regions today and whether they appear to serve the cause of individual freedom and democracy.

10.11 Students analyze the integration of countries into the world economy and the information, technological, and communications revolutions (e.g., television, satellites, computers).

Course
Descriptions

Grade Eleven

Grade Eleven— United States History and Geography: Continuity and Change in the Twentieth Century

In this course students examine major turning points in American history in the twentieth century. During the year certain themes should be emphasized: the expanding role of the federal government and federal courts; the continuing tension between the individual and the state and between minority rights and majority power; the emergence of a modern corporate economy; the role of the federal government and Federal Reserve System in the economy; the impact of technology on American society and culture; change in the ethnic composition of American society; the movements toward equal rights for racial minorities and women; and the role of the United States as a major world power. In each unit students should examine American culture, including religion, literature, art, drama, architecture, education, and the mass media.

The year begins with a selective review of United States history, with an emphasis on two major themes—*the nation's beginnings,* linked to the tenth-grade retrospective on the Enlightenment and the rise of democratic ideas; *and the industrial transformation of the new nation,* linked to the students' tenth-grade studies of the global spread of industrialism during the nineteenth century.

Connecting with Past Learnings: The Nation's Beginnings

In this first review unit, students should draw on their earlier studies (in grades seven, eight, and ten) of the Enlightenment and the rise of democratic ideas as the context in which this nation was founded. Special attention should be given to the ideological origins of the American Revolution and its grounding in the democratic political tradition, Judeo-Christian ideals, and the natural rights philosophy of the Founding Fathers. Special attention also should be given to the framing of the Constitution as background for understanding the contemporary constitutional issues raised throughout this course.

Connecting with Past Learnings: The United States to 1900

In this second review unit, students should concentrate on the testing of the new nation through the Civil War and the nineteenth-century growth of the nation as an industrial power. First, students should review the history of the Constitution after 1787, with particular attention given to the issue of federal versus state authority, a question that was resolved only by the Civil War.

Standard 11.3.

Students analyze the role religion played in the founding of America, its lasting moral, social, and political impacts, and issues regarding religious liberty.

Standard 11.1.

Students analyze the significant events in the founding of the nation and its attempts to realize the philosophy of government described in the Declaration of Independence.

Standard 11.1.3.

Understand the history of the Constitution after 1787 with emphasis on federal versus state authority and growing democratization.

The war and the Reconstruction of the federal union that followed should be highlighted.

Second, students should review the growth of the United States as an industrial and world power. A brief retrospective of the grade ten study of the industrial revolution should set the global context for America's development. Other emphases in this review unit should include the significance of immigration in producing ethnic diversity, the demographic shifts of the nineteenth century, and the emergence of the United States in the late nineteenth century as a world power. Again, reference should be made to grade ten studies of nineteenth century European imperialism as the global context in which America's growing influence as a world power was established.

The Progressive Era

In the first in-depth study of the year, students learn about the Progressive Era, a period rich with controversy and change. Students should understand the combination of massive immigration and industrialization that produced vast urban slums with intolerable living and working conditions and crowded, inadequate schools. They should examine the corporate mergers that produced trusts and cartels, industrial giants, "robber barons," and the gaudy excesses of the Gilded Age. They should study examples of the corrupt big-city machines that delivered services to the immigrant poor in exchange for votes. They should discuss the philosophy of Social Darwinism as well as the religious reformism associated with the ideal of the Social Gospel. The work of social reformers such as Jane Addams to improve living conditions for the poor and downtrodden should be noted. Excerpts from the works of muckrakers such as Lincoln Steffens, Jacob Riis, Ida Tarbell, and Joseph Mayer Rice and novels by writers such as Theodore Dreiser, Upton Sinclair, and Frank Norris will help set the scene. These social conditions should be seen as background for the progressive reform movement that challenged big-city bosses; rallied public indignation against "the trusts"; led successful campaigns for social and economic legislation at the city, state, and federal levels; and played a major role in national politics in the pre–World War I era. Students should examine the impact of mining and agriculture on the laws concerning water rights during these years. As a result of progressive legislation, the role of the federal government in regulating business and commerce was expanded during the administrations of Theodore Roosevelt and Woodrow Wilson.

Students should analyze the nation's foreign policy, especially President Theodore Roosevelt's "big stick" policies and the United States' involvement in World War I. They should review their tenth-grade study of the causes and consequences of World War I and its projection of the United States into world affairs. Students should learn about President Woodrow Wilson's Fourteen Points and the League of Nations. They should discuss domestic opposition to

Grade Eleven

Standard 11.1.4.

Examine the effects of
the Civil War and
Reconstruction and of
the industrial revolution,
including demographic
shifts and the emergence
in the late nineteenth
century of the United
States as a world power.

Standard 11.2.

Students analyze the
relationship among the
rise of industrialization,
large-scale rural-to-urban
migration, and massive
immigration from
Southern and Eastern
Europe.

**Historical
Interpretation 3.**

Students interpret past
events and issues within
the context in which an
event unfolded rather
than solely in terms
of present-day norms
and values.

Standard 11.4.

Students trace the rise of
the United States to its
role as a world power in
the twentieth century.

Grade Eleven

Standard 11.5.4.

Analyze the passage of the Nineteenth Amendment and the changing role of women in society.

Standard 11.5.

Students analyze the major political, social, economic, technological, and cultural developments of the 1920s.

Historical Research, Evidence, and Point of View 3.

Students evaluate major debates among historians concerning alternative interpretations of the past, including an analysis of authors' use of evidence and the distinctions between sound generalizations and misleading oversimplifications.

Historical Interpretation 1.

Students show the connections, causal and otherwise, between particular historical events and larger social, economic, and political trends and developments.

the war, prejudice toward German Americans, and the nation's reversion to isolationism.

Popular fears of communism and anarchism associated with the Russian Revolution and World War I provoked attacks on civil liberties and industrial unionists; for example, the postwar Palmer Raids, the "Red Scare," the Sacco-Vanzetti case, and legislation restraining individual expression and privacy. Legal challenges to these activities produced major Supreme Court decisions defining the right to dissent and freedom of speech. By reading some of the extraordinary decisions of Justices Louis Brandeis and Oliver Wendell Holmes, students will understand the continuing tension between the rights of the individual and the power of government. Students can consider such questions as: Who speaks for unpopular causes in American society? Is such a voice needed in a society controlled by majority vote? This is an appropriate point to discuss the founding of organizations such as the American Civil Liberties Union (ACLU) and the National Association for the Advancement of Colored People (NAACP) to defend unpopular views and minority rights.

As the Progressive Era ended, women won the right to vote with the passage of a constitutional amendment establishing women's suffrage. What were the arguments for and against female suffrage? How is the Constitution amended?

The Jazz Age

The 1920s had no single event such as a war or a depression around which to organize its story, but the decade was nonetheless colorful and important. It is usually characterized as a period of Prohibition, gangsters, speakeasies, jazz bands, and flappers, living frivolously as the economic disaster of the 1930s inexorably drew near. This in-depth study should be used to test the complex realities of this era. Students should recognize the change from the reformism of the Progressive Era to the desire for "normalcy" in the 1920s as evidenced by the election of Warren Harding, Calvin Coolidge, and Herbert Hoover. What was normalcy to some was reaction to others, however, as Congress restricted immigration on the basis of nationality quotas, Ku Klux Klan activities increased in the South and Midwest, farm income declined precipitously, and labor unrest spread throughout the country.

For most Americans, however, the standard of living rose, and new consumer goods such as automobiles, radios, and household appliances became available. Students should learn how the widespread adoption of mass production techniques such as the assembly line helped to make American workers highly efficient. The emergence of the mass media created new markets, new tastes, and a new popular culture. Movies, radio, and advertising spread styles, raised expectations, and promoted interest in fads and sports. At the same time, major new writers began to appear, such as William Faulkner, F. Scott Fitzgerald, and Sinclair Lewis.

A migration of many blacks from the South helped to create the "Harlem Renaissance," the literary and artistic flowering of black artists, poets, musicians, and scholars, such as W. E. B. Du Bois, Langston Hughes, Richard Wright, and Zora Neale Hurston. Examples of their work should be read. Marcus Garvey, the black nationalist leader of a Back to Africa movement, reached the peak of his popularity during this period.

The Great Depression

The collapse of the national and international economies in 1929 led to the Great Depression of the 1930s and major changes in American politics, society, and culture. Although the political culture of the 1920s exuded self-confidence and optimism, the Depression caused many people to question the viability of American institutions. One reaction to the economic crisis and the rise of fascism in Europe was the growth of extremist political movements on the right and the left.

Students should assess the likely causes of the Depression and examine its effects on ordinary people in different parts of the nation through use of historical materials. They should recognize the way in which natural drought combined with unwise agricultural practices to cause the Dust Bowl, a major factor in the economic and cultural chaos of the 1930s. They should see the linkage between severe economic distress and social turmoil. Photographs, videotapes, newspaper accounts, interviews with persons who lived in the period, as well as paintings and novels (such as John Steinbeck's *Grapes of Wrath*) will help students understand this critical era.

The administration of Franklin D. Roosevelt and his New Deal should be studied as an example of the government's response to economic crisis. The efforts of the Roosevelt administration to alleviate the crisis through the creation of social welfare programs, regulatory agencies, and economic planning bureaus should be carefully assessed. President Roosevelt's dominance of American politics should not obscure the significant opposition to his policies. Students should have an accurate sense of the controversy generated by the New Deal and of the attacks on Roosevelt. Students should read excerpts from Roosevelt's memorable inaugural addresses and fireside chats in order to perceive the president's efforts to rally the nation's spiritual energy. Events during Roosevelt's presidency mark the beginning of what some historians have called the "Imperial Presidency." The crisis of the Depression, World War II, and postwar international tensions have caused a dramatic expansion of the power of the presidency. Students should analyze the risk to separation of powers caused by this phenomenon and the continuing danger to representative government that this trend implies.

Standard 11.6.

Students analyze the different explanations for the Great Depression and how the New Deal fundamentally changed the role of the federal government.

Historical Research, Evidence, and Point of View 4.

Students construct and test hypotheses; collect, evaluate, and employ information from multiple primary and secondary sources; and apply it in oral and written presentations.

Course
Descriptions

Grade Eleven

Standard 11.7.

Students analyze
America's participation
in World War II.

Standard 11.7.5.

Discuss the constitutional
issues and impact of events on
the U.S. home front, including
the internment of Japanese
Americans (e.g., *Fred Korematsu
v. United States of America*) and
the restrictions on German
and Italian resident aliens; the
response of the administration
to Hitler's atrocities against
Jews and other groups; the
roles of women in military
production; and the roles and
growing political demands of
African Americans.

Standard 11.9.

Students analyze U.S. foreign
policy since World War II.

World War II

In this unit students examine the role of the United States in World War II. Students should review the rise of dictatorships in Germany, the Soviet Union, and Japan; and they should examine the events in Europe and Asia in the 1930s that led to war. Students should understand the debate between isolationists and interventionists in the United States as well as the effect on American public opinion of the Nazi-Soviet pact and the bombing of Pearl Harbor. Students should look again at the Holocaust and consider the response of Franklin D. Roosevelt's administration to Hitler's atrocities against Jews and other groups.

By reading contemporary accounts in newspapers and popular magazines, students should understand the extent to which this war taught Americans to think in global terms. By studying wartime strategy and major military operations, students should grasp the geopolitical implications of the war and its importance for postwar international relations. The controversy over President Harry S. Truman's decision to drop atomic bombs on Japan should be analyzed fully, considering both his rationale and differing historical judgments.

Attention should be paid to the effect of the war on the home front. Industrial demands fueled by war needs contributed to ending the Depression and set a model for an expanded governmental role after the war. Wartime factory work created new job opportunities for unskilled women and blacks. The racial segregation of the armed forces, combined with the egalitarian ideology of the war effort, produced a strong stimulus for civil rights activism when the war ended. The relocation and internment of 110,000 Japanese Americans during the war on grounds of national security was a governmental decision that should be analyzed as a violation of their human rights.

The Cold War

In this unit students focus on the postwar relations between the United States and the Soviet Union. Students should examine the Soviet conquest of Eastern Europe and its takeover of Poland, Hungary, and Czechoslovakia. As part of their study of President Truman's policy of containment of communism, students should examine the Truman Doctrine, the Marshall Plan, the creation of the North Atlantic Treaty Organization, and the Berlin blockade and airlift. They should be aware of the Soviet Union's violations of human rights during this period. The controversy among historians over the causes of the Cold War should be discussed.

The domestic political response to the spread of international communism should receive attention as part of the study of the Cold War. Students should learn about the investigations of domestic communism at the federal and state levels and about the celebrated spy trials of the period. As part of this unit, students should discuss the censure of Senator Joseph McCarthy by his colleagues in the U.S. Senate. Students should debate the appropriateness of loyalty oaths (an important issue at the University of California in the 1950s) and legislative investigations of people's beliefs. During this era there were significant Supreme Court decisions that protected citizens' rights to dissent and freedom of speech.

The study of the foreign policy consequences of the Cold War should be extended to an examination of the major events of the administrations of Dwight D. Eisenhower, John F. Kennedy, and Lyndon B. Johnson. Students should examine the United Nations' intervention in Korea, Eisenhower's successful conclusion of that conflict, and his administration's defense policies based on nuclear deterrence and massive retaliation. Foreign policy during the Kennedy and Johnson administrations represents a continuation of Cold War strategy, with the emphasis shifting to guerrilla warfare in Southeast Asia and leading to the Vietnam War. Students should be aware of U.S. support of anticommunist governments, including burgeoning democracies and authoritarian governments. These events should be placed within the context of continuing tensions between the Soviet Union and the United States.

President Eisenhower's warning about the rise of a "military-industrial complex," created during World War II and maintained to meet the military threat of Soviet expansionism, raises important issues for students to discuss: What is the role of conventional forces in a nuclear age? How important to the economy of states and localities are defense industries? What effect does research for military purposes have on our economic productivity and competitiveness? What is the appropriate balance between "guns and butter" or between military and civilian needs? How are these questions decided in our political system?

Chronological and Spatial Thinking 1.

Students compare the present with the past, evaluating the consequences of past events and decisions and determining the lessons that were learned.

Hemispheric Relationships in the Postwar Era

In this unit students should consider the nation's postwar relationships with Latin America and Canada. Students should examine the events leading to the Cuban Revolution of 1959; the political purges and the economic and social changes enforced by Castro; the introduction of Soviet influence and military aid in the Caribbean; the 1961 Bay of Pigs invasion and the 1962 Missile Crisis; the 1965 crisis in the Dominican Republic; the 1978 Panama Canal Treaty; and the spread of Cuban influence, indigenous revolution, and counterrevolution in Nicaragua and El Salvador in the 1980s. Students should analyze the continuing involvement of the United States in this region.

An analysis of U.S. economic relationships with the nations of Latin America today should include the international as well as domestic causes of mounting third world debt in Latin America and the global interrelatedness of the economies of this hemisphere and the world.

A study of postwar relationships between the United States and Canada should note the long history of peaceful, negotiated settlement of problems

Standard 11.9.3.

Trace the origins and geopolitical consequences (foreign and domestic) of the Cold War and containment policy, including the following:
• The Bay of Pigs Invasion and the Cuban Missile Crisis
• Latin American policy

Course
Descriptions

Grade Eleven

Standard 11.8.6.

Discuss the diverse environmental regions of North
America, their relationship
to local economies, and
the origins and prospects
of environmental problems
in those regions.

Standard 11.10.

Students analyze the
development of federal
civil rights and voting
rights.

between these nations. To understand certain problems, students should become sensitive to the Canadian perspective and to Canada's heavy economic dependence on its forest products and its oceanic fishing grounds. In turning to the World Court to settle fishing rights to the prolific Georges Bank fishing grounds off Nova Scotia, the United States and Canada provide an important case study in peaceful arbitration between nations. Among the unresolved problems confronting these two nations is the problem of acid rain, an issue of global interdependence that concerns other nations in the industrialized world today.

The Civil Rights Movement in the Postwar Era

In this unit students should focus on the history of the civil rights movement in the 25 years after World War II and on the dramatic social and political transformations that it brought. The emphasis in this unit is on the application of the Constitution and the Bill of Rights in modern times to the resolution of human rights issues. Students should understand the central role black Americans have played in this century in expanding the reach of the Constitution to include all Americans.

A review of earlier learnings should help students grasp the enormous barriers black Americans had to overcome in their struggle for their rights as citizens. Attention should be given to the provisions enacted into the Constitution in 1787 that preserved slavery; the post–Civil War laws and practices that reduced the newly freed slaves to a state of peonage; and the Jim Crow laws that were upheld by the Supreme Court in a series of decisions in the late nineteenth century. Students should be aware of Booker T. Washington, the founder of Tuskegee Institute. Excerpts from his 1895 Atlanta Exposition address will show his efforts to adjust to the handicaps of racial segregation. Discrimination continued to confront black citizens who migrated to northern cities and who served in world wars I and II.

Readings from Gunnar Myrdal's *An American Dilemma* will help students analyze the contrast between the American creed and the practices of racial segregation throughout the nation in the years preceding World War II. What was the dilemma? What is the creed that Myrdal stressed? As background, students must understand the meaning of "separate but equal," both as a legal term and as a reality that effectively limited the life chances of black Americans by denying them equal opportunity for jobs, housing, education, health, and voting rights.

Students should learn about the rise of the civil rights movement and the legal battle to abolish segregation. The battle in the courts began with challenges to racial segregation in higher education and achieved a signal victory in 1954 with the *Brown* v. *Board of Education of Topeka* decision. This important decision should be read and discussed. Students should analyze why one of the first demands of the civil rights movement was for equal educational opportunity. Why is education so important in the life chances of an individual? What happens to people who are not educated in America today? What kinds of jobs can they get? How does mass illiteracy affect an entire society? (Here students should review what they learned in the tenth-grade unit "Nationalism in the Contemporary World.") What would life in the United States be like if there were no public schools? Interviews and case studies can be made of successful men and women from minority groups whose lives have changed because of their education.

The *Brown* decision and its slow acceptance by local and state governments stimulated a generation of political and social activism led by black Americans pursuing their civil rights. Momentous events in this story illumine the process of change: the commitment of white people in the South to "massive resistance" against desegregation; the Montgomery bus boycott, which was started by Rosa Parks and then led by the young Martin Luther King, Jr.; the clash in Little Rock, Arkansas, between federal and state power; the student sit-in demonstrations that began in Greensboro, North Carolina; the "freedom rides"; the march on Washington in 1963; the Mississippi Summer Project of 1964; and the march in Selma, Alabama, in 1965. Students should recognize how these dramatic events influenced public opinion and enlarged the jurisdiction of the federal courts. They should understand Dr. King's philosophical and religious dedication to nonviolence by reading documents such as his "Letter from a Birmingham Jail," and they should recognize the leadership of the black churches in the movement. By viewing films of this period, students should recognize both the extraordinary moral courage of ordinary black men, women, and children and the interracial character of the civil rights movement.

The expansion of the role of the federal government as a guarantor of civil rights should be examined, especially during the administrations of Presidents Kennedy and Johnson. After President Kennedy's assassination, Congress enacted landmark federal programs in civil rights, education, and social welfare. Students should examine the historical significance of the Civil Rights Act of 1964 and the Elementary and Secondary Education Act of 1965.

The peak of legislative activity in 1964-65 was accompanied by a dramatic increase in civil unrest and protest among urban blacks, and 1966 saw the emergence of the Black Power movement. The assassination of Dr. King in 1968 deprived the civil rights movement of its best-known leader, but not its enduring effects on American life. In considering issues such as school busing and group quotas, students can discuss the continuing controversy between group rights to a fair share as opposed to individual rights to equal treatment. Well-chosen readings should heighten students' sensitivity to the issues raised in this unit, such as *The Autobiography of Malcolm X*, Lerone Bennett's *Before the Mayflower: A History of Black America*, Ralph Ellison's *Invisible Man*, Richard Wright's *Native Son*, and Lorraine Hansberry's *A Raisin in the Sun*.

**Historical
Interpretation 4.**

Students understand the
meaning, implication,
and impact of historical
events and recognize
that events could have
taken other directions.

Course
Descriptions

Grade Eleven

Standard 11.8.

Students analyze the
economic boom and social
transformation of post–
World War II America.

The success of the black civil rights movement encouraged other groups—including women, Hispanics, American Indians, Asians, Pacific Islanders, and individuals with disabilities—in their campaigns for legislative and judicial recognition of their civil equality. Students should study how Cesar Chavez and the United Farm Workers' movement used nonviolent tactics, educated the general public about the working conditions in agriculture, and worked to improve the lives of farmworkers. Major events in the development of all these movements and their consequences should be noted.

American Society in the Postwar Era

In this unit students focus on other significant social, economic, and political changes of the 25 years following World War II. Having emerged from the war with a strong industrial base, the nation experienced rapid economic growth and a steady increase in the standard of living. The GI Bill of Rights opened college doors to millions of returning veterans who contributed to the nation's technological capacity. The economic surge was extended during the Eisenhower era, which was marked by low inflation, social calm, and political quiescence.

Students should examine the significance of the Supreme Court under the leadership of former California Governor Earl Warren. Decisions of this court made sweeping changes in many areas of American life. Beyond the *Brown* decision (already studied), consideration should be given to decisions affecting criminal due process, voting rights, freedom of speech, and other areas of expression that have affected our lives dramatically. Students should be prepared to debate the question of the role of the courts in overturning laws passed by Congress and state legislatures. Historical depth should be provided by comparing the Warren Court to the Hughes Court of the 1930s, both of which used judicial power to invalidate statutes passed by democratically elected legislatures.

Students should read about the beginning of the environmental movement in the 1960s and the environmental protection laws that were passed. The expansion of the war in Vietnam provoked antiwar protests that reflected and contributed to a deep rift within American culture. From within the protest movement, a "counterculture" emerged with its own distinctive style of music, dress, language, and films. When the war ended, the counterculture was absorbed in the mainstream.

The Nixon administration (1968–1974) was notable for establishing relations with the People's Republic of China, opening a period of detente with the Soviet Union, and negotiating a withdrawal of American troops from Vietnam. Despite his skill in managing foreign affairs, Richard Nixon's administration was marred by a political scandal called Watergate that led to his resignation in 1974. Students should understand the events that led to President Nixon's resignation, and they should assess the roles of the courts, the press, and the Congress. Students can discuss the continuing issue of unchecked presidential power. Are the president and his staff above the law?

The study of this fascinating period should include an examination of the continuing economic contractions and expansions and the use of monetary and fiscal policy in influencing business cycles. Students should learn about the growth of the middle class, with poverty concentrated among minority groups, the elderly, and single-parent families. Major attention should be given to demographic changes, such as the Baby Boom, white flight to the newly developing suburbs, the migration to the Sunbelt, the decline of the family farm, the entry of women into the labor force in large numbers, the rise of the women's movement, increasing divorce rates, and the changing family structure. Students should consider the connections between the modern women's movement and the women's rights movement of earlier decades. Which issues created the women's movement of the 1970s? Why did the Equal Rights Amendment fail? Selections from the writings of leading feminists and their opponents can be read and discussed. Attention should be paid to the major gains by women in education and in the workplace.

Finally, consideration should be given to the major social problems of contemporary America, including juvenile and adult crime, illegal use of drugs and alcohol, teenage pregnancy, and child neglect. Issues inherent in these problems can be debated, and experts from the community can be invited as speakers.

**Chronological and
Spatial Thinking 4.**

Students relate current
events to the physical
and human characteris-
tics of places and
regions.

The United States in Recent Times

In this concluding unit students can place the recent past in historical perspective. At the end of this year's study, students should be able to discuss long-term trends and to assess their meaning. They should be aware of the influence of the Constitution on daily events in their community and nation and its continuing importance in defining the rights and freedoms of Americans.

The teacher should review the major events of the last quarter of the twentieth century, including the presidencies of Jimmy Carter, Ronald Reagan, George Bush, and William Clinton, and set them in historical perspective. What are the electoral patterns of contemporary times, and how has voting behavior changed over the last 10, 20, or 50 years? To what extent is foreign policy bipartisan? How might a president from another party handle a particular crisis; for example, the Middle East or the Iranian hostage crisis? What should be done about the national debt and deficit spending?

Much of the national political debate of recent decades has been concerned with the expansion of the power of the federal government and the federal courts. This unit is intended to help students understand the extent to which such issues are rooted in the Progressive Era, the New Deal, and the civil rights movement. This is an appropriate time to reflect on the redefinition of the Bill of Rights during the twentieth century, particularly the tension between the

Standard 11.11.

Students analyze the
major social problems
and domestic policy
issues in contemporary
American society.

Grade Eleven

**Historical
Interpretation 1.**

Students show the
connections, causal and
otherwise, between
particular historical events
and larger social,
economic, and political
trends and developments.

rights of the individual and the power of the state. By examining major social controversies, students should consider how the Constitution works today and compare contemporary practices to the vision of the Founding Fathers.

Contemporary economic and social conditions in the United States can be viewed with historical perspective. Students might examine census data to examine basic demographic changes and predict future patterns of growth and decline. Students might compare the status of minorities in 1900 to that of the present and reflect on changes in job opportunities, educational opportunities, and legal protections available to minorities and women. How does the life of a new immigrant to the United States today compare with what it was in 1900? What is the condition of women's rights today compared to 1900? By viewing three generations of social and economic change, students can begin to assess the collective effects of the political and legal reforms that have been enacted since the Progressive Era.

Students should recognize that under our democratic political system the United States has achieved a level of freedom, political stability, and economic prosperity that has made it a model for other nations, the leader of the world's democratic societies, and a magnet for people all over the world who yearn for a life of freedom and opportunity. Students should understand that our rights and freedoms are not accidents of history. They are the result of a carefully defined set of political principles that are embodied in the Constitution. Students should recognize that our ability to debate our current and historical problems and to freely criticize our government is not a sign of weakness but is one of the hallmarks of a free society.

Students should see that the history of the United States has had special significance for the rest of the world, both because of its free political system and its pluralistic nature. In a world struggling with ethnic, racial, and religious hatred, the United States has demonstrated the strength and dynamism of a racially, religiously, and culturally diverse people. All citizens of the United States enjoy a democratic republic, rule of law, and guaranteed constitutional rights.

Students should perceive these historic achievements in a global context. They should recognize the cynicism with which undemocratic regimes use the rhetoric of democracy while violating its most basic principles. They should understand that most nations today do not rest on the consent of the governed and do not guarantee their citizens basic rights and freedoms.

By the end of grade eleven, students should see the relevance of history to their daily lives and understand how the ideas and events of the past shape the institutions and debates of contemporary America. Living in a free society is a precious inheritance; it should not be taken for granted. Students should recognize that our democratic political system depends on them—as educated citizens—to survive and prosper.

History–Social Science Standards

Grade Eleven
United States History and Geography:
Continuity and Change in the Twentieth Century

11.1 Students analyze the significant events in the founding of the nation and its attempts to realize the philosophy of government described in the Declaration of Independence.

1. Describe the Enlightenment and the rise of democratic ideas as the context in which the nation was founded.

2. Analyze the ideological origins of the American Revolution, the Founding Fathers' philosophy of divinely bestowed unalienable natural rights, the debates on the drafting and ratification of the Constitution, and the addition of the Bill of Rights.

3. Understand the history of the Constitution after 1787 with emphasis on federal versus state authority and growing democratization.

4. Examine the effects of the Civil War and Reconstruction and of the industrial revolution, including demographic shifts and the emergence in the late nineteenth century of the United States as a world power.

11.2 Students analyze the relationship among the rise of industrialization, large-scale rural-to-urban migration, and massive immigration from Southern and Eastern Europe.

1. Know the effects of industrialization on living and working conditions, including the portrayal of working conditions and food safety in Upton Sinclair's *The Jungle*.

2. Describe the changing landscape, including the growth of cities linked by industry and trade, and the development of cities divided according to race, ethnicity, and class.

3. Trace the effect of the Americanization movement.

4. Analyze the effect of urban political machines and responses to them by immigrants and middle-class reformers.

5. Discuss corporate mergers that produced trusts and cartels and the economic and political policies of industrial leaders.

6. Trace the economic development of the United States and its emergence as a major industrial power, including its gains from trade and the advantages of its physical geography.

7. Analyze the similarities and differences between the ideologies of Social Darwinism and Social Gospel (e.g., using biographies of William Graham Sumner, Billy Sunday, Dwight L. Moody).

8. Examine the effect of political programs and activities of Populists.

9. Understand the effect of political programs and activities of the Progressives (e.g., federal regulation of railroad transport, Children's Bureau, the Sixteenth Amendment, Theodore Roosevelt, Hiram Johnson).

11.3 Students analyze the role religion played in the founding of America, its lasting moral, social, and political impacts, and issues regarding religious liberty.

1. Describe the contributions of various religious groups to American civic principles and social reform movements (e.g., civil and human rights, individual responsibility and the work ethic, antimonarchy and self-rule, worker protection, family-centered communities).

2. Analyze the great religious revivals and the leaders involved in them, including the First Great Awakening, the Second Great Awakening, the Civil War revivals, the Social Gospel Movement, the rise of Christian liberal theology in the nineteenth century, the impact of the Second Vatican Council, and the rise of Christian fundamentalism in current times.

3. Cite incidences of religious intolerance in the United States (e.g., persecution of Mormons, anti-Catholic sentiment, anti-Semitism).

4. Discuss the expanding religious pluralism in the United States and California that resulted from large-scale immigration in the twentieth century.

5. Describe the principles of religious liberty found in the Establishment and Free Exercise clauses of the First Amendment, including the debate on the issue of separation of church and state.

11.4 Students trace the rise of the United States to its role as a world power in the twentieth century.

1. List the purpose and the effects of the Open Door policy.

2. Describe the Spanish-American War and U.S. expansion in the South Pacific.

3. Discuss America's role in the Panama Revolution and the building of the Panama Canal.

4. Explain Theodore Roosevelt's Big Stick diplomacy, William Taft's Dollar Diplomacy, and Woodrow Wilson's Moral Diplomacy, drawing on relevant speeches.

5. Analyze the political, economic, and social ramifications of World War I on the home front.

6. Trace the declining role of Great Britain and the expanding role of the United States in world affairs after World War II.

11.5 Students analyze the major political, social, economic, technological, and cultural developments of the 1920s.

1. Discuss the policies of Presidents Warren Harding, Calvin Coolidge, and Herbert Hoover.

2. Analyze the international and domestic events, interests, and philosophies that prompted attacks on civil liberties, including the Palmer Raids, Marcus Garvey's "back-to-Africa" movement, the Ku Klux Klan, and immigration quotas and the responses of organizations such as the American Civil Liberties Union, the National Association for the Advancement of Colored People, and the Anti-Defamation League to those attacks.

3. Examine the passage of the Eighteenth Amendment to the Constitution and the Volstead Act (Prohibition).

4. Analyze the passage of the Nineteenth Amendment and the changing role of women in society.

5. Describe the Harlem Renaissance and new trends in literature, music, and art, with special attention to the work of writers (e.g., Zora Neale Hurston, Langston Hughes).

6. Trace the growth and effects of radio and movies and their role in the worldwide diffusion of popular culture.

7. Discuss the rise of mass production techniques, the growth of cities, the impact of new technologies (e.g., the automobile, electricity), and the resulting prosperity and effect on the American landscape.

11.6 Students analyze the different explanations for the Great Depression and how the New Deal fundamentally changed the role of the federal government.

1. Describe the monetary issues of the late nineteenth and early twentieth centuries that gave rise to the establishment of the Federal Reserve and the weaknesses in key sectors of the economy in the late 1920s.

2. Understand the explanations of the principal causes of the Great Depression and the steps taken by the Federal Reserve, Congress, and Presidents Herbert Hoover and Franklin Delano Roosevelt to combat the economic crisis.

3. Discuss the human toll of the Depression, natural disasters, and unwise agricultural practices and their effects on the depopulation of rural regions and on political movements of the left and right, with particular attention to the Dust Bowl refugees and their social and economic impacts in California.

4. Analyze the effects of and the controversies arising from New Deal economic policies and the expanded role of the federal government in society and the economy since the 1930s (e.g., Works Progress

Administration, Social Security, National Labor Relations Board, farm programs, regional development policies, and energy development projects such as the Tennessee Valley Authority, California Central Valley Project, and Bonneville Dam).

5. Trace the advances and retreats of organized labor, from the creation of the American Federation of Labor and the Congress of Industrial Organizations to current issues of a postindustrial, multinational economy, including the United Farm Workers in California.

11.7 Students analyze America's participation in World War II.

1. Examine the origins of American involvement in the war, with an emphasis on the events that precipitated the attack on Pearl Harbor.

2. Explain U.S. and Allied wartime strategy, including the major battles of Midway, Normandy, Iwo Jima, Okinawa, and the Battle of the Bulge.

3. Identify the roles and sacrifices of individual American soldiers, as well as the unique contributions of the special fighting forces (e.g., the Tuskegee Airmen, the 442nd Regimental Combat team, the Navajo Code Talkers).

4. Analyze Roosevelt's foreign policy during World War II (e.g., Four Freedoms speech).

5. Discuss the constitutional issues and impact of events on the U.S. home front, including the internment of Japanese Americans (e.g., *Fred Korematsu* v. *United States of America*) and the restrictions on German and Italian resident aliens; the response of the administration to Hitler's atrocities against Jews and other groups; the roles of women in military production; and the roles and growing political demands of African Americans.

6. Describe major developments in aviation, weaponry, communication, and medicine and the war's impact on the location of American industry and use of resources.

7. Discuss the decision to drop atomic bombs and the consequences of the decision (Hiroshima and Nagasaki).

8. Analyze the effect of massive aid given to Western Europe under the Marshall Plan to rebuild itself after the war and the importance of a rebuilt Europe to the U.S. economy.

11.8 Students analyze the economic boom and social transformation of post–World War II America.

1. Trace the growth of service sector, white collar, and professional sector jobs in business and government.

2. Describe the significance of Mexican immigration and its relationship to the agricultural economy, especially in California.

3. Examine Truman's labor policy and congressional reaction to it.

4. Analyze new federal government spending on defense, welfare, interest on the national debt, and federal and state spending on education, including the California Master Plan.

5. Describe the increased powers of the presidency in response to the Great Depression, World War II, and the Cold War.

6. Discuss the diverse environmental regions of North America, their relationship to local economies, and the origins and prospects of environmental problems in those regions.

7. Describe the effects on society and the economy of technological developments since 1945, including the computer revolution, changes in communication, advances in medicine, and improvements in agricultural technology.

8. Discuss forms of popular culture, with emphasis on their origins and geographic diffusion (e.g., jazz and other forms of popular music, professional sports, architectural and artistic styles).

11.9 Students analyze U.S. foreign policy since World War II.

1. Discuss the establishment of the United Nations and International Declaration of Human Rights, International Monetary Fund, World Bank, and General Agreement on Tariffs and Trade (GATT) and their importance in shaping modern Europe and maintaining peace and international order.

2. Understand the role of military alliances, including NATO and SEATO, in deterring communist aggression and maintaining security during the Cold War.

3. Trace the origins and geopolitical consequences (foreign and domestic) of the Cold War and containment policy, including the following:

   • The era of McCarthyism, instances of domestic Communism (e.g., Alger Hiss) and blacklisting
   • The Truman Doctrine
   • The Berlin Blockade
   • The Korean War
   • The Bay of Pigs Invasion and the Cuban Missile Crisis
   • Atomic testing in the American West, the "mutual assured destruction" doctrine, and disarmament policies
   • The Vietnam War
   • Latin American policy

4. List the effects of foreign policy on domestic policies and vice versa (e.g., protests during the war in Vietnam, the "nuclear freeze" movement).

5. Analyze the role of the Reagan administration and other factors in the victory of the West in the Cold War.

6. Describe U.S. Middle East policy and its strategic, political, and economic interests, including those related to the Gulf War.

7. Examine relations between the United States and Mexico in the twentieth century, including key economic, political, immigration, and environmental issues.

11.10 Students analyze the development of federal civil rights and voting rights.

1. Explain how demands of African Americans helped produce a stimulus for civil rights, including President Roosevelt's ban on racial discrimination in defense industries in 1941, and how African Americans' service in World War II produced a stimulus for President Truman's decision to end segregation in the armed forces in 1948.

2. Examine and analyze the key events, policies, and court cases in the evolution of civil rights, including *Dred Scott* v. *Sandford, Plessy* v. *Ferguson, Brown* v. *Board of Education, Regents of the University of California* v. *Bakke,* and California Proposition 209.

3. Describe the collaboration on legal strategy between African American and white civil rights lawyers to end racial segregation in higher education.

4. Examine the roles of civil rights advocates (e.g., A. Philip Randolph, Martin Luther King, Jr., Malcolm X, Thurgood Marshall, James Farmer, Rosa Parks), including the significance of Martin Luther King, Jr.'s "Letter from Birmingham Jail" and "I Have a Dream" speech.

5. Discuss the diffusion of the civil rights movement of African Americans from the churches of the rural South and the urban North, including the resistance to racial desegregation in Little Rock and Birmingham, and how the advances influenced the agendas, strategies, and effectiveness of the quests of American Indians, Asian Americans, and Hispanic Americans for civil rights and equal opportunities.

6. Analyze the passage and effects of civil rights and voting rights legislation (e.g., 1964 Civil Rights Act, Voting Rights Act of 1965) and the Twenty-Fourth Amendment, with an emphasis on equality of access to education and to the political process.

7. Analyze the women's rights movement from the era of Elizabeth Cady Stanton and Susan B. Anthony and the passage of the Nineteenth Amendment to the movement launched in the 1960s, including differing perspectives on the roles of women.

11.11 **Students analyze the major social problems and domestic policy issues in contemporary American society.**

1. Discuss the reasons for the nation's changing immigration policy, with emphasis on how the Immigration Act of 1965 and successor acts have transformed American society.

2. Discuss the significant domestic policy speeches of Truman, Eisenhower, Kennedy, Johnson, Nixon, Carter, Reagan, Bush, and Clinton (e.g., with regard to education, civil rights, economic policy, environmental policy).

3. Describe the changing roles of women in society as reflected in the entry of more women into the labor force and the changing family structure.

4. Explain the constitutional crisis originating from the Watergate scandal.

5. Trace the impact of, need for, and controversies associated with environmental conservation, expansion of the national park system, and the development of environmental protection laws, with particular attention to the interaction between environmental protection advocates and property rights advocates.

6. Analyze the persistence of poverty and how different analyses of this issue influence welfare reform, health insurance reform, and other social policies.

7. Explain how the federal, state, and local governments have responded to demographic and social changes such as population shifts to the suburbs, racial concentrations in the cities, Frostbelt-to-Sunbelt migration, international migration, decline of family farms, increases in out-of-wedlock births, and drug abuse.

Grade Twelve—
Principles of American Democracy
(One Semester)

In this course students apply knowledge gained in previous years of study to pursue a deeper understanding of the institutions of American government. In addition, they draw on their studies of American history and of other societies to compare different systems of government in the world today. This course should be viewed as the culmination of the civic literacy strand that prepares students to vote, to reflect on the responsibilities of citizenship, and to participate in community activities.

The Constitution and the Bill of Rights

In this first study of the course, students focus on the philosophy of those who framed the Constitution and the Bill of Rights. Both documents are used in conjunction with selected portions of the *Federalist Papers.* Teachers should use the latter to illustrate such major constitutional concepts as separation of powers, checks and balances, and enumerated powers as well as the framers' understanding of human nature and the political process. For example, when dealing with the rationale for checks and balances and separation of powers, students should study *Federalist Paper Number 51;* or when dealing with the role of the judiciary, they should study *Federalist Paper Number 78.* Students should read substantive selections from these and other federalist essays.

The *Federalist Papers* should be presented as arguments intended to dispel Antifederalist reservations and to persuade a skeptical public, rather than as holy writ, so that students can understand that the ideas now taken for granted had to survive close scrutiny. In addition, students should study the Declaration of Independence, Washington's Farewell Address, Lincoln's Gettysburg Address and the Emancipation Proclamation for deeper understanding of the fundamental principles and moral values of American democracy.

The Courts and the Governmental Process

In this unit students examine the role of the courts s a major element the governmental process. They should concentrate on how the courts have interpreted the Bill of Rights over time, with emphasis on themes such as due process of law and equal protection as guaranteed by the Fourteenth Amendment. Whenever possible, students should be given illustrations of the kinds of controversies that have arisen because of challenges or differing interpretations of the Bill of Rights. The unit should be organized around case studies of specific issues, such as the First Amendment's cases on free speech,

Standard 12.1.

Students explain the fundamental principles and moral values of American democracy as expressed in the U.S. Constitution and other essential documents of American democracy.

Chronological and Spatial Thinking 1.

Students compare the present with the past, evaluating the consequences of past events and decisions and determining the lessons that were learned.

Standard 12.2.

Students evaluate and take and defend positions on the scope and limits of rights and obligations as democratic citizens, the relationships among them, and how they are secured.

religious liberty, separation of church and state, academic freedom, and the right of assembly. Supreme Court decisions may be debated or simulated in the classroom, following readings of original source materials, including significant excerpts from the specific cases. Students should understand not only that rights and societal interests were in conflict, but also that each case involved real people and that our present laws have resulted from the debates, trials, and sacrifices of ordinary people.

In examining the evolution of the civil rights issue under the equal protection clause, students should draw on their knowledge of the Civil War and the passage of the Reconstruction amendments. Students should examine the changing interpretation of civil rights law from the *Plessy* v. *Ferguson* decision of 1896 to the *Brown* decision of 1954. Although it is not possible to analyze every decision that marked the shift of the Supreme Court from 1896 to 1954, critical reading of the *Yick Wo* and *Korematsu* v. *United States* decisions should serve to remind students that racial discrimination affected not only blacks but other groups as well, including Asians and Hispanics. A study of the higher education cases (for example, *Sweatt* v. *Painter* or *McLaurin* v. *Oklahoma*) should prepare the ground for the Court's switch in *Brown*. The *Brown* decision provides the opportunity to debate whether the law should be color blind or color conscious. Students can use materials from these cases to simulate a trial of the issues.

Our Government Today: The Legislative and Executive Branches

In this unit students examine the work of modern legislatures and the executive branch of government.

Each generation of Americans has made contributions to our governmental system, and citizens in each era have created mechanisms to deal with new problems and address inequities. Case studies of recent issues (for example, tax reform, social security reform, and environmental protection laws) should be used to explore the process and issues of lawmaking, such as the committee system, lobbying, and the influence of the media and special interests on legislation. Through critical reading of primary documents and the use of simulations, role play, and other interactive learning strategies, students can practice critical thinking and apply these skills to assess proposed legislation, candidates for office, and the practices of legislatures.

Students should examine the workings of the executive branch. Through a critical reading of primary documents and the use of simulations, role play, and other interactive learning strategies, students can practice critical thinking and apply these skills to assess proposed legislation, candidates for office, and the practices of legislatures.

Students should examine the workings of the executive branch. Through a critical reading of primary and secondary sources, students should be able to

Standard 12.5.

Students summarize landmark U.S. Supreme Court interpretations of the Constitution and its amendments.

Historical Research, Evidence, and Point of View 1.

Students distinguish valid arguments from fallacious arguments in historical interpretations.

Standard 12.4.

Students analyze the unique roles and responsibilities of the three branches of government as established by the U.S. Constitution.

Historical Research, Evidence, and Point of View 4.

Students construct and test hypotheses; collect, evaluate, and employ information from multiple primary and secondary sources; and apply it in oral and written presentations.

Course
Descriptions

Grade Twelve

Standard 12.8.

Students evaluate and take and defend positions on the influence of the media on American political life.

Standard 12.7.

Students analyze and compare the powers and procedures of the national, state, tribal, and local governments.

Standard 12.3.

Students evaluate and take and defend positions on what the fundamental values and principles of civil society are (i.e., the autonomous sphere of voluntary personal, social, and economic relations that are not part of government), their interdependence, and the meaning and importance of those values and principles for a free society.

document the evolution of the Presidency and the growth of the power to cope with war, economic crisis, and America's role in world affairs. Through selected case studies, students can analyze presidential campaigns, the handling of international crises, and the scope and limits of presidential power (both foreign and domestic). Examples might include the Steel Crisis, the Cuban Missile Crisis, or the Iran Hostage Crisis. Students should explore the process of presidential decision making through role play, simulation, and interactive learning.

Federalism: State and Local Government

In this unit students analyze the principles of federalism. Students should learn how power is divided among federal, state, and local governments. Student should understand that local governments are the legal creations of state governments. What kinds of issues does each level of government handle? What happens when there is overlapping jurisdiction; for example, on matters such as transportation and housing? How do people get involved in state and local government? How do state and local regulatory agencies differ form those at the federal level? Students should become aware of the important areas (for example, criminal justice, family law, environmental protection, and education) that remain largely under state and county control. They should discuss the important functions that are retained by localities, such as police and fire protection, sanitation, local public schools, and other services.

By analyzing a significant school policy issue, students should learn how public education is governed and financed and how policies that affect schools are influenced and decided. Students should examine topics such as the role of the local school board, state legislation, California initiatives affecting the schools such as Proposition 13, and the budgetary priorities of elected state officials. Students should analyze the importance of their vote in influencing the quality and future of public education in California and consider ways of becoming actively involved in issues that affect education.

Time should be devoted to a study of the ways in which individuals can become participatory citizens through voting, jury service, volunteerism, and involvement in community organizations. Resource people from local agencies and organizations can be invited to visit classrooms and facilitate site visits to demonstrate the work they do and reinforce the vital role the individual plays in community life. In addition, students should be given opportunities to volunteer for community service in their schools and communities.

Comparative Governments, with Emphasis on Communism in the World

This unit begins with a review of the major philosophies encountered by students during their previous studies: socialism, fascism, communism,

Course
Descriptions

Grade Twelve

Standard 12.9.

Students analyze the
origins, characteristics,
and development of
different political systems
across time, with
emphasis on the quest
for political democracy,
its advances, and its
obstacles.

capitalism, and democratic pluralism. Students should understand the way in which these different philosophies influence governments, economic policies, social welfare policies, and human rights practices. They should recognize that most nations combine aspects of different philosophies.

The varieties of democracies should be explored, so that students understand the fundamental features of democratic governments. At the same time, students should examine how some Western democracies have "mixed" systems of capitalism and state socialism and that contemporary politics has been marked by movements toward more market-based systems.

The fundamental differences between democracies and dictatorships of the right and the left should be understood. Critical thinking skills should be used to analyze the nature of a dictatorial regime in which no social contract exists between the state and those it governs and in which citizens have no rights nor means of redressing wrongs. Does such a government rest on the consent of the governed? Do citizens have rights that the state must respect?

A review of pre–World War II fascism in Germany, Italy, Spain, and Portugal should be updated with a survey of contemporary dictatorships of the right. Attention should be given to the arbitrary rulings, torture, imprisonment, and executions without trials that attend fascist takeovers and help to maintain their control. Students should examine the social, economic, and political conditions that have given rise to such regimes. They should analyze the support given to such regimes by people who would protect or restore the status quo at any cost and by people who seek a military end to internal and imported revolutionary terrorism that their civilian governments have been unable to control. Attention also should be given to the movement to democratic government and the effects of the end of the Cold War in such countries as Spain, Argentina, Chile, the Philippines, South Korea, Guatemala, El Salvador, and South Africa.

The main focus of this unit is on dictatorship because it is the antithesis of democracy. Understanding the nature of dictatorship should be enhanced by map study and identification of antidemocratic governments in Asia, Africa, Latin America, and Eastern Europe. In discussing dictatorship students should use what they learned in grade ten about communism, with specific reference to the Russian Revolution, Marxist ideology, the dictatorship of Joseph Stalin, and the expansion of Soviet power after World War II. The nature of dictatorial communist rule in the Soviet Union should be compared to communism today in Cuba, Cambodia, Vietnam, and China with attention to similarities and differences.

Students should examine the means by which communist regimes have come to power and the appeal that these regimes have for groups of the left who believe that only revolution or radical change can reform their societies. Students should understand the appeal of communist ideology to intellectuals and the poor.

Course
Descriptions

Grade Twelve

Students should understand the concept of the total state where the government, the military, the educational system, all social organizations, the media, and the economy are controlled by the communist party. They should analyze the methods used by communist regimes to maintain control; for example, the repression of political opposition and dissident minorities through the use of internal controls such as the KGB and forced labor camps in the Gulag Archipelago, where critics and dissident intellectuals are treated as criminals.

Students should examine the condition of human rights in communist societies: Why have communist revolutions been followed by purges of dissidents, mass arrests of political opponents, murder of "class enemies," suppression of free speech, abolition of private property, and attacks on religious groups? Why do many artists and intellectuals defect to non-communist nations? Why do communist governments spy on their citizens and prevent them from emigrating? Why do they jail or harass critics of their government? Why is only one party allowed in a communist state? What significance does a one-party election have in a communist state? Why are independent trade unions not tolerated in a communist state? Why do ordinary people risk their lives to flee a communist state? To assess the Soviet Union's pattern of dominating other nations, students should review the overthrow of the Czech government, the mass deportations and Russification of the Baltic populations, the Hungarian Revolution, the Berlin Wall, the suppression of the Solidarity movement in Poland, and the invasion of Afghanistan. Students should analyze why communism collapsed and study the governments that arose in the former Soviet Union and Eastern Europe.

The economic record of communism should be assessed: What have been the effects of centralized planning? Students should analyze the effects of an economic system in which greater effort does not result in greater reward for the individual; in which individuals are not allowed to accumulate capital for future productivity; in which prices are not allowed to rise in order to reduce quantities demanded; and in which consumers have no control over allocation policies affecting the tradeoff between consumer goods on one hand and military, defense, and police activities on the other. Recent changes in China to encourage entrepreneurial activities and modernize its economy should be analyzed.

Historical

Interpretation 6.

Students conduct cost-benefit analyses and apply basic economic indicators to analyze the aggregate economic behavior.

Contemporary Issues in the World Today

This course should conclude with an activity in which students analyze a major social issue. This activity might be a research paper in which students analyze a problem, marshal historical and social science evidence, provide a critique of alternative positions, use available electoral and polling data to make a prediction of popular support for positions, and present their own position on the issue. A student could prepare this research as if it were a background paper for candidates in local, state, or national elections or as if the student were developing reasons for choosing among candidates.

Among the topics that might be addressed are technological issues, such as nuclear arms proliferation and arms control; environmental issues, such as acid rain, toxic waste disposal, and resource depletion; human rights issues; economic issues, such as competition from abroad, either because of cheap labor or advanced technology; health issues, such as drug abuse and the spread of AIDS; international economic issues, such as the movement to decentralize socialist economies; and international political issues stemming from the demand for democratic government in nations of Central and South America, Africa, and Asia. Students should pay attention to the global context of these issues as well as their importance in local, state, or national affairs.

At the conclusion of this unit, a schoolwide consortium might be planned in which students present their papers in open forum and debate or discuss the issues from alternative viewpoints.

Grade Twelve

Standard 12.10.

Students formulate questions about and defend their analyses of tensions within our constitutional democracy and the importance of maintaining a balance between the following concepts: majority rule and individual rights; liberty and equality; state and national authority in a federal system; civil disobedience and the rule of law; freedom of the press and the right to a fair trial; the relationship of religion and government.

Standard 12.6.

Students evaluate issues regarding campaigns for national, state, and local elective offices.

Chronological and Spatial Thinking 3.

Students use a variety of maps and documents to interpret human movement, including major patterns of domestic and international migration, changing environmental preferences and settlement patterns, the frictions that develop between population groups, and the diffusion of ideas, technological innovations, and goods.

History–Social Science Standards

Grade Twelve
Principles of American Democracy

12.1 Students explain the fundamental principles and moral values of American democracy as expressed in the U.S. Constitution and other essential documents of American democracy.

1. Analyze the influence of ancient Greek, Roman, English, and leading European political thinkers such as John Locke, Charles-Louis Montesquieu, Niccolò Machiavelli, and William Blackstone on the development of American government.

2. Discuss the character of American democracy and its promise and perils as articulated by Alexis de Tocqueville.

3. Explain how the U.S. Constitution reflects a balance between the classical republican concern with promotion of the public good and the classical liberal concern with protecting individual rights; and discuss how the basic premises of liberal constitutionalism and democracy are joined in the Declaration of Independence as "self-evident truths."

4. Explain how the Founding Fathers' realistic view of human nature led directly to the establishment of a constitutional system that limited the power of the governors and the governed as articulated in the *Federalist Papers.*

5. Describe the systems of separated and shared powers, the role of organized interests *(Federalist Paper Number 10),* checks and balances *(Federalist Paper Number 51),* the importance of an independent judiciary *(Federalist Paper Number 78),* enumerated powers, rule of law, federalism, and civilian control of the military.

6. Understand that the Bill of Rights limits the powers of the federal government and state governments.

12.2 Students evaluate and take and defend positions on the scope and limits of rights and obligations as democratic citizens, the relationships among them, and how they are secured.

1. Discuss the meaning and importance of each of the rights guaranteed under the Bill of Rights and how each is secured (e.g., freedom of religion, speech, press, assembly, petition, privacy).

2. Explain how economic rights are secured and their importance to the individual and to society (e.g., the right to acquire, use, transfer, and dispose of property; right to choose one's work; right to join or not join labor unions; copyright and patent).

165

Course
Descriptions

**Grade Twelve
Content
Standards**

3. Discuss the individual's legal obligations to obey the law, serve as a juror, and pay taxes.

4. Understand the obligations of civic-mindedness, including voting, being informed on civic issues, volunteering and performing public service, and serving in the military or alternative service.

5. Describe the reciprocity between rights and obligations; that is, why enjoyment of one's rights entails respect for the rights of others.

6. Explain how one becomes a citizen of the United States, including the process of naturalization (e.g., literacy, language, and other requirements).

12.3 Students evaluate and take and defend positions on what the fundamental values and principles of civil society are (i.e., the autonomous sphere of voluntary personal, social, and economic relations that are not part of government), their interdependence, and the meaning and importance of those values and principles for a free society.

1. Explain how civil society provides opportunities for individuals to associate for social, cultural, religious, economic, and political purposes.

2. Explain how civil society makes it possible for people, individually or in association with others, to bring their influence to bear on government in ways other than voting and elections.

3. Discuss the historical role of religion and religious diversity.

4. Compare the relationship of government and civil society in constitutional democracies to the relationship of government and civil society in authoritarian and totalitarian regimes.

12.4 Students analyze the unique roles and responsibilities of the three branches of government as established by the U.S. Constitution.

1. Discuss Article I of the Constitution as it relates to the legislative branch, including eligibility for office and lengths of terms of representatives and senators; election to office; the roles of the House and Senate in impeachment proceedings; the role of the vice president; the enumerated legislative powers; and the process by which a bill becomes a law.

2. Explain the process through which the Constitution can be amended.

3. Identify their current representatives in the legislative branch of the national government.

4. Discuss Article II of the Constitution as it relates to the executive branch, including eligibility for office and length of term, election to and removal from office, the oath of office, and the enumerated executive powers.

5. Discuss Article III of the Constitution as it relates to judicial power, including the length of terms of judges and the jurisdiction of the Supreme Court.

6. Explain the processes of selection and confirmation of Supreme Court justices.

12.5 Students summarize landmark U.S. Supreme Court interpretations of the Constitution and its amendments.

1. Understand the changing interpretations of the Bill of Rights over time, including interpretations of the basic freedoms (religion, speech, press, petition, and assembly) articulated in the First Amendment and the due process and equal-protection-of-the-law clauses of the Fourteenth Amendment.

2. Analyze judicial activism and judicial restraint and the effects of each policy over the decades (e.g., the Warren and Rehnquist courts).

3. Evaluate the effects of the Court's interpretations of the Constitution in *Marbury* v. *Madison, McCulloch* v. *Maryland,* and *United States* v. *Nixon,* with emphasis on the arguments espoused by each side in these cases.

4. Explain the controversies that have resulted over changing interpretations of civil rights, including those in *Plessy* v. *Ferguson, Brown* v. *Board of Education, Miranda* v. *Arizona, Regents of the University of California* v. *Bakke, Adarand Constructors, Inc.* v. *Pena, and United States* v. *Virginia* (VMI).

12.6 Students evaluate issues regarding campaigns for national, state, and local elective offices.

1. Analyze the origin, development, and role of political parties, noting those occasional periods in which there was only one major party or were more than two major parties.

2. Discuss the history of the nomination process for presidential candidates and the increasing importance of primaries in general elections.

3. Evaluate the roles of polls, campaign advertising, and the controversies over campaign funding.

4. Describe the means that citizens use to participate in the political process (e.g., voting, campaigning, lobbying, filing a legal challenge, demonstrating, petitioning, picketing, running for political office).

5. Discuss the features of direct democracy in numerous states (e.g., the process of referendums, recall elections).

6. Analyze trends in voter turnout; the causes and effects of reapportionment and redistricting, with special attention to spatial districting and the rights of minorities; and the function of the Electoral College.

167

Course
Descriptions

Grade Twelve
Content
Standards

12.7 **Students analyze and compare the powers and procedures of the national, state, tribal, and local governments.**

1. Explain how conflicts between levels of government and branches of government are resolved.
2. Identify the major responsibilities and sources of revenue for state and local governments.
3. Discuss reserved powers and concurrent powers of state governments.
4. Discuss the Ninth and Tenth Amendments and interpretations of the extent of the federal government's power.
5. Explain how public policy is formed, including the setting of the public agenda and implementation of it through regulations and executive orders.
6. Compare the processes of lawmaking at each of the three levels of government, including the role of lobbying and the media.
7. Identify the organization and jurisdiction of federal, state, and local (e.g., California) courts and the interrelationships among them.
8. Understand the scope of presidential power and decision making through examination of case studies such as the Cuban Missile Crisis, passage of Great Society legislation, War Powers Act, Gulf War, and Bosnia.

12.8 **Students evaluate and take and defend positions on the influence of the media on American political life.**

1. Discuss the meaning and importance of a free and responsible press.
2. Describe the roles of broadcast, print, and electronic media, including the Internet, as means of communication in American politics.
3. Explain how public officials use the media to communicate with the citizenry and to shape public opinion.

12.9 **Students analyze the origins, characteristics, and development of different political systems across time, with emphasis on the quest for political democracy, its advances, and its obstacles.**

1. Explain how the different philosophies and structures of feudalism, mercantilism, socialism, fascism, communism, monarchies, parliamentary systems, and constitutional liberal democracies influence economic policies, social welfare policies, and human rights practices.
2. Compare the various ways in which power is distributed, shared, and limited in systems of shared powers and in parliamentary systems, including the influence and role of parliamentary leaders (e.g., William Gladstone, Margaret Thatcher).
3. Discuss the advantages and disadvantages of federal, confederal, and unitary systems of government.

4. Describe for at least two countries the consequences of conditions that gave rise to tyrannies during certain periods (e.g., Italy, Japan, Haiti, Nigeria, Cambodia).

5. Identify the forms of illegitimate power that twentieth-century African, Asian, and Latin American dictators used to gain and hold office and the conditions and interests that supported them.

6. Identify the ideologies, causes, stages, and outcomes of major Mexican, Central American, and South American revolutions in the nineteenth and twentieth centuries.

7. Describe the ideologies that give rise to Communism, methods of maintaining control, and the movements to overthrow such governments in Czechoslovakia, Hungary, and Poland, including the roles of individuals (e.g., Alexander Solzhenitsyn, Pope John Paul II, Lech Walesa, Vaclav Havel).

8. Identify the successes of relatively new democracies in Africa, Asia, and Latin America and the ideas, leaders, and general societal conditions that have launched and sustained, or failed to sustain, them.

12.10 Students formulate questions about and defend their analyses of tensions within our constitutional democracy and the importance of maintaining a balance between the following concepts: majority rule and individual rights; liberty and equality; state and national authority in a federal system; civil disobedience and the rule of law; freedom of the press and the right to a fair trial; the relationship of religion and government.

Grade Twelve—
Economics (One Semester)

In a one-semester course in economics, students should deepen their understanding of the economic problems and institutions of the nation and world in which they live. They should learn to make reasoned decisions on economic issues as citizens, workers, consumers, business owners and managers, and members of civic groups. In this capstone course students should add to the economic understandings they acquired in previous grades and apply tools (such as graphs, statistics, and equations) learned in other subject fields to their understanding of our economic system.

This course primarily is a course in social science, enriching students' understanding of the operations and institutions of economic systems, rather than a course in household or business management or budgeting. Throughout this course, measurement concepts and methods should be introduced; for example, tables, charts, graphs, ratios, percentages, and index numbers. Behind every graph is an equation or set of equations that specifies a relationship among economic variables. Thus, to master the economic method, students must use graphs and understand, at the appropriate level, the mathematical equations they represent.

Fundamental Economic Concepts

The basic economic problem facing all individuals, groups, and nations is the problem of scarcity. Scarcity results from the limited natural resources, such as water, land, and minerals, that are available to produce the variety of goods and services that we need and want. Because of scarcity, choices must be made concerning how to utilize limited resources. At the same time, students should understand how the market economy spurs innovation and growth, tends toward cycles, and distributes income and wealth. In this unit students should learn the difference between the final goods and services that any economy produces and the productive resources, including human resources, capital goods, and natural resources that are used to produce these final goods and services. They should learn and then apply a reasoned approach to making decisions.

Economic reasoning relies in part on mastering cost-benefit analysis. Through this skill, students will be able to explain actions of individuals in product and labor markets. Using cost-benefit analysis, individuals are able to weigh alternatives, compare costs and benefits, and make decisions using economic reasoning. A consumption decision would compare the benefits and costs of buying one product instead of another, or buying on credit, or not buying at all. A production decision would compare the benefits and costs of

Historical
Interpretation 6.

Students conduct cost-benefit analyses and apply basic economic indicators to analyze the aggregate economic behavior of the U.S. economy.

Standard 12.1

Students understand common economic terms and concepts and economic reasoning.

Course
Descriptions

Grade Twelve

producing one product instead of another, or producing more or less of one product, or not producing a product at all. An educational decision would compare the benefits and costs of college, technical school, apprenticeship, or immediate entrance into the workforce. Through cost-benefit analysis, students will be able to understand strengths and weaknesses of decisions made by individuals in the market. Economic reasoning helps students to apply analytical economic skills to the decisions they are making and will be making and to recognize the constraints and opportunities of the U.S. economy in the world economy of the twenty-first century.

The basic choices that producers in any economic system must make involve determining what goods and services to produce, how to produce these goods and services, and for whom to produce them. Students should be introduced to our largely free market system that uses prices and levels of supply and demand in markets to answer these basic questions. Households, including individuals, demand the goods and services that give them the most satisfaction, given their income and the prices of these goods. Business firms try to maximize profits by supplying at the least cost the goods and services that households demand.

Businesses allocate factors of production based on the demand for the goods and services they produce. This "derived demand" for factors is a major determinant of distribution of income in a market economy.

Economic efficiency requires that individuals and business firms specialize in the performance of particular tasks or the manufacture of particular goods and that they exchange their surpluses of goods for the goods they want to consume. Money was developed to facilitate this exchange. Thus, specialization, exchange, and money are the results of our interdependence, which, in turn, results in efficient production of the final goods and services of our economy.

Comparative Economic Systems

Standard 12.2

Students analyze the elements of America's market economy in a global setting.

A market system is characterized by decentralized decision making on the part of households and businesses. In this free enterprise system, most of the goods and services are produced by the private sector, by firms owned and operated for profit. The decisions of individuals influence market prices that reflect the preferences of all participants and that act as signals to producers and as rationing devices. Thus, to answer the basic economic questions, decision makers in the market system rely primarily on the preferences and choices of the members of the society.

Students should learn about alternatives to the market system, such as traditional and command economies, and learn how decisions in these economies rely on mechanisms other than the choices of the members of these societies. Students should learn that no real world economy is a pure form of any of these economies. They should understand that decentralized decision making in a market is most evident in the economies of the United States,

Canada, and Western Europe, whereas elements of a command economy are most evident in the former Soviet Union. They should learn that economic systems change to reflect changes in values or technology and in the role of the market and the government. Students should study the strengths and weaknesses of each society and its values regarding the objectives of an economic system.

Microeconomics

In this unit students should examine the operations of markets. They should learn how prices and the quantity demanded and supplied are determined in the markets for goods and factors of production. They should study how prices provide information and incentives and serve to ration limited resources. Students should learn about the interaction of the demand schedule and the curve which represents it together with the supply schedule and its graphic representation in determining prices and output. They also should learn what events lead to changes in demand and supply and how these changes influence prices.

Students should learn about alternative forms of business organizations, including single proprietorships, partnerships, and corporations, and their impact on the economy. They should consider in detail the operations of the labor market. Students should analyze the determinants of the levels of employment and wages in different occupations and the impact of unionization, the minimum wage, unemployment insurance, and the effects of international mobility of capital and labor.

Standard 12.4.

Students analyze the elements of the U.S. labor market in a global setting.

Students should focus specifically on the distribution of income in our economy, the differing costs of living across the United States, and the determination of income and cost distribution. Students should be aware of alternative measures of this distribution and the methods that federal, state, and local governments use to influence income distribution through transfer payments and taxes.

Our market economy is characterized by different market structures, including monopolies and oligopolies, and various economic principles, such as monopolistic competition and perfect competition. Students should learn how less than perfectly competitive markets operate and examine their impact on the economy. They should also learn that a pure market economy has disadvantages, including its failure to provide goods and services that are consumed jointly or that benefit people who do not have to pay for them directly. These goods and services include clean air, education, national defense, and roads. Students should consider the role of the government in a largely free market economy. Students should examine other responsibilities of the government, including establishing trade regulations and price controls and influencing the market's equilibrium. The role of the government in agriculture can be introduced as a case study of government intervention in a market.

Historical Research, Evidence, and Point of View 4.

Students construct and test hypotheses; collect, evaluate, and employ information from multiple primary and secondary sources; and apply it in oral and written presentations.

Course
Descriptions

Grade Twelve

Standard 12.5.

Students analyze the aggregate economic behavior of the U.S. economy.

Chronological and Spatial Thinking 2.

Students analyze how change happens at different rates at different times; understand that some aspects can change while others remain the same; and understand that change is complicated and affects not only technology and politics but also values and beliefs.

Standard 12.3.

Students analyze the influence of the federal government on the American economy.

Standard 12.6.

Students analyze issues of international trade and explain how the U.S. economy affects, and is affected by, economic forces beyond the United States's borders.

Macroeconomics

Macroeconomics is the functioning of our economy as a whole. To facilitate their understanding of macroeconomics and deepen their understanding of the nature and history of our economy, students should learn about the statistics that have been developed to measure the functioning of our economy, including measures of national income (such as the gross national product) and measures of change in the price level (such as the consumer price index and the gross national product deflator). Students should use these statistics and measures of employment and unemployment to study the business cycle, unemployment, inflation, and economic growth.

Aggregate demand in our economy is determined by decisions of households on consumption, of businesses on investment, of purchasers of our goods abroad, and of the government. Students should learn about the factors that determine each of these components of aggregate demand. Teachers should emphasize that fiscal policy involves government spending and taxing actions to stabilize the economy. Students should understand how this policy is determined and how it operates. They should understand the federal budget process. They should be able to discuss the meaning of the government budget deficit and the government debt and how these factors influence the economy.

Monetary policy influences aggregate demand. The course covers the creation of money, the role of the Federal Reserve in the creation of money and monetary policy, and the role of financial intermediaries in our economy. Students should understand the purposes and economic effects of these financial institutions.

Aggregate supply is the total amount of goods and services produced in the economy during a given period of time. The upper limit on aggregate supply is the productive capacity of our economy. Increasing this capacity requires giving up consumption today for future benefits; for example, a student postponing working to acquire more education, a business retaining earnings to reinvest rather than distributing these earnings as dividends, and government acting to raise taxes.

International Economic Concepts

In this final unit students should concentrate on the differences between intranational and international trade. They should learn about foreign exchange and how exchange rates are determined. Students should learn why nations trade internationally, and they should understand comparative and absolute advantage. They should apply what they learned about specialization and exchange in the first unit of the course to the field of international trade.

The balance of payments and the balance of trade are measures of the performance of countries in the international market. Students should learn about the meaning of these measures and what is included in them. Governments influence the pattern of imports and exports by tariffs, quotas, and other trade restrictions. Students should learn the reasons for these policies and how such policies affect the sectors of the economy that are being protected and the nation as a whole.

Finally, students might review their tenth-grade studies of developing nations and consider what factors, conditions, and policies help them to achieve sustained economic growth. They should apply to other nations what they have learned about supply and growth in our economy.

Chronological and Spatial Thinking 3. Students use a variety of maps and documents to interpret human movement, including major patterns of domestic and international migration, changing environmental preferences and settlement patterns, the frictions that develop between population groups, and the diffusion of ideas, technological innovations, and goods.

History–Social Science Standards

Grade Twelve
Principles of Economics

12.1 **Students understand common economic terms and concepts and economic reasoning.**

1. Examine the causal relationship between scarcity and the need for choices.
2. Explain opportunity cost and marginal benefit and marginal cost.
3. Identify the difference between monetary and nonmonetary incentives and how changes in incentives cause changes in behavior.
4. Evaluate the role of private property as an incentive in conserving and improving scarce resources, including renewable and non-renewable natural resources.
5. Analyze the role of a market economy in establishing and preserving political and personal liberty (e.g., through the works of Adam Smith).

12.2 **Students analyze the elements of America's market economy in a global setting.**

1. Understand the relationship of the concept of incentives to the law of supply and the relationship of the concept of incentives and substitutes to the law of demand.
2. Discuss the effects of changes in supply and/or demand on the relative scarcity, price, and quantity of particular products.
3. Explain the roles of property rights, competition, and profit in a market economy.
4. Explain how prices reflect the relative scarcity of goods and services and perform the allocative function in a market economy.
5. Understand the process by which competition among buyers and sellers determines a market price.
6. Describe the effect of price controls on buyers and sellers.
7. Analyze how domestic and international competition in a market economy affects goods and services produced and the quality, quantity, and price of those products.
8. Explain the role of profit as the incentive to entrepreneurs in a market economy.
9. Describe the functions of the financial markets.
10. Discuss the economic principles that guide the location of agricultural production and industry and the spatial distribution of transportation and retail facilities.

12.3 Students analyze the influence of the federal government on the American economy.

1. Understand how the role of government in a market economy often includes providing for national defense, addressing environmental concerns, defining and enforcing property rights, attempting to make markets more competitive, and protecting consumers' rights.

2. Identify the factors that may cause the costs of government actions to outweigh the benefits.

3. Describe the aims of government fiscal policies (taxation, borrowing, spending) and their influence on production, employment, and price levels.

4. Understand the aims and tools of monetary policy and their influence on economic activity (e.g., the Federal Reserve).

12.4 Students analyze the elements of the U.S. labor market in a global setting.

1. Understand the operations of the labor market, including the circumstances surrounding the establishment of principal American labor unions, procedures that unions use to gain benefits for their members, the effects of unionization, the minimum wage, and unemployment insurance.

2. Describe the current economy and labor market, including the types of goods and services produced, the types of skills workers need, the effects of rapid technological change, and the impact of international competition.

3. Discuss wage differences among jobs and professions, using the laws of demand and supply and the concept of productivity.

4. Explain the effects of international mobility of capital and labor on the U.S. economy.

12.5 Students analyze the aggregate economic behavior of the U.S. economy.

1. Distinguish between nominal and real data.

2. Define, calculate, and explain the significance of an unemployment rate, the number of new jobs created monthly, an inflation or deflation rate, and a rate of economic growth.

3. Distinguish between short-term and long-term interest rates and explain their relative significance.

12.6 Students analyze issues of international trade and explain how the U.S. economy affects, and is affected by, economic forces beyond the United States's borders.

1. Identify the gains in consumption and production efficiency from trade, with emphasis on the main products and changing geographic patterns of twentieth-century trade among countries in the Western Hemisphere.

2. Compare the reasons for and the effects of trade restrictions during the Great Depression compared with present-day arguments among labor, business, and political leaders over the effects of free trade on the economic and social interests of various groups of Americans.

3. Understand the changing role of international political borders and territorial sovereignty in a global economy.

4. Explain foreign exchange, the manner in which exchange rates are determined, and the effects of the dollar's gaining (or losing) value relative to other currencies.

177

Course
Descriptions

**Grades Nine
Through Twelve**
Historical
and Social Sciences
Analysis Skills

Grades Nine Through Twelve
Historical and Social Sciences Analysis Skills

The intellectual skills noted below are to be learned through, and applied to, the content standards for grades nine through twelve. They are to be assessed *only in conjunction with* the content standards in grades nine through twelve.

In addition to the standards for grades nine through twelve, students demonstrate the following intellectual, reasoning, reflection, and research skills.

Chronological and Spatial Thinking

1. Students compare the present with the past, evaluating the consequences of past events and decisions and determining the lessons that were learned.
2. Students analyze how change happens at different rates at different times; understand that some aspects can change while others remain the same; and understand that change is complicated and affects not only technology and politics but also values and beliefs.
3. Students use a variety of maps and documents to interpret human movement, including major patterns of domestic and international migration, changing environmental preferences and settlement patterns, the frictions that develop between population groups, and the diffusion of ideas, technological innovations, and goods.
4. Students relate current events to the physical and human characteristics of places and regions.

Historical Research, Evidence, and Point of View

1. Students distinguish valid arguments from fallacious arguments in historical interpretations.
2. Students identify bias and prejudice in historical interpretations.
3. Students evaluate major debates among historians concerning alternative interpretations of the past, including an analysis of authors' use of evidence and the distinctions between sound generalizations and misleading over-simplifications.
4. Students construct and test hypotheses; collect, evaluate, and employ information from multiple primary and secondary sources; and apply it in oral and written presentations.

Historical Interpretation

1. Students show the connections, causal and otherwise, between particular historical events and larger social, economic, and political trends and developments.
2. Students recognize the complexity of historical causes and effects, including the limitations on determining cause and effect.

Course
Descriptions

**Grades Nine
Through Twelve**
Historical
and Social Sciences
Analysis Skills

3. Students interpret past events and issues within the context in which an event unfolded rather than solely in terms of present-day norms and values.

4. Students understand the meaning, implication, and impact of historical events and recognize that events could have taken other directions.

5. Students analyze human modifications of landscapes and examine the resulting environmental policy issues.

6. Students conduct cost-benefit analyses and apply basic economic indicators to analyze the aggregate economic behavior of the U.S. economy.

Criteria for Evaluating Instructional Materials

Kindergarten Through Grade Eight

Criteria for Evaluating Instructional Materials: Kindergarten Through Grade Eight

This document provides criteria for evaluating the alignment of instructional materials with the *History–Social Science Content Standards for California Public Schools* (2000) and the *History–Social Science Framework for California Public Schools (2001 Updated Edition).* The content standards were adopted by the California State Board of Education in October 1998. They describe what students should know and be able to do at each grade level. The updated framework was adopted by the State Board of Education in October 2000. It incorporates the standards and includes instructional guidelines. The framework, together with the standards, defines the essential skills and knowledge in history–social science that will enable all California students to enjoy a world-class education.

The instructional materials must provide guidance for the teacher to present the content standards and curriculum at each grade level and to teach students all the analysis skills required for the grade spans. Students should be able to demonstrate reasoning, reflection, and research skills. These skills are to be learned through, and applied to, the content standards and are to be assessed only in conjunction with the content standards. Special attention should also be paid to the appendixes in the framework, which address important overarching issues.

In 2005 the State Board of Education will adopt a new list of history–social science instructional materials for use in kindergarten through grade eight. This adoption and any follow-up adoption prior to 2011 will be guided by the criteria described below. To be adopted, materials must first meet *in full* Category 1, History–Social Science Content/Alignment with Standards. Materials will be evaluated holistically in the other categories of Program Organization, Assessment, Universal Access, and Instructional Planning and Support. (These criteria may also be used by publishers and local educational agencies as a guide for developing and selecting instructional materials for

Criteria
for Evaluating
Instructional
Materials:
Kindergarten
Through
Grade Eight

grades nine through twelve.) To assist the State Board in the evaluation of instructional materials, publishers will use a standards map template supplied by the California Department of Education to demonstrate a program's alignment with the standards.

The criteria are organized into five categories:

1. **History–Social Science Content/Alignment with Standards:** The content as specified in the *Education Code,* the *History–Social Science Content Standards,* and the *History–Social Science Framework (2001 Updated Edition)*

2. **Program Organization:** The sequence and organization of the history–social science program

3. **Assessment:** The strategies presented in the instructional materials for measuring what students know and are able to do

4. **Universal Access:** Instructional materials that are understandable to all students, including students eligible for special education, English learners, and students whose achievement is either below or above that typical of the class or grade level

5. **Instructional Planning and Support:** The instructional planning and support information and materials, typically including a separate edition specially designed for use by teachers in implementing the *History–Social Science Content Standards* and *History–Social Science Framework*

History–social science instructional materials must support teaching aligned with the standards and framework. Materials that are contrary to or inconsistent with the standards, framework, and criteria are not allowed. Extraneous materials should be minimal and clearly purposeful.

Category 1: History–Social Science Content/Alignment with Standards

1. Instructional materials, as defined in *Education Code* Section 60010(h), provide instruction designed to ensure that students master all the *History–Social Science Content Standards* for the intended grade level. Analysis skills of the pertinent grade span must be covered at each grade level.

2. Instructional materials reflect and incorporate the content of the *History–Social Science Framework.*

3. Instructional materials shall use proper grammar and spelling (*Education Code* Section 60045).

4. Instructional materials present accurate, detailed content and a variety of perspectives.

5. History is presented as a story well told, with continuity and narrative coherence (a beginning, a middle, and an end), and based on the best

Criteria
for Evaluating
Instructional
Materials:
Kindergarten
Through
Grade Eight

recent scholarship. Without sacrificing historical accuracy, the narrative is rich with the forceful personalities, controversies, and issues of the time. Primary sources, such as letters, diaries, documents, and photographs, are incorporated into the narrative to present an accurate and vivid picture of the times.

6. Materials include sufficient use of primary sources appropriate to the age level of students so that students understand from the words of the authors the way people saw themselves, their work, their ideas and values, their assumptions, their fears and dreams, and their interpretation of their own times. These sources are to be integral to the program and are carefully selected to exemplify the topic. They serve as a voice from the past, conveying an accurate and thorough sense of the period. When only an excerpt of a source is included in the materials, the students and teachers are referred to the entire primary source. The materials present different perspectives of participants, both ordinary and extraordinary people, in world and U.S. history.

7. Materials include the study of issues and historical and social science debates. Students are presented with different perspectives and come to understand the importance of reasoned debate and reliable evidence, recognizing that people in a democratic society have the right to disagree.

8. Throughout the instructional resources the importance of the variables of time and place, when and where, and history and geography is stressed repeatedly. In examining the past and present, the instructional resources consistently help students recognize that events and changes occur in a specific time and place. Instructional resources also consistently help students judge the significance of the relative location of place.

9. The history–social science curriculum is enriched with various genres of fiction and nonfiction literature of and about the historical period. Forms of literature such as diaries, essays, biographies, autobiographies, myths, legends, historical tales, oral literature, poetry, and religious literature richly describe the issues or the events studied as well as the life of the people, including both work and leisure activities.

10. Materials on religious subject matter remain neutral; do not advocate one religion over another; do not include simulation or role playing of religious ceremonies or beliefs; do not include derogatory language about a religion or use examples from sacred texts or other religious literature that are derogatory, accusatory, or instill prejudice against other religions or those who believe in other religions.

11. Numerous examples are presented of women and men from different demographic groups who used their learning and intelligence to make important contributions to democratic practices and society and to science and technology. Materials emphasize the importance of education in a democratic society.

Criteria
for Evaluating
Instructional
Materials:
Kindergarten
Through
Grade Eight

12. For grades six through eight, the breadth and depth of world history to be covered are described in the updated *History–Social Science Framework* in Appendix D, "The World History Sequence at Grades Six, Seven, and Ten: Content, Breadth/Depth, and Coverage Issues with Some Local Options." In addition to the content called for at grade six, instructional materials shall include the grade seven content standards on the Roman Empire (standard 7.1 and its sequence) and Mayan civilization (standard 7.7 and the applicable Mayan aspects of the sequence). In addition to the content called for at grade eight, materials shall include the grade seven content standards on the Age of Exploration, the Enlightenment, and the Age of Reason (standard 7.11 and its sequence).

13. For kindergarten through grade three, instructional materials are distinguished by the inclusion of literature that brings alive people and events for children and teaches ethics, values, and civic responsibility. The literary selections are broadly representative of varied cultures, ethnic groups, men, women, and children and, where appropriate, provide meaningful connections to the other content standards: English–language arts, mathematics, science, and visual and performing arts.

14. Student writing assignments are aligned with the grade-level expectations in the *English–Language Arts Content Standards* (adopted by the State Board of Education in 1997) under the strands "Writing" and "Written and Oral English Language Conventions."

15. Instructional materials use biography to portray the experiences of men, women, children, and youths. Where the standards call for examples (or use "e.g."), materials shall go beyond the listed examples and include the roles and contributions of people from different demographic groups: American Indians, African Americans, Mexican Americans, Asian Americans, European Americans, and members of other ethnic and cultural groups (*Education Code* Section 60040).

16. Instructional materials, where appropriate, present the contributions of the entrepreneur and labor in the total development of California and the United States (*Education Code* sections 51009 and 60040).

17. Instructional materials, where appropriate and called for in the standards, include examples of religious and secular thinkers in history. All materials must be in accordance with the guidance provided in the updated *History–Social Science Framework*, Appendix C, "Religion and the Teaching of History–Social Science," and *Education Code* sections 51500, 51501, 51511, and 51513. The rites and practices of religions must be respected and must not be reenacted or simulated in any manner. When U.S. history is examined, religious matters, both belief

Criteria
for Evaluating
Instructional
Materials:
Kindergarten
Through
Grade Eight

and nonbelief, must be treated respectfully and be explained as protected by the U.S. Constitution.

18. Instructional materials, where appropriate, examine humanity's place in ecological systems and the necessity for the protection of the environment (*Education Code* Section 60041).

19. Instructional materials for grades five and eight shall include a discussion of the Great Irish Famine of 1845–1850 and the effect of the famine on American history (*Education Code* Section 51226.3[c]).

20. Emphasis is placed on civic values, democratic principles, and democratic institutions, including frequent opportunities for discussion of the fundamental principles embodied in the U.S. Constitution and the Bill of Rights. When appropriate to the comprehension of pupils, instructional materials shall include a copy of the U.S. Constitution and the Declaration of Independence (*Education Code* Section 60043).

21. Materials emphasize America's multiethnic heritage and its contribution to this country's development while explaining how American civic values provide students with a foundation for understanding their rights and responsibilities in this pluralistic society (*Education Code* sections 51226.5 and 60200.6).

22. Materials on American life and history give significant attention to the principles of morality, truth, justice, and patriotism and to a comprehension of the rights, duties, and dignity of American citizenship, inspiring an understanding of and a commitment to American ideals. Examples of memorable addresses by historical figures are presented in their historical context, including the effect of those addresses on people then and now (*Education Code* sections 52720 and 60200.5).

23. Materials for studying the life and contributions of Cesar E. Chavez and the history of the farm labor movement and of Martin Luther King, Jr., and the civil rights movement shall be included at each grade level, with suggestions for supporting the respective holidays in honor of those men and the accompanying activities (*Education Code* sections 51008 and 60200.6, respectively).

24. Any gross inaccuracies or deliberate falsifications revealed during the review process will result in disqualification, and any found during the adoption cycle will be subject to removal of the program from the list of state-adopted textbooks. Gross inaccuracies and deliberate falsifications are defined as those requiring changes in content.

25. All authors listed in the instructional program are held responsible for the content. If requested, the authors must be willing to supply proof of authorship. Beyond the title and publishing company's name, the only name to appear on a cover and title page shall be the actual author or authors.

Criteria
for Evaluating
Instructional
Materials:
Kindergarten
Through
Grade Eight

Category 2: Program Organization

1. Sequential organization of the material provides structure concerning what students should learn each year and allows teachers to convey the history–social science content efficiently and effectively.

2. The content is well organized and presented in a manner consistent with providing all students an opportunity to achieve the essential knowledge and skills described in the standards and framework. The academic language (i.e., vocabulary) specific to the content is presented in a manner that provides explicit instructional opportunities for teachers and appropriate practice for all students.

3. A detailed, expository narrative approach providing for in-depth study is the predominant writing mode and focuses on people and their ideas, thoughts, actions, conflicts, struggles, and achievements.

4. Explanations are provided so that students clearly understand the likely causes of the events, the reasons the people and events are important, why things turned out as they did, and the connections of those results to events that followed.

5. The narrative unifies and interrelates the many facts, explanations, visual aids, maps, and literary selections included in the topic or unit. Those components clearly contribute directly to students' deeper understanding and retention of the events.

6. The relevant grade-level standards shall be explicitly stated in both the teacher and student editions. Topical headings reflect the framework and standards and clearly indicate the content that follows.

7. Each topic builds clearly on the preceding one(s) in a systematic manner.

8. Topics selected for in-depth study are enriched with a variety of materials and content-appropriate activities and reflect the framework's course descriptions.

9. Each unit presents strategies for universal access, including ways in which to improve the vocabulary and reading and language skills of English learners in the context of history–social science.

10. Materials explain how history–social science instruction may be improved by the effective use of library media centers and information literacy skills.

11. The tables of contents, indexes, glossaries, content summaries, and assessment guides are designed to help teachers, parents/guardians, and students.

Category 3: Assessment

1. Assessment tools measure what students know and are able to do, including their analysis skills, as defined by the standards.

Criteria
for Evaluating
Instructional
Materials:
Kindergarten
Through
Grade Eight

2. Assessment tools that publishers include as a part of their instructional materials should provide evidence of students' progress toward mastering the content called for in the standards and framework and should yield information teachers can use in planning and modifying instruction to help all students meet or exceed the standards.

3. Materials provide frequent assessments at strategic points of instruction by such means as pretests, unit tests, chapter tests, and summative tests.

4. Materials assess students' progress toward meeting the instructional goals of history–social science, most notably by expository writing. Student writing assessments are aligned with the grade-level requirements in the *English–Language Arts Content Standards* under the strands "Writing" and "Written and Oral English Language Conventions."

5. Materials include analytical rubrics that are content-specific and provide an explanation of the use of the rubrics by teachers and students to evaluate and improve skills in writing, analysis, and the use of evidence.

6. Assessment tools include multiple-choice, short answer, essay, and oral presentation.

7. Assessment tools measure how students are able to use library media centers and information literacy skills when studying history–social science topics.

Category 4: Universal Access

1. Instructional materials shall provide access to the curriculum for all students. Therefore, the following design principles for perceptual alternatives shall be used:

   • To be consistent with federal copyright law, all text for students must be in digital format so that it can easily be transcribed, reproduced, modified, and distributed in braille, large print (only if the publisher does not offer such an edition), recordings, American Sign Language videos for the deaf, or other specialized accessible media exclusively for use by pupils with visual disabilities or other disabilities that prevent the use of standard materials.

   • Written captions and written descriptions must be in digital format for audio portions of visual instructional materials, such as videotapes (for those students who are deaf or hearing impaired).

   • Educationally relevant descriptions must be provided for those images, graphic devices, or pictorial information essential to the teaching of key concepts. (When key information is presented solely in graphic or pictorial form, it limits access for students who are blind or who have low vision. Digital images with an oral description provide not only access for those students but also flexibility for instructional emphasis, clarity, and direction.)

187

Criteria
for Evaluating
Instructional
Materials:
Kindergarten
Through
Grade Eight

2. Instructional materials present comprehensive guidance for teachers in providing effective, efficient instruction for all students. Instructional materials should provide access to the standards and framework-based curriculum for all students, including those with special needs: English learners, advanced learners, students below grade level in reading and writing skills, and special education students.

3. Materials for kindergarten through grade three focus on the content called for in the *History–Social Science Content Standards* and the *History–Social Science Framework* while complementing the goals of the *English–Language Arts Content Standards* and the *Reading/Language Arts Framework for California Public Schools* (adopted in 1999).

4. Materials for grades four through eight provide suggestions to further instruction in history–social science while assisting students whose reading and writing skills are below grade level.

5. Instructional materials are designed to help meet the needs of students whose reading, writing, listening, and speaking skills fall below the level prescribed in the English–language arts content standards and to assist in accelerating students' skills to grade level. Those students whose skills are *significantly* below grade level in reading (two years or more) should be directed to intensive reading instruction.

6. Materials must address the needs of students who are at or above grade level. Although materials are adaptable to each student's point of entry, such differentiated instruction is focused on the history–social science content standards.

7. All suggestions and procedures for meeting the instructional needs of all students are ready to use with minimum modifications.

8. Materials provide suggestions for enriching the program or assignments for advanced learners by:
   - Studying a topic, person, place, or event in more depth
   - Conducting a more complex analysis of a topic, person, place, or event
   - Reading and researching related topics independently
   - Emphasizing the rigor and depth of the analysis skills to provide a challenge for all students

9. Materials provide suggestions to help teach English learners the *History–Social Science Content Standards* while reinforcing instruction based on the *English–Language Arts Content Standards*—notably to read, write, comprehend, and speak at academically proficient levels.

10. Materials use the following design principles for "considerate" text:
    - Adequate titles for each selection
    - Introductory subheadings for chapter sections
    - Introductory paragraphs

Criteria
for Evaluating
Instructional
Materials:
Kindergarten
Through
Grade Eight

- Concluding or summary paragraphs
- Complete paragraphs, including a clear topic sentence, relevant support, and transitional words and expressions (e.g., *furthermore, similarly*)
- Effective use of typographical aids, such as boldface print, italics
- Relevant, standards-aligned visual aids connected to the print: illustrations, photographs, charts, graphs, maps
- Manageable instead of overwhelming visual and print stimuli
- Identification and highlighting of important terms
- List of objectives or focus questions at the beginning of each selection
- List of follow-up comprehension and application questions

Category 5: Instructional Planning and Support

1. Teacher support materials, including the required teacher edition, are built into the instructional materials and contain suggestions and illustrative examples of how teachers can implement the instructional program.

2. The teacher and student editions present ways for all students to learn the content and analysis skills called for in the standards.

3. Directions are explicit regarding how the analysis skills are to be taught and assessed in the context of the content standards.

4. Instructional materials provide a clear road map for teachers to follow when they are planning instruction.

5. Teacher and student editions have correlating page numbers.

6. Instructional materials include a teacher-planning guide describing the relationships between the components of the program and how to use all the components to meet all the standards.

7. Publishers provide teachers with easily accessible and workable instructional examples and with practice opportunities for students as they develop their understanding of the content and analysis skills.

8. Black line masters are accessible in print and in digitized formats and are easily reproduced. Black areas shall be minimal to require less toner when printing or photocopying.

9. The teacher's edition describes what to teach, how to teach, and when to teach.

10. Terms from the standards are used appropriately and accurately in the instructions.

11. All assessment tools, instructional tools, and informational technology resources include technical support and suggestions for appropriate use of technology.

189

Criteria
for Evaluating
Instructional
Materials:
Kindergarten
Through
Grade Eight

12. Electronic learning resources, when included, support instruction and connect explicitly to the standards.

13. The teacher resource materials provide background information about important events, people, places, and ideas appearing in the standards and framework.

14. Instructional practices recommended in the materials are based on the content in the standards and on current and confirmed research.

15. Materials discuss and address common misconceptions held by students.

16. Homework extends and reinforces classroom instruction and provides additional practice of skills that have been taught.

17. Materials include suggestions on how to explain students' progress toward attaining the standards.

18. Materials include suggestions for parents on how to support student achievement.

19. The format clearly distinguishes instructions for teachers from those for students.

20. Answer keys are provided for all workbooks and other related student activities.

21. Publishers provide charts of the time requirements and cost of staff development services available for preparing teachers to implement fully the program.

22. Materials provide teachers with instructions on how outside resources (e.g., guest speakers, museum visits, and electronic field trips) are to be incorporated into a standards-based lesson.

23. Materials provide guidance on the effective use of library media centers to improve instruction and on the materials in library media centers that would best complement the history–social science content standards.

Selected References

History–Social Science Content Standards for California Public Schools, Kindergarten Through Grade Twelve. Sacramento: California Department of Education, 2000.

History–Social Science Framework for California Public Schools, Kindergarten Through Grade Twelve, 2001 Updated Edition. Sacramento: California Department of Education, 2001.

English–Language Arts Content Standards for California Public Schools, Kindergarten Through Grade Twelve. Sacramento: California Department of Education, 1998.

Reading/Language Arts Framework for California Public Schools, Kindergarten Through Grade Twelve. Sacramento: California Department of Education, 1999.

Criteria
for Evaluating
Instructional
Materials:
Kindergarten
Through
Grade Eight

Mathematics Content Standards for California Public Schools, Kindergarten Through Grade Twelve. Sacramento: California Department of Education, 1999.

Mathematics Framework for California Public Schools, Kindergarten Through Grade Twelve, 2000 Revised Edition. Sacramento: California Department of Education, 2000.

Science Content Standards for California Public Schools, Kindergarten Through Grade Twelve. Sacramento: California Department of Education, 2000.

Science Framework for California Public Schools, Kindergarten Through Grade Twelve. Sacramento: California Department of Education, 2003.

Visual and Performing Arts Content Standards for California Public Schools, Prekindergarten Through Grade Twelve. Sacramento: California Department of Education, 2001.

Appendixes

Introduction to the Appendixes

*B*oth in the nation and in the world, the end of the twentieth century has brought about fundamental and sometimes painful reappraisal, as old assumptions are being reexamined and new ones are taking shape.

In the United States, elected officials and editorialists debated the proper role of government and the appropriate allocation of responsibility among federal, state, and local governments; books such as Philip Howard's *The Death of Common Sense** drew attention to the problems of counterproductive government regulation. Thoughtful commentators expressed concern about the state of civil and civic society in the United States. Two of the most widely discussed works of the decade are *The Tragedy of American Compassion,** by Marvin Olasky, and "Bowling Alone," an article by Robert D. Putnam that first appeared in the *Journal of Democracy* in January, 1995. (The latter work is reprinted in Appendix G of this framework.) These works use Tocqueville's *Democracy in America* as a benchmark and provide insight into the factors contributing to the decline in civic engagement.

In the international sphere, the end of the Cold War led to the dissolution of not only the Soviet Union but also the predictability of a bipolar world. The upheavals of the late 1980s and early 1990s were followed by the formation of new governments, resurgence of nationalism, outbreaks of political violence, and pressure on the United Nations to restrain civil wars. These events indicate uncertainty and confusion about the future that should remind teachers and students of our generation's enormous responsibilities and opportunities in that future. They should also serve as the basis for understanding the issues that lie ahead, issues only dimly perceived today.

These appendixes are intended to help curriculum developers and teachers ensure in local planning that students are prepared for the responsibilities and challenges of the future.

- The papers titled "Nationalism, Free Markets, and Democracy in the Contemporary World" and "U.S. History and Geography" are designed to update the framework for grades ten and eleven with respect to recent events.
- "Religion and the Teaching of History–Social Science" introduces statements that are found in *Finding Common Ground: A First Amend-*

---

*Bibliographical information for these documents appears in Appendix B.

ment Guide to Religion and Public Education produced by The Freedom Forum First Amendment Center. It provides support to educators regarding teaching about religion.

- "The World History Sequence at Grades Six, Seven, and Ten: Content, Breadth/Depth, and Coverage Issues with Some Local Options" discusses several options for teachers of world history to consider when planning coverage and articulation of world history across the three grade levels.

- The "Examples of Careers in History–Social Science" paper provides insights into careers in the twenty-first century and is intended to assist school counselors, teachers, and others in helping students identify the full range of possible future careers.

- "Using Primary Sources in the Study of History," by Amanda Podany, will assist teachers in using primary resources in the classroom to enhance students' learning.

- As noted above, the Putnam article documents the decline in civic participation and serves as a serious reminder of the importance of the skills and concepts learned through the study of history–social science.

- As an antidote to Putnam's analysis, "History–Social Science and Service-Learning" provides examples of how history–social science curriculum is able to foster civic participation.

Together, the body of the framework and these appendixes lay the foundation for development of history–social science curriculum that prepares students for the challenges of the twenty-first century.

Appendix A
Nationalism, Free Markets, and Democracy in the Contemporary World

This appendix offers some alternatives to the case studies that appear in the last unit of the framework's course description for grade ten.

The collapse of the Soviet Union has been followed by what may prove to be a new historical era, marked by resurgence of nationalism (sometimes of a virulent type), world trading blocs, and new democratic governments on every continent.

Four case studies involving related pairs of nations will illustrate these contemporary phenomena. "Post–Russia and Germany" presents contrasting examples of national dissolution and reunification in the wake of communism's collapse. "Ukraine and Yugoslavia" reveals another crucial effect of Soviet communism's fall, namely the resurgence of long-suppressed nationalist movements. "Japan and Mexico" points to the growing importance of multinational trading blocs in Asia and North America and highlights the relationship between economic change and the end of one-party rule. Finally, "Argentina and South Africa" provides excellent examples of nations that have begun the transition from authoritarianism to democracy.

This appendix concludes with sections titled "Democracy and Development in the Contemporary World," "The Role of Women in the Contemporary World," "The United Nations in the Contemporary World," and "The Future of Democracy." In each section several primary sources or readings are recommended, and full bibliographical information appears at the end of the appendix. Students are also encouraged to access a variety of print materials, nonprint media, and Web sites.

Post–Soviet Union Russia and Germany

The changes that have taken place in the former Soviet Union since 1987 are nothing short of revolutionary. The centralized command economy collapsed. Authoritarian government gave way to a hybrid presidential and parliamentary regime that grants Russians unprecedented civil liberties and democratic rights. The Soviet empire vanished, giving independence to states that, in some cases, had not known autonomy for more than a millennium. And perhaps most important, the fall of communism brought an end to the Cold War that held the world hostage to the threat of nuclear annihilation for more than 40 years. The danger of nuclear and other forms of military conflict, has not, of course, vanished. Students should be aware of the problems that remain.

Students should reflect on the historic significance of the developments described above, especially in light of the Russian Revolution of 1917 (studied earlier at this grade level). They should analyze the aspects of the Soviet Union's economy, technological progress, political system, and foreign relations that led to the collapse of communism. It is crucial, moreover, for them to understand the nationalist aspirations of non-Russian peoples within Russia itself, and they should consider the opportunities and dangers that confront this region.

Whereas the fall of communism caused the Soviet Union to dissolve into its component parts, that same development enabled Germany to become a single unified state for the first time since 1945. When East and West Germans came together to tear down the Berlin Wall in 1989, their act symbolized the removal of barriers that had divided Europeans into two distinct blocs for nearly half a century. But once Berliners finished celebrating the demise of East Germany's police state, the hard work of reunification began. Many East Germans resented being included as poor cousins in the larger and far more prosperous West German family. And West German taxpayers disliked the astronomical cost of modernizing East Germany's backward economy, cleaning up its environmental pollution, and updating its antiquated infrastructure of transport and communications. As students study the process of reunification, they should consider the extent to which the institutions of the newly reunified Germany have been shaped by the experiences of West Germany.

The strains of unification and other internal tensions contributed to a xenophobic reaction by some Germans against people originally from other countries. Students need to understand these and other political, cultural, and economic obstacles facing Germans as they complete the reunification of their country. Students should consider the meaning of the postreunification attacks against Turks and members of other immigrant groups and how they relate to examples of racial and ethnic hatred elsewhere.

As background reading, Mary Fulbrook's *The Divided Nation: A History of Germany, 1918–1990* provides information and insight. Amity Shlaes's *Germany: The Empire Within* is another important resource, and selections from Robert Darnton's *Berlin Journal* will provide students with an eyewitness account of the collapse of the Berlin Wall. For studying Russia (the largest part of the former Soviet Union), the following resources are useful: Robert V. Daniels's *Soviet Communism from Reform to Collapse* and his translation of *A Documentary History of Communism from Lenin to Gorbachev; Lenin's Tomb,* by David Remnick; and *Perestroika: New Thinking for Our Country and the World,* by Mikhail Gorbachev.

In the former Soviet Union, and especially in Russia, there continues to be nostalgia for the order and security of the old regime; the electoral support for communists and former communists, not only in Russia but also throughout Eastern Europe, suggests that the transition to democracy and a market economy presents continuing challenges. Some commentators fear that frustration with the slow pace of change will strengthen efforts to reestablish a failed system. Students should follow the transition carefully, paying particular attention to the fragility of democracy and the challenges citizens face as they seek to achieve and maintain political rights. These considerations could lead into appropriate time for students to compare a market economy and a command economy and to consider the relationship between a market economy and political democracy.

Ukraine and Yugoslavia

The collapse of communism unleashed nationalistic passions that had been suppressed since the Russian Revolution in Ukraine and the end of World War II in Yugoslavia. These passions have been channeled into relatively peaceful ends in the former and extraordinarily destructive ones in the latter.

Students should keep in mind that the antecedent of the first Ukrainian state, Kyivan Rus, was centered in Kyiv, now the capital of Ukraine and a locus of religion and culture since perhaps the eighth century. Kyiv (formerly referred to as Kiev in maps and atlases) fell in the thirteenth century to Mongol invaders and later to Lithuania and then Poland. To escape harsh Polish rule, Ukrainians allied themselves with Moscow in the mid-seventeenth century. Most of Ukraine was incorporated into the czarist Russian empire at that time and, except for brief periods, remained under Russian domination until the collapse of the Soviet Union in the late 1980s. Under the Czar and later under the Soviet regime, Ukrainians fared little better than they had under the Poles. Students should explore the brutal legacy of Stalinism, including the collectivization campaign of the 1930s. According to some historians, Stalin approved a campaign of political murder designed to stamp out Ukrainian culture and imposed a famine on the entire region. Because Ukraine and Russia were closely linked for centuries, Ukraine's establishment as an independent state in 1990 has profoundly affected both countries.

Ukraine is by far the largest of the republics to separate from Russia, and it encompasses some of the most fertile farmland in Europe. It also possesses rich mineral resources. Students should consider the implications of disassociation for citizens of both countries; students should also think about the conflict and ultimate resolution about control of the atomic weapons deployed by the former Soviet Union on Ukrainian territory. Eastern parts of Ukraine have traditionally leaned more toward Moscow than western ones; students should analyze the extent to which this historical division creates obstacles to the maintenance of a strong independent state.

The collapse of the Soviet Union enabled Ukrainian nationalists to peacefully establish a new political entity. It also freed the USSR's other satellite countries in Eastern Europe to pursue their own independent paths. Poland, Hungary, and Czechoslovakia—itself divided into the Czech and Slovak Republics—have made largely nonviolent transitions to noncommunist rule. Romania and Bulgaria have experienced somewhat more difficulty, while in Yugoslavia the fall of communism unleashed a virulent nationalism that has led to political disunion and brutal ethnic strife.

Students should study the reasons for the end of communist rule in Eastern Europe and how it has affected and will continue to affect the economic and political development of Europe. They should also examine the problem of moving from a state-owned or state-managed economy to one in which most enterprise belongs to private citizens and corporations. In particular, they should consider the problem of privatization: Who owns the land? How should state-owned enterprises be transferred to private ownership? What is the role of foreign investors? In answering these questions, students should analyze the ways that the former communist countries have used to meet the challenges of moving from democracy to capitalism.

Students should also examine why Yugoslavia disintegrated into nationalistic conflict. They should do so, in part, by comparing Yugoslavia's tragic experience with Czechoslovakia's peaceful division into separate Czech and Slovak Republics.

As they consider Yugoslavia, students should remember that this country—translated literally as the land of the South Slavs—has existed only since the end of the First World War. As part of the peace settlement that ended that war, the creation of

Yugoslavia brought together a variety of different groups—Albanians, Bosnian Muslims, Croats, Montenegrans, Serbs, and Slovenes. For centuries, most of these peoples had been ruled by the Ottoman Empire, whose Muslim religion the Bosnians, in particular, had adopted. A series of Balkan wars fought in the late nineteenth and early twentieth centuries resulted in an independent Serbian state and the annexation of Bosnia and Herzegovina by Austria-Hungary. With the collapse of both the Ottoman and Austro-Hungarian Empires at the end of World War I, Serbia was able to dominate the formation of a new Yugoslav state. In doing so, it created religious and ethnic animosities that continue to this day.

Study of contemporary Yugoslavia should focus on why the Slovenes, Croats, and Bosnians have established independent states, and why their efforts to do so have resulted in wars with Serbia and Serbian forces in Croatia and Bosnia. Students should pay particular attention to the process by which nationalist passions have led to *ethnic cleansing,* the effort to expel from a given area all those who do not belong to a particular ethnic group. This process has resulted in death, injury, and exile for hundreds of thousands of Balkan people. It has also destroyed what in some parts of the region appeared to be successful, functioning multiethnic societies. As they study this troubled region, students should consider why the United States and its European allies were reluctant to intervene militarily in these conflicts. They should also examine the role of the United Nations in these events and compare that role to the UN's recent interventions in Africa and other parts of the world. Appropriate questions for students to consider are: What conditions are necessary for a multiethnic or multiracial society to function: a common language? a meaningful commitment to *e pluribus unum?* Why does one multiethnic society slip into civil war, while another does not? What kinds of bonds hold such a society together?

Resources for students include Kuzio and Wilson's *Ukraine from Perestroika to Independence;* Conquest's *Harvest of Sorrow* (and a documentary based on it); Subtelny's *Ukraine—A History;* Sjelten's *Sarajevo Daily: A City and Its Newspaper Under Siege;* and Glenny's *The Fall of Yugoslavia.*

Japan and Mexico

The comparison of these two countries begins with a brief overview of Japan's modern history. Students should consider how the leaders of the Meiji Restoration of the 1860s responded to the challenge of the West by rapidly transforming their country into an industrialized power. They should also evaluate the reasons that Japan was able to join the ranks of imperial countries and why it sought, in particular, to dominate China. Japan's aims in World War II need to be considered, as do the nature and implications of the United States' postwar occupation of that country. This discussion then leads to a consideration of Japan's post-1945 economic miracle: emergence from the devastation of the war to develop the world's second-strongest economy.

In considering Japan's remarkable economic development, students should analyze its evolving relationship with the United States as well as its rise as the leader of a potent Asian and Pacific trading bloc that includes South Korea, China, Hong Kong, Taiwan, and Singapore. Recently, Japan has experienced some economic difficulties, the effects of a high yen abroad and recession at home. It is important to examine the reasons for these problems and to consider their relationship to the political changes

Japan experienced in the early 1990s. After being governed by a single political party for most of its postwar history, Japan seems now to be moving toward a more pluralistic system. In addition, Japan's home market may be increasingly open to foreign competition as a result of international trade pacts.

Like Japan, Mexico appears to be developing a considerably more open and pluralistic political order, as well as moving from a state-managed economy toward free markets. To understand the importance of current political ferment in Mexico, students need to supplement the work they did in Unit 8 with a brief review of Mexico's modern history. They should begin with Mexico's prolonged period of revolution early in the twentieth century and evaluate the process by which the Institutional Revolutionary Party (PRI) consolidated power in the 1930s and proceeded to rule the country for the next 60 years. Recently, PRI has faced mounting challenges both to its political monopoly and economic control. The government has responded by allowing more genuine electoral competition and scaling back government involvement in the economy. Students should evaluate the implications of these developments in terms of Mexico's political landscape, economic opportunities, and relationship both to the United States and Latin America. They should pay particular attention to efforts to reform PRI, the economic consequences of Mexico's partici-pation in the North American Free Trade Agreement, the Indian rebellion in the state of Chiapas, and emigration to the United States.

Recommended readings on Japan and Mexico are Edward Lincoln's *Japan's New Global Role;* John Ross's *Rebellion from the Roots: Indian Uprising in Chiapas;* Jorge Castaneda's *The Mexican Shock: Its Meaning for the United States;* and Robert A. Pastor and Jorge Castaneda's *Limits to Friendship: The United States and Mexico.*

Argentina and South Africa

A comparative study of these two countries highlights the process of transforma-tion from authoritarian rule to democratic government. It emphasizes how difficult the transition is from a society governed by a narrow elite to one in which control over politics, culture, and economic life is broadly decentralized. After a long and violent period of military dictatorship, Argentina's voters elected a democratic government in the early 1980s. The transition was far from easy. The new Alfonsin government had not only to confront Argentina's long-standing problems with hyperinflation and economic inequality but also to undertake the delicate task of seeking justice for victims of the former regime. Students should examine how the civilian government approached these problems and compare its experiences with those of neighboring Chile, another South American nation that has recently made its own transformation from authoritarianism to democracy. Chileans had to endure a harsh military dictator-ship in the 1970s and 1980s, but in 1989, free elections returned the country to civilian and democratic rule. In comparing Argentina and Chile, students should examine the relationship of these countries to the world's major trading blocs and consider the extent to which the economic concept of comparative advantage is important to understanding their international commerce.

To place Argentina's recent democratic achievements in perspective, students should study its political history beginning with the strongman Juan Peron's rise to power in the 1940s and proceeding through its alternating series of civilian and military governments. In this context, it is extremely significant that Argentina was able in the early 1990s to move peacefully from one democratically elected government to another.

Although students may have considered South Africa in Unit 8 of the Grade Ten course description in the framework, "Nationalism in the Contemporary World," the remarkable changes that have occurred in that country in recent years merit further study. Students should supplement their earlier work with an examination of the fall of South Africa's apartheid regime. They should consider the pivotal roles played by the Republic's former president F. W. de Klerk and former African National Congress leader Nelson Mandela in preparing the way for the country's first genuinely democratic elections. Thanks to their efforts, South Africa's black majority won the right to vote and elected Mandela to the presidency. In evaluating South Africa's new democracy, students need to consider the ways in which the legacy of apartheid creates obstacles to achieving political and economic progress.

To get a sense of the human toll taken by Argentina's military dictatorship, students should consult Jacobo Timerman, *Prisoner Without a Name, Cell Without a Number.* Nelson Mandela's "Rivonia Trial Speech to the Court" provides a vivid portrait of apartheid and of the future president's alternative vision for his country.*

Democracy and Development in the Contemporary World

Efforts to build democracy in Argentina and South Africa have coincided with a flowering of democratic government and democratic movements throughout the world. From El Salvador in Latin America to Poland, the Czech Republic, and Hungary in Eastern Europe, democracy is on the rise. Even where governments resist political change, as in China, democratic movements have seriously shaken the regimes in question. To examine this resurgence of democracy, students will find it helpful to compare the different political paths these countries have followed. Such an effort will help them evaluate the extent to which social, cultural, and economic problems present challenges to the persistence of democratic government.

The Czech Republic is an example of a country that in a short period of time has developed democratic institutions and private enterprise. In consideration of this and other transitions to democracy, an essential issue for students to ponder is power: Who makes decisions? Who has control of the economy, the state, and the culture? Concentration of political and economic power is typical of an authoritarian regime; dispersion and decentralization of power are common features of a democracy.

Unlike the Czech Republic, many of the world's emerging democracies are not blessed with strong economies, and their economic fragility may, in the years to come, threaten their democratic government and economic development, recognizing that the two do not always coincide. Whereas the Czech Republic and Poland have achieved prosperity under their democratic governments and free market economic policies, new democracies elsewhere in Eastern Europe and in Latin America have not done so well.

---

*Teachers of world history at the high school level are also referred to *Course Models for the History– Social Science Framework, Grade 10—World History, Culture, and Geography: The Modern World* (Sacramento: California Department of Education, 1995), pages 321–326, for additional case studies that teach the concept of nationalism in the contemporary world. The options specified in this framework (pages 89–92) are the Soviet Union and China, Israel and Syria, Ghana and South Africa, and Mexico and Brazil. The course models will be available online at <http://www.cde.ca.gov/statetests/history/models.html>.

To gain perspective on the experience of the successful fledgling democracies described above, students should compare the recent histories of those democracies with those of three countries of the Pacific Rim, where remarkable economic development has occurred with an authoritarian government in power. These countries are South Korea, Singapore, and the Republic of China (Taiwan). South Korea and Singapore were colonies of Japan and England, respectively, until after World War II, and Taiwan was an island province of China that separated politically from the mainland after the Revolution of 1949. Students should examine the postwar decolonization of Korea and Singapore and consider the circumstances under which the Chinese Nationalists created a separate state on the island of Taiwan.

Having achieved independence, the three Asian nations embarked on a course of rapid economic development fostered by powerful government regulation and direction of the economy. Their economies remained capitalist, but they were guided capitalist systems organized by the state. By the 1970s these countries had achieved rates of economic growth several times those of the developed West. Such success was due in part, perhaps, to restriction of political opposition and independent labor unions by their muscular states.

A fourth Pacific Rim power, Hong Kong, is important to study as well. Ceded by the Chinese to England in 1842, Hong Kong was a British crown until England returned it to China in 1997. After World War II, the English granted Hong Kong almost complete autonomy, and its economy grew at the extraordinary pace set by South Korea, Singapore, and Taiwan, though with considerably less state intervention. Students should study the agreement between the People's Republic of China and Great Britain that established the conditions of the transfer back to China.

Students should compare the economies of each of these four Pacific Rim nations to that of Japan and consider the advantages and disadvantages of their governments' roles in economic and political life. They should also examine the significance of the turn toward free elections in Taiwan and South Korea and consider the relationship in those two states between economic prosperity and the democratization of political life.

Suggested readings on contemporary democracy are *Stabilizing Fragile Democracies: New Party Systems in Southern and Eastern Europe* and *From Dictatorship to Democracy: Rebuilding Political Consensus in Chile*. For reading on the Pacific Rim, students should consult Staffan B. Linder's *Pacific Century: Economic and Political Consequences of Asian-Pacific Dynamism*. For information on Korea, students will benefit from reading David Rees's *A Short History of Modern Korea*. An excellent study of Singapore is Janet W. Salaff's *State and Family in Singapore: Restructuring an Industrial Society*.

The Role of Women in the Contemporary World

As they study the emergence of new democratic governments, students should recognize that women have been prominent in all these developments and that they have sought political rights at the same time as men. The new South African constitution, for example, explicitly acknowledges women's equality with men and prohibits discrimination on the basis of gender. One measure of the progress of gender equality is the number of women who have become heads of state or government since the 1960s. These women leaders include Indira Gandhi (India, 1966–84), Benazir Bhutto (Pakistan, 1980s and 1990s), Sirimavo Bandaranaike (Sri Lanka, 1960s and

1970s), Corazon Aquino (Philippines, 1986–92), Isabel Peron (Argentina, 1974–76), Golda Meir (Israel, late 1960s and 1970s), and Margaret Thatcher (Great Britain, 1980s). In addition, women have been prime ministers or presidents of France, Ireland, Lithuania, Nicaragua, Norway, and Turkey. Students should become familiar with the careers of these women leaders and analyze the nature of their political accomplishments.

Although women's participation in politics is a healthy sign of gender equality, women leaders are not necessarily more democratic in practice than their male counterparts. In this connection, students should explore the differing political opportunities open to women in presidential and parliamentary systems of government. They should also consider why relatively few women have been elected to state or national office in the United States. Finally, students should evaluate the extent to which democratic movements have improved the position of women and consider the obstacles that remain to the achievement of equal opportunities between the sexes.

An excellent resource for the study of women is *Women, the Family, and Freedom: The Debate in Documents,* an important collection of primary source documents. Another useful volume is *Women's Rights in International Documents: A Sourcebook with Commentary.* Helpful as well are publications by the National Women's History Project.

The United Nations in the Contemporary World

Students should understand the reasons for the establishment of the United Nations and its roles in the contemporary world. Students should be aware that the United Nations' charter was signed in San Francisco and the reasons for which nations signed the charter. Students should familiarize themselves with the functions of the United Nations' "principal organs," or main bodies, including the General Assembly, the Security Council, and the Secretariat. In addition, students should understand the varied functions of the United Nations in promoting respect for human rights and individual freedoms, fostering environmental protection and health, maintaining peace and security, aiding in conflict resolution, eradicating famine, fighting disease, providing disaster relief, helping refugees, and fostering economic improvement. Students should be aware of how the Cold War shaped the workings of the United Nations and how the post–Cold War era has placed new demands and expectations on the United Nations. Students should consider how this international organization faces the challenges presented by contemporary nationalism and globalization.*

The Future of Democracy

To conclude this course of study, students should think about what makes a society democratic and free. Is our society democratic? How important is political participation? Should everyone have the right to vote (what about children, prisoners, and so forth)? What kind of social contract exists between a state and its governed? What rights of citizens must the state respect? What evidence is there of "consent of the governed" and "balance of power"? What is the right balance of power between government and citizens? Thinking about the spread of democratic governments and freedom throughout the world provides an opportunity to reflect on our own democracy and the responsibility of citizens to preserve and improve democracy.

---

*The activities of the United Nations can be found at *<http://www.un.org/>*.

Throughout these case studies students are reminded that building and sustaining a democratic society is hard work that is never finished. Comparing challenges to democratic processes in the United States over the past two centuries to current challenges is worthwhile. An excellent collection of primary sources and literary selections is *The Democracy Reader: Classic and Modern Speeches, Essays, Poems, Declarations, and Documents on Freedom and Human Rights Worldwide,* edited by Diane Ravitch and Abigail Thernstrom. The readings help students understand that democracy is not a foregone conclusion; its rights are reversible, and citizens are continually responsible for maintaining a democratic society.

Suggested Resources

Russia and Germany

Daniels, Robert V. *Soviet Communism from Reform to Collapse.* Lexington, Mass.: D. C. Heath and Co., 1995.

Darnton, Robert. *Berlin Journal.* New York: W. W. Norton, 1993.

A Documentary History of Communism from Lenin to Gorbachev. Translated by Robert V. Daniels. Hanover, N.H.: University Press of New England, 1993.

Fulbrook, Mary. *The Divided Nation: A History of Germany, 1918–1990.* New York: Oxford University Press, 1992.

Gorbachev, Mikhail. *Perestroika: New Thinking for Our Country and the World.* San Bernardino, Calif.: Borgo Press, 1991.

Remnick, David. *Lenin's Tomb: The Last Days of the Soviet Empire.* New York: Random House, Inc., 1994.

Shlaes, Amity. *Germany: The Empire Within.* New York: Farrar, Straus, and Giroux, Inc., 1991.

Ukraine and Yugoslavia

Conquest, Robert. *Harvest of Sorrow: Soviet Collectivization and the Terror—Famine.* New York: Oxford University Press, 1986.

Glenny, Misha. *The Fall of Yugoslavia: Yugoslavia at War.* New York: Viking Penguin, 1993.

Kuzio, Taras, and Andrew Wilson. *Ukraine from Perestroika to Independence.* New York: St. Martin's Press, 1994.

Sjelten, Tom. *Sarajevo Daily: A City and Its Newspaper Under Siege.* New York: HarperCollins, 1995.

Subtelny, Orest. *Ukraine—A History.* Toronto: Toronto University Press, 1993.

Japan and Mexico

Castaneda, Jorge. *The Mexican Shock: Its Meaning for the United States.* New York: New Press, 1995.

Lincoln, Edward. *Japan's New Global Role.* Washington, D.C.: Brookings Institution, 1995.

Pastor, Robert A., and Jorge Castaneda. *Limits to Friendship: The United States and Mexico.* New York: Random House, Inc., 1989.

Ross, John. *Rebellion at the Roots: Indian Uprising in Chiapas.* Monroe, Me.: Common Courage Press, 1994.

Argentina and South Africa

Mandela, Nelson. "Rivonia Trial Speech to the Court," in *The Human Record: Sources of Global History, Vol. II.* Edited by Alfred J. Andrea and James H. Overfield. Boston: Houghton Mifflin Co., 1994, p. 505.

Timerman, Jacobo. *Prisoner Without a Name, Cell Without a Number.* New York: Random House, Inc., 1988.

Contemporary Democracy

From Dictatorship to Democracy: Rebuilding Political Consensus in Chile. Edited by Joseph S. Tulchin and Augusto Varas. Boulder, Colo.: Lynne Rienner Publications, Inc., 1991.

Linder, Staffan B. *Pacific Century: Economic and Political Consequences of Asian-Pacific Dynamism.* Stanford, Calif.: Stanford University Press, 1986.

Rees, David. *A Short History of Modern Korea.* New York: Hippocrene Books, 1988.

Salaff, Janet W. *State and Family in Singapore: Restructuring an Industrial Society.* Ithaca, N.Y.: Cornell University, 1988.

Stabilizing Fragile Democracies: New Party Systems in Southern and Eastern Europe. Edited by Geoffrey Pridham and Paul Lewis. New York: Routledge, 1995.

Study of Women

Women's Rights in International Documents: A Sourcebook with Commentary. Edited by Winston E. Langley. Jefferson, N.C.: McFarland & Co., Inc., 1991.

Women, the Family, and Freedom: The Debate in Documents, Vol. II, 1880–1950. Edited by Karen M. Offen and Susan G. Bell. Stanford, Calif.: Stanford University Press, 1983.

Primary Sources

The Democracy Reader: Classic and Modern Speeches, Essays, Poems, Declarations, and Documents on Freedom and Human Rights Worldwide. Edited by Diane Ravitch and Abigail Thernstrom. New York: HarperCollins, 1993.

Appendix B
U.S. History and Geography

This appendix augments the last unit in the course description for grade eleven with studies to extend the chronology to current times. In this final unit of American history studies, teachers should take every opportunity to draw connections between the issues of the present and those that students have previously learned about.

The students should review the major political trends of the recent past, paying particular attention to the enduring issue of federalism, that is, how political power is exercised by different levels of government. They should discuss the differences *between* the two major parties and differences *within* the parties on such issues as the role of the federal government, taxes, the deficit, and affirmative action.

In examining contemporary issues, students should draw upon their knowledge of American history to consider the influence of third parties on the political process. They should also read arguments and debates expressing differing points of view. They may also wish to explore a variety of other print and nonprint materials, including Web sites.

In studying federalism, students should analyze efforts at the state and national levels to revise laws and programs shaped during the New Deal and the Great Society. Students should become familiar with debates in California and other states about the financing and control of health care, welfare, education, crime and public safety, and other social programs.

The following multimedia programs, monographs, and books provide helpful student resources for studying contemporary issues:

Bloom, Allan. *The Closing of the American Mind.* New York: Simon and Schuster Trade, 1988.

Burns, James, and L. Marvin Overby. *Cobblestone Leadership: Majority Rule, Minority Power.* Norman: University of Oklahoma Press, 1990.

Crime. Edited by James Q. Wilson and Joan Petersilia. San Francisco: ICS Press, 1996. Twenty-eight leading experts look at the most pressing problem of our time.

Howard, Philip K. *The Death of Common Sense: How Law Is Suffocating America.* New York: Random House, Inc., 1995.

Lasch, Christopher. *The Revolt of the Elites and the Betrayal of Democracy.* New York: W. W. Norton & Co., Inc., 1995.

The New Civil War. ABC News Video Library, 1990. A 50-minute videocassette on the national debate over abortion.

Peterson, Paul. *The Price of Federalism.* Washington, D.C.: Brookings Institution, 1995.

Rauch, Jonathan. *Demosclerosis: The Silent Killer of American Government.* New York: Random House, Inc., 1994.

Rodriguez, Richard. *Hunger of Memory—The Education of Richard Rodriguez: An Autobiography.* New York: Bantam Books, Inc., 1983.

Samuelson, Robert J. *The Good Life and Its Discontents: How the American Dream Became a Fantasy, 1945–1995.* New York: Random House, Inc., 1996.

Simhealth: A Tool for National Debate. Monterey, Calif.: Thinking Tools, Inc., 1994. A software simulation on health care issues.

Sowell, Thomas. *Vision of the Anointed: Self-Congratulation as a Basis for Social Policy.* New York: Basic Books, 1995.

Sykes, Charles J. *A Nation of Victims: The Decay of the American Character.* New York: St. Martin's Press, Inc., 1992.

Students should discuss and debate the events that led to the end of the Cold War and the problems of shaping a post–Cold War foreign policy. They should also explore the different uses of American military and economic power in the world today. The following resources are appropriate for student research:

Beschloss, Michael R., and Strobe Talbott. *At the Highest Levels: The Inside Story of the End of the Cold War.* New York: Little, Brown & Co., 1994.

Nixon, Richard. *Seize the Moment: America's Challenge in a One-Superpower World.* New York: Simon and Schuster Trade, 1992.

"Rise and Fall of the Soviet Empire," in *Live from the Past.* New York: *New York Times,* 1995. This material is Part Six in the series and consists of four modules, the fourth of which, "The Demise of Communism and the Soviet Empire, 1991," is of special interest. It contains reproducible archival sheets of *New York Times* articles, a teaching guide, classroom poster, and video with historical film footage, background information, and commentary by *New York Times* journalists.

Schweizer, Peter. *Victory: The Reagan Administration's Secret Strategy That Hastened the Collapse of the Soviet Union.* New York: Grove/Atlantic, Inc., 1996.

Students should assess important social trends that are changing American society, including changes in the family; women's roles in the workplace; migration; legal and illegal immigration patterns; increased violence; and the new uses of modern technology at work, at home, and at school. They should also analyze the transformation of the economy by international trade and new technologies, including the decline of traditional industries, the downsizing of manufacturing, and the growing importance of education in the postindustrial world.

Another focus for this capstone unit is the issue of national identity. Students should draw upon their earlier studies of American history to consider competing visions of pluralism, assimilation, and separatism in American life. What is the role of race and ethnicity in American life? Is affirmative action necessary or is it unfair? Under what circumstances does a multiracial, multiethnic society function best?

The following resources are a sampling from a variety of perspectives:

Schlesinger, Arthur, Jr. *The Disuniting of America.* New York: W. W. Norton & Co., Inc., 1993.

Steele, Shelby. *The Content of Our Character: A New Vision of Race in America.* New York: HarperCollins, 1991.

Steinberg, Stephen. *Turning Back: The Retreat from Racial Justice in American Thought and Policy.* Boston: Beacon Press, 1995.

Other contemporary topics are covered in the following materials:

Chiras, Daniel. *Beyond the Fray: Reshaping America's Environmental Movement.* Boulder, Colo.: Johnson Books, 1990.

Olasky, Marvin. *The Tragedy of American Compassion.* Wheaton, Ill.: Crossway Books, 1995.

Rifkin, Jeremy. *End of Work: The Decline of the Global Labor Force and the Dawn of the Post-Market Era.* New York: Jeremy P. Tarcher, Inc., 1996.

Unequal Protection: Environmental Justice and Communities of Color. Edited by Robert D. Bullard. San Francisco: Sierra Club Books, 1994.

Ungar, Sanford. *Fresh Blood: The New American Immigrant.* New York: Simon and Schuster Trade, 1995.

Oral histories such as the following help to humanize the study of U.S. history by providing personal accounts of individuals who took part in major events in this century:

Terkel, Studs. *Coming of Age: The Story of Our Century by Those Who've Lived It.* New York: New Press, 1995.

All teachers should read Putnam's "Bowling Alone: America's Declining Social Capital" (*Journal of Democracy,* January 1995), which appears as Appendix G of this publication. It documents declining participation in civic and social organizations, which Putnam describes as a serious problem for our democracy. This article can lead to probing questions for students to ask: Are we in danger of becoming a society of consumers and spectators? What are the indicators? The reasons? What can be done?

Throughout their study of United States history of both the distant and recent past, students and teachers alike will find documentary and literary resource materials of interest and use. Among those available are the following:

The American Reader: Words That Moved a Nation. Edited by Diane Ravitch. New York: HarperCollins, 1992.

Charting Democracy in America: Landmarks from History and Political Thought. Edited by Alfred Fernbach and Charles J. Bishko. Washington, D.C.: American University Press, 1995. A compilation of documents, essays, court decisions, and speeches about democracy and its origins, as well as challenges to democracy.

Appendix C

Religion and the Teaching of History–Social Science

Few issues have stirred greater controversy in Americans' attitudes toward public education than the role of religion and values in public schools. In California the official response to this controversy is expressed in this framework.

On pages 5-6, this framework "supports the frequent study and discussion of the fundamental principles embodied in the United States Constitution and the Bill of Rights . . . including the right to freedom of religion." On page 7, this framework asserts the importance of religion in human history: "When studying world history, students must become familiar with the basic ideas of the major religions and the ethical traditions of each time and place. Students are expected to learn about the role of religion in the founding of this country."

This appendix is intended to assist educators as they implement the framework and as they respond to community concerns. To this end, "Religious Liberty, Public Education, and the Future of American Democracy: A Statement of Principles" and "Guidelines for Teaching About Religion" are printed below to help educators address issues of religious liberty and public education.*

"Religious Liberty, Public Education, and the Future of American Democracy: A Statement of Principles" was released by the Freedom Forum's First Amendment Center in March 1995. Using the civic principles of rights, responsibilities, and respect (three Rs) to guide them, members of 20 other national organizations and religious bodies, representing different points of view, formulated the statement. In that statement Americans are called upon to recognize, affirm, and guarantee every citizen's right to religious freedom and to treat each other with respect and dignity as they seek to live together amid their deeply held differences.

Understanding the role of religion in public schools also requires the discernment between the teaching of religion (religious education) and teaching *about* religion. In 1988 a broad coalition of 17 religious and educational organizations published "Guidelines for Teaching About Religion," in *Religion in the Public School Curriculum: Questions and Answers*. These guidelines distinguish between instruction about religion and religious indoctrination. The guidelines' significant statements are excellent resources for all individuals and groups to use in their work to bring people together, ensure the survival of democracy in our nation, and teach about religion in an academic way that is constitutionally permissible and educationally sound. The guidelines also demonstrate

---

*"Religious Liberty, Public Education, and the Future of American Democracy: A Statement of Principles" can be found at <*http://www.fac.org/publicat/principles/ambles1.htm*>. Both of these documents are reprinted in *Finding Common Ground: A First Amendment Guide to Religion and Public Education* (Third edition). Edited by Charles C. Haynes and Oliver Thomas, Legal Editor. Nashville, Tenn.: The Freedom Forum First Amendment Center, 1998. Copies are available from The Freedom Forum First Amendment Center, 1207 18ᵗʰ Ave., South, Nashville, TN 37212, or by telephone at 800-830-3733 or at their Web site at <*http://www.freedomforum.org/*>.

how the three Rs can enable persons of differing persuasions to work together peaceably for the common good.

Religious Liberty, Public Education, and the Future of American Democracy: A Statement of Principles

. . . The rights and responsibilities of the Religious Liberty clauses [of the First Amendment] provide the civic framework within which we are able to debate our differences, to understand one another, and to forge public policies that serve the common good in public education.

Today, many American communities are divided over educational philosophy, school reform, and the role of religion and values in our public schools. Conflict and debate are vital to democracy. Yet, if controversies about public education are to advance the best interests of the nation, then *how* we debate, and not only *what* we debate, is critical.

In the spirit of the First Amendment, we propose the following principles as civic ground rules for addressing conflicts in public education:

I. **Religious Liberty for All**

Religious liberty is an inalienable right of every person.

As Americans, we all share the responsibility to guard that right for every citizen. The Constitution of the United States with its Bill of Rights provides a civic framework of rights and responsibilities that enables Americans to work together for the common good in public education.

II. **The Meaning of Citizenship**

Citizenship in a diverse society means living with our deepest differences and committing ourselves to work for public policies that are in the best interest of all individuals, families, communities, and our nation.

The framers of our Constitution referred to this concept of moral responsibility as civic virtue.

III. **Public Schools Belong to All Citizens**

Public schools must model the democratic process and constitutional principles in the development of policies and curricula.

Policy decisions by officials or governing bodies should be made only after appropriate involvement of those affected by the decision and with due consideration for the rights of those holding dissenting views.

IV. **Religious Liberty and Public Schools**

Public schools may not inculcate nor inhibit religion. They must be places where religion and religious conviction are treated with fairness and respect.

Public schools uphold the First Amendment when they protect the religious liberty rights of students of all faiths or none. Schools demonstrate fairness when they ensure that the curriculum includes study about religion, where appropriate, as an important part of a complete education.

V. **The Relationship Between Parents and Schools**

Parents are recognized as having the primary responsibility for the upbringing of their children, including education.

Parents who send their children to public schools delegate to public school educators some of the responsibility for their children's education. In so doing, parents acknowledge the crucial role of educators without abdicating their parental duty. Parents may also choose not to send their children to public schools and have their children educated at home or in private schools. However, private citizens, including business leaders and others, also have the right to expect public education to give students tools for living in a productive democratic society. All citizens must have a shared commitment to offer students the best possible education. Parents have a special responsibility to participate in the activity of their children's schools. Children and schools benefit greatly when parents and educators work closely together to shape school policies and practices and to ensure that public education supports the societal values of their community without undermining family values and convictions.

VI. **Conduct of Public Disputes**

Civil debate, the cornerstone of a true democracy, is vital to the success of any effort to improve and reform America's public schools.

Personal attacks, name-calling, ridicule, and similar tactics destroy the fabric of our society and undermine the educational mission of our schools. Even when our differences are deep, all engaged in public disputes should treat one another with civility and respect, and should strive to be accurate and fair. Through constructive dialogue we have much to learn from one another.

The Statement of Principles is not an attempt to ignore or minimize differences that are important and abiding, but rather a reaffirmation of what we share as American citizens across our differences. Democratic citizenship does not require a compromise of our deepest convictions. We invite all men and women of good will to join us in affirming these principles and putting them into action. The time has come for us to work together for academic excellence, fairness, and shared civic values in our nation's schools.

"A Statement of Principles" is sponsored jointly by the following entities:

American Association of School Administrators
American Center for Law and Justice
American Federation of Teachers
Anti-Defamation League
Association for Supervision and Curriculum Development
Carnegie Foundation for the Advancement of Teaching
Catholic League for Religious and Civil Rights
Central Conference of American Rabbis
Christian Coalition
Christian Educators Association International
Christian Legal Society
Citizens for Excellence in Education

Council on Islamic Education
The Freedom Forum First Amendment Center
National Association of Elementary School Principals
National Association of Evangelicals
National Association of Secondary School Principals
National Congress of Parents and Teachers
National Council of Churches of Christ in the U.S.A.
National Education Association
National School Boards Association
People for the American Way
Phi Delta Kappa
Union of American Hebrew Congregations

Guidelines for Teaching About Religion

In 1988 a broad coalition of 17 religious and education organizations endorsed *Religion in the Public School Curriculum: Questions and Answers,* which contains "Guidelines for Teaching About Religion." These guidelines distinguish between teaching about religion and indoctrinating or advocating religion.

1. The school's approach to religion is academic, not devotional.
2. The school may strive for student awareness of religions, but should not press for student acceptance of any one religion.
3. The school may sponsor study about religion, but may not sponsor the practice of religion.
4. The school may expose students to a diversity of religious views, but may not impose any particular view.
5. The school may educate about all religions, but may not promote or denigrate any religion.
6. The school may inform students about various beliefs, but should not seek to conform students to any particular belief.

The "Guidelines for Teaching About Religion" are sponsored jointly by the following entities:

American Academy of Religion
American Association of School Administrators
American Federation of Teachers
American Jewish Congress
Americans United (formerly Americans United Research Foundation)
Association for Supervision and Curriculum Development
Baptist Joint Committee on Public Affairs
Christian Legal Society
The Church of Jesus Christ of Latter-day Saints
The Islamic Society of North America
National Association of Evangelicals
National Conference for Community and Justice (formerly National Conference of Christians and Jews)
National Council for the Social Studies
National Council of Churches of Christ in the U.S.A.

National Council on Religion and Public Education
National Education Association
National School Boards Association

Legal Basis for Religious Liberty and Teaching About Religion

U.S. Constitution

First Amendment: Congress shall make no law respecting an establishment of religion, or prohibiting the free exercise thereof. . . .

California Constitution

Article 1 Declaration of Rights

Section 4. Free exercise and enjoyment of religion without discrimination or preference are guaranteed. This liberty of conscience does not excuse acts that are licentious or inconsistent with the peace or safety of the State. The Legislature shall make no law respecting an establishment of religion. . . .

Article 9 Education

Section 8. No public money shall ever be appropriated for the support of any sectarian or denominational school, or any school not under the exclusive control of the officers of the public schools; nor shall any sectarian or denominational doctrine be taught, or instruction thereon be permitted, directly or indirectly, in any of the common schools of this State.

Education Code

51500. No teacher shall give instruction nor shall a school district sponsor any activity which reflects adversely upon persons because of their race, sex, color, creed, handicap, national origin, or ancestry.

51501. No textbook, or other instructional materials shall be adopted by the state board or by any governing board for use in the public schools which contains any matter reflecting adversely upon persons because of their race, sex, color, creed, handicap, national origin, or ancestry.

51511. Nothing in this code shall be construed to prevent, or exclude from the public schools, references to religion or references to or the use of religious literature, art, or music or other things having a religious significance when such references or uses do not constitute instruction in religious principles or aid to any religious sect, church, creed, or sectarian purpose and when such references or uses are incidental to or illustrative of matters properly included in the course of study.

51513. No test, questionnaire, survey, or examination containing any questions about the pupil's personal beliefs or practices in sex, family life, morality, and religion, or any questions about the pupil's parents' or guardians' beliefs and practices in sex, family life, morality, and religion, shall be administered to any pupil in kindergarten or grades 1 to 12, inclusive, unless the parent or guardian of the pupil is notified in writing that this test, questionnaire, survey, or examination is to be administered and the parent or guardian of the pupil gives written permission for the pupil to take this test, questionnaire, survey, or examination.

Appendix D

The World History Sequence at Grades Six, Seven, and Ten: Content, Breadth/Depth, and Coverage Issues with Some Local Options

Teachers and curriculum specialists who reviewed the *History–Social Science Framework* soon after its publication in 1988 applauded the new document for its increased emphasis on world history, culture, and geography. The Bradley Commission for History in the Schools had recommended three years of history-related study in a report published in 1987, and the State Board of Education adopted the framework the same year. Thus, California became a leader in the nation in its emphasis on a history- and geography-centered curriculum.

The 17 characteristics in the framework identify points of emphasis; the goals and strands delineate the literacies to be developed at each grade. The course descriptions identify content units that allow for breadth of coverage in world history across grades six, seven, and ten and in literature and studies of cultures in the primary grades. Also presented in the course descriptions are in-depth studies at each grade level that make learning understandable and memorable. The studies are connected to United States history units of study in grades five, eight, and eleven and to relevant issues in the world today.

California teachers have responded enthusiastically to the framework's increased attention to world history; however, many have found that combining appropriate chronological coverage with in-depth studies of important issues is a difficult challenge. Teachers and students appear to enjoy the in-depth studies so much that important course content may be never fully covered; this dilemma is a testament to the inherent appeal of the subject as well as to the skill of the teachers.

Field surveys conducted in 1994 revealed gaps in student learning when only in-depth studies were emphasized. For example, in some sixth grade classrooms students never reached the study of ancient Rome because of the extended time they spent on the study of Mesopotamia and Egypt earlier in the year. Some seventh graders never studied about Europe during the Renaissance, the Reformation, and the Scientific Revolution—the Age of Exploration to the Enlightenment. In both cases, the balance within the world history curriculum was skewed, particularly in relation to the influence of religion and the rise of democratic ideals. When the teaching of chronological eras was divided among three grade levels, it was anticipated that there would be more time for coverage as well as for in-depth studies. To make such an expectation a reality, however, teachers must give serious thought to prioritization of topics for in-depth studies and the selection of time-efficient strategies and curriculum integration.

Both in-depth studies and coverage are important. When students do not receive the benefit of chronological coverage, their teachers in the subsequent grades feel a tremendous imposition on their responsibilities, whether United States history or world history is the subject. This situation emphasizes the need for curriculum specialists and history–social science teachers, both within grade levels and across the grades, to plan together and articulate the curriculum, resources to be used, and selected areas for important in-depth studies.

In-depth studies are engaging to students, but selectivity is key and reasonableness in duration is imperative to ensure that essential units and topics are also covered each year. Curriculum specialists and teachers are referred to the *Course Models* for grades six, seven, and ten for teachers' recommendations regarding appropriate amounts of time to spend on each unit and topic. Those publications also suggest some resources for in-depth studies that extend beyond a single instructional resource.

Implementation of the 1988 framework was a primary topic of field inquiry in 1994, when the publication was scheduled for updating. Coverage of the world history chronology was a major issue, and the challenge of content coverage for teachers of grade seven, in particular, was identified. The following strategies were suggested by teachers as local options for the world history sequence. The strategies allow for coverage, incorporate the content, and continue to provide for selected in-depth studies. Each option is intended to support the distinguishing characteristics of the framework, in particular those enumerated in the introduction and indicated below in parentheses:

- The centering in the chronological study of history (1)
- An integrated and correlated approach to the teaching of history–social science (2)
- The importance of history as a story well told (3)
- The enrichment of the study of history with the use of literature (4)
- The importance of studying major historical events and periods in depth as opposed to superficial skimming of enormous amounts of material (6)
- A sequential curriculum (7)
- Three years of world history (9)
- The frequent study and discussion of the principles of democracy and the presence or absence of the rights of the individual (12)
- The presentation of controversial issues honestly and accurately within their historical or contemporary context (13)
- The importance of religion in human history (14)
- The inclusion of critical thinking skills (15)
- A variety of content-appropriate teaching methods that engage students actively in the learning process (16)

Because of the disparity in the numbers of units addressed at each grade in which world history is taught (five units at grade six, eleven units at grade seven, and eight units at grade ten), the following options are offered to address the coverage issue at grade seven with additional suggestions for the other grade levels affected:

1. Move the unit "Connecting with Past Learnings: The Fall of Rome" to grade six to follow "East Meets West: Rome." Sixth-grade students can then study the rise and the fall of the Roman Empire in the same year.
2. In the unit "Civilizations of the Americas," move the portion of the unit that examines the period before A.D. from grade seven to grade six. Students would learn that civilizations were developing in both the eastern and western hemispheres during that period.
3. Move the unit "Early Modern Europe: The Age of Exploration to the Enlightenment" from grade seven to grade eight where it can become the preface to the study of the political ideas and institutions of the United States. The Enlightenment receives further emphasis at grade ten in the unit "Connecting with Past Learnings: The Rise of Democratic Ideas."

4. To compensate for the addition at grade eight, move the grade eight unit "The Rise of Industrial America: 1877–1914" (the studies of the Gilded Age, Social Darwinism, and Progressives) to grade eleven where it is already suggested in *Course Models for Grade Ten* as a unit for in-depth focus.

5. Among the history–social science elective course offerings at grade nine, include a semester of in-depth studies in world history of the kind loved by students at grades six and seven that could not be included for all units because of the need for chronological coverage.

6. Add a fourth year of world history at grade nine instead of the suggested year of electives. This addition would allow for the distribution of the units/historical chronology across four grades (six, seven, nine, ten) instead of only three (six, seven, ten). With this new distribution, teachers would be able to explore more units in depth.

7. As an alternative to the deletion of a year of varied electives at grade nine, include the opportunities for varied electives described in the framework throughout the high school years. This alternative is suggested as an addition to, not a replacement for, any of the required courses: one year of world history, cultures, and geography; one year of U.S. history, cultures, and geography; a semester of American government and civics; and a semester of economics. In high schools where students can take six or seven courses per semester, elective options can be further augmented. This possibility is highly desirable for an educated citizenry.

In addition to the options cited above, it is strongly recommended that teachers of history and geography work closely with teachers of English–language arts and teachers of visual and performing arts to plan core programs or integrated curricula. When teachers provide a careful selection of resources and activities that support a thinking, meaning-centered approach for each discipline, they help students make meaningful connections and learn important concepts in several curricular areas. This interdisciplinary approach is a more efficient use of instructional time as well. The previously mentioned *Course Models* give many examples that use this technique.

In conclusion, teachers who use the cited options must articulate and agree on strategies across grades and share their resources. Decisions should not be made arbitrarily, but if coverage is not addressed, key eras, events, and issues may be lost. By working collaboratively across grade levels, teachers can establish reasonable agreements about what is to be covered at each grade. Appropriate teaching strategies can then be developed to ensure a balance between engaging in-depth study and sufficient coverage.

References Cited

Course Models for the History–Social Science Framework, Grade Seven—World History and Geography: Medieval and Early Modern Times. Sacramento: California Department of Education, 1994.

Course Models for the History–Social Science Framework, Grade Six—World History and Geography: Ancient Civilizations. Sacramento: California Department of Education, 1993.

Course Models for the History–Social Science Framework, Grade Ten—World History, Culture, and Geography: The Modern World. Sacramento: California Department of Education, 1995.

Appendix E

Examples of Careers in History–Social Science

The knowledge and ways of thinking and problem solving that students learn through the study of history–social science in kindergarten through grade twelve provide skills for effective citizenship in a democratic society. Those skills also open the door to a variety of career possibilities.

Today's job market is in rapid transition. The restructuring, downsizing, and reconfiguring of businesses and professional services are reshaping the American workplace to address a global, interdependent economy. Emerging technologies are redefining how we discover, store, and use information. According to Willard Daggett, Director of the International Center for Leadership in Education, three of five jobs that will be available in the twenty-first century are not yet known. Recent research also indicates that workers in the twenty-first century will change occupations at least five to seven times throughout their lifetimes. Such changes will require workers to demonstrate adaptability, flexibility, and creativity; resiliency in a changing job market will be a necessity.

Today, and in the emerging workplace, why study history–social science? Career titles in the *Occupational Outlook Handbook, 1994–1995 Edition** fall into five possible categories: information specification; educational services (provided by environmental and governmental entities, among others); business administration and management; teaching; and technology services. The knowledge and skills gained from a rigorous history-centered curriculum—integrated with geography, the other social sciences, and the humanities—contribute to a wide range of career choices in these categories. The following is a limited list of job titles which characterize the expanding field of information specialization:

Admissions officer	Employment interviewer
Administrative assistant	Library and information specialist
Assistant editor	Market researcher
Assistant planner	Media specialist
Claims adjudicator	Paralegal
Communications assistant	Planner
Computer programmer	Policy analyst
Counselor	Research assistant, public policies
Corporate historian	Securities information researcher
Customer service representative	Software specialist
Database network coordinator	System analyst
Database/records manager	Teacher
Development associate for research	Travel agent
Economic researcher	

The challenge of helping students identify the full range of employment possibilities must be met by school counselors and teachers; persons in business, industry, and public

---

*Bureau of Labor Statistics Staff. Washington, D.C.: U.S. Department of Labor, 1994.

service; and researchers. The preceding list and the following chart serve as starting points.

The chart reflects a sample of today's possibilities for careers in history–social science or places for employment. Although a linear list does not present inter-disciplinary connections—knowledge and skills beneficial to full competency in the role—the examples do represent a broad range of important and meaningful careers.

Civics	Economics	Geography	History
Education	*Education*	*Education*	*Education*
Primary teacher	Primary teacher	Primary teacher	Primary teacher
Secondary teacher	Secondary teacher	Secondary teacher	Secondary teacher
Higher education instructor	Higher education instructor	Higher education instructor	Higher education instructor
Adult education	Adult education	Adult education	Adult education
Corporate training programs	Corporate training programs	Research	Corporate training programs
Research	Research	Climate	Research librarian
		Land form	
Government and Business	*Finance*	Marketing	*Applied History*
Elected official	Financial planning	Minerals	Archives management
Staff to elected officials or governing bodies	Investment services	Soil	Business and corporate history
	Accounting	Urban systems	
	Auditing	Vegetation	Cultural resource management
Policy analysis	Business and corporate finance	Water	Foreign service
Foreign service	Insurance	*Cartography*	Historic preservation and restoration
Law	Banking	Cartographer	
Records management	Securities	Cartographic draftsperson	Historic site archaeology
Publishing	Appraiser	Cartographic illustrator	Library science
Banking	Credit representative, analyst, manager	Map analyst	Museum operations
Communications media		Map librarian	Historical analysis
Insurance	Benefits analyst	Environment	Research
Human services worker	Business management	Environmental planner	Genealogical services
Marketing	Human services worker	Soil conservationist	Publishing
Real estate	Fashion buyer/ designer	Soil geographer	Banking
Speech writer	Research	Surveyor	Communications media
Columnist	Communications media	Park ranger	Insurance
Court reporter	Journalism	Oil companies	Investment services
Police officer	Utilities	Geographic information systems (GIS) analyst/ technician	Journalism
Technical writer	Law		Law
Customer service representative	Labor relations	Geologist	Manufacturing
	Fiscal policy analysis	Industrial developer	Marketing and advertising
	Real estate	Intelligence analyst	
	Elected official	International economist	Mineral extraction industries
	Staff to elected officials or governing bodies	Librarian	Public relations
		Meteorologist	Utilities
		Climatologist	Antiques
		Oceanographer	Architecture
		Political analyst	Audiovisual productions
		Urban planner	Engineering
		Archives and records services	Environmental sciences
		Aerial photo interpreter	Finance
		Marketing analyst	Tourism
		Travel consultant	Military

Appendix F

Using Primary Sources in the Study of History

Introduction

Teachers of history at all grade levels have recently begun to encourage their students not just to study history but to investigate it, in much the same way that professional historians engage in research into the past. Teachers attest that this is one of the best ways to make history exciting for their students, and also to increase students' retention and understanding of the material.

Fundamental to this process are primary sources, which lie as much at the heart of history as experiments lie at the heart of science. Students of history should be given opportunities to read and analyze primary sources, to wrestle with their meanings, and to attempt to interpret them and place them in context. They need to see that observers of events in the past often disagreed with one another, and that a single primary source from a period provides only part of a picture. They need to become critical, to wonder if an account was written by an eyewitness or as hearsay, to look for clues to the author's particular intent in writing a certain way.

To begin to deal with primary sources, students need to develop an understanding of what they are, and how to read them. Primary sources include written documents, images, and artifacts from the period being studied; secondary sources, on the other hand, are interpretations and syntheses of primary sources, such as textbooks.

The distinction between a primary source and a secondary source is not always clear-cut, and sometimes a single document might be both. Not all documents written long ago are primary sources; they may be syntheses based on yet earlier material. For example, Edward Gibbons's *Decline and Fall of the Roman Empire,* written around the time of the American Revolution, is a secondary source for understanding ancient history, but a primary source for understanding intellectual movements of the eighteenth century.

Historians tend to begin their research by finding and reading up-to-date secondary sources, both books and articles, on their chosen topic. In this way they learn what has already been discovered, what the main schools of thought are about their topic, and what has yet to be investigated. They decide which arguments are compelling and which seem grounded on weak evidence, and in so doing, they refine their research topics and begin to identify the primary sources they will need to consult.

Most primary sources are unpublished. They are found in archives, or in special collections at libraries or historical societies. A historian working from a specific group of sources such as these works like a detective, piecing together strands of evidence to understand what happened and why it happened. The historian's conclusions are written up as a book or article that is very specific in terms of the time period, region,

This appendix was written by Amanda Podany, former executive director of the California History–Social Science Project and an associate professor of history at California State Polytechnic University, Pomona.

and subject matter covered. This type of work is called a monograph. The author of a textbook synthesizes the findings from many monographs to create a narrative covering a longer period of time.

Types of Primary Sources

Documents make up most, but not all, of the primary source materials used by historians. These fall into a number of categories. Public documents include such items as congressional records, royal inscriptions, peace treaties, censuses, codes of law, and diplomatic correspondence. These documents can be found in state archives and help to shed light on, for example, politics, the government, and international relations. Private documents include personal letters, diaries, and other personal records. Personal documents from "average citizens" can tell us a great deal about society, giving us insights into matters such as family structure, relations between men and women, possibilities for social mobility, and daily life.

Works of literature can also be seen in some cases as primary sources for the period in which they were written, if they are set in the author's own time and place. The characters in a novel may be the author's own creations, but he or she is likely to have cast them in a social, economic, political, religious, and physical environment that was true to life.

One needs to be cautious, however, in using works of literature to illuminate historical periods. If the work is modern and purports to describe life long ago, there is a good chance that the author has recreated a past that suits the story, rather than portraying the past as a historian would see it. Works such as these are clearly not primary sources. They may be wonderful stories, but they cannot be analyzed for insights into history.

Religious writings also enrich our understanding about the past. Parts of the Bible can be considered to be a primary source for the history of the ancient Israelites, and they give us particular insights into the religious views of men and women of that civilization. In the same way the Analects of Confucius and the Koran are primary sources for understanding Confucianism and Islam. Hymns, myths, and legends tell us about the beliefs of the people for whom they were sacred literature.

Nonwritten sources are also vital for the reconstruction of history. These include buildings, objects, and works of art that have remained in use or continued to be appreciated since they were made, along with those that have fallen into disuse and been rediscovered (sometimes through archaeological excavation). For the history of the last century, photographs, films, and videos can all be analyzed as primary sources. All aspects of the material environment tell us something about the history of the time that produced them.

Historical Critique of Sources

Each primary source consulted must be subjected to criticism to assess its value for the reconstruction of the history of its period. One needs to ask a number of probing questions: Is the document or image authentic? For whom was it written or produced and why? Did the author create it as propaganda for a particular cause? Was it written by an eyewitness? Has the document been translated, and has the format been changed in translation (from poetry into prose, for example)? Most primary sources reflect their author's particular point of view; this does not make them less valuable. The reader simply needs to be aware of the author's perspective and to avoid taking the source at face value.

Problems of Translation

Historical documents that were written in English tend to be published in their original form. This practice can create problems of interpretation for early documents because the language has changed significantly over the centuries. Any type of paraphrase or attempt to render the document in modern English is an interpretation and compromises the authenticity of the document. However, students can often learn to develop their own paraphrasing so that they may understand the meaning of text.

Some primary sources from other cultures have been translated into English so that students and other general readers can understand them. The translated document is not a carbon copy of the original; it is an interpretation by the translator so that it makes sense to an English-speaking audience.

Poetry is singularly difficult to translate, because the effectiveness of the original depends so much on the sounds and rhythms of the language in which it was written. Sometimes a translation will also be in a poetic form, but it often contains subtle changes in meaning that are required to adapt the forms of English to the original poetic structure. On the other hand, it may be translated into prose, with less change in meaning but with a complete loss of the poetic structure.

Finally, translation can be misleading in its style. A classic example is the King James Version of the New Testament. This work includes some of the most eloquent literature available in English. The Greek original, however, was written in *koine,* the dialect of the streets. A translation that reflected the style of the original would have to include colloquialisms that one would never suspect from reading the King James Version.

Conclusion

Interpreting primary sources can be an excellent way to increase historical understanding in the classroom. After gaining a general sense of the historical background of a particular period or event, students can look at several primary sources, both written and visual, from the same time period, to understand the era in greater depth.

Understanding a primary source depends on asking the right questions of the text and analyzing it more deeply than simply summarizing the contents. Interpretation first involves criticism of the document. Following this initial step, students can ask what the document tells us about the time in which it was written. Similar questions can be asked about an object or image. In such a process, details that may not initially seem informative may yield interesting insights when analyzed. After consulting one source, students should look at others to see if the original analyses are confirmed, and, if not, what areas may need to be investigated further.

The type of analysis described above can be done on any primary source, ancient or modern. Such an exercise allows students to work as historians; it prevents them from simply relying on the narrative history presented in the textbook. Students begin to question their assumptions about the past. They also observe that many possible interpretations can be made of a group of documents, and hence of a historical event or era; and that no single, final, and true interpretation preempts all others. In working with primary sources, students can formulate their own interpretations of the past, supported by sound historical evidence.

Appendix G

Bowling Alone: America's Declining Social Capital

Many students of the new democracies that have emerged over the past decade and a half have emphasized the importance of a strong and active civil society to the consolidation of democracy. Especially with regard to the postcommunist countries, scholars and democratic activists alike have lamented the absence or obliteration of traditions of independent civic engagement and a widespread tendency toward passive reliance on the state. To those concerned with the weakness of civil societies in the developing or postcommunist world, the advanced Western democracies and above all the United States have typically been taken as models to be emulated. There is striking evidence, however, that the vibrancy of American civil society has notably declined over the past several decades.

Ever since the publication of Alexis de Tocqueville's *Democracy in America,* the United States has played a central role in systematic studies of the links between democracy and civil society. Although this is in part because trends in American life are often regarded as harbingers of social modernization, it is also because America has traditionally been considered unusually "civic" (a reputation that, as we shall later see, has not been entirely unjustified).

When Tocqueville visited the United States in the 1830s, it was the Americans' propensity for civic association that most impressed him as the key to their unprecedented ability to make democracy work. "Americans of all ages, all stations in life, and all types of disposition," he observed, "are forever forming associations. There are not only commercial and industrial associations in which all take part, but others of a thousand different types—religious, moral, serious, futile, very general and very limited, immensely large and very minute. . . . Nothing, in my view, deserves more attention than the intellectual and moral associations in America."[1]

Recently, American social scientists of a neo-Tocquevillean bent have unearthed a wide range of empirical evidence that the quality of public life and the performance of social institutions (and not only in America) are indeed powerfully influenced by norms and networks of civic engagement. Researchers in such fields as education, urban poverty, unemployment, the control of crime and drug abuse, and even health have discovered that successful outcomes are more likely in civically engaged communities. Similarly, research on the varying economic attainments of different ethnic groups in the United States has demonstrated the importance of social bonds within each group. These results are consistent with research in a wide range of settings that demonstrates the vital importance of social networks for job placement and many other economic outcomes.

Meanwhile, a seemingly unrelated body of research on the sociology of economic development has also focused attention on the role of social networks. Some of this

Note: This article was written by Robert Putnam for the *Journal of Democracy,* Vol. 6, No. 1 (January 1995), 65–78. Reprinted by permission of the Johns Hopkins University Press.

work is situated in the developing countries, and some of it elucidates the peculiarly successful "network capitalism" of East Asia.[2] Even in less exotic Western economies, however, researchers have discovered highly efficient, highly flexible "industrial districts" based on networks of collaboration among workers and small entrepreneurs. Far from being paleoindustrial anachronisms, these dense interpersonal and interorganizational networks undergird ultramodern industries, from the high tech of Silicon Valley to the high fashion of Benetton.

The norms and networks of civic engagement also powerfully affect the performance of representative government. That, at least, was the central conclusion of my own 20-year, quasi-experimental study of subnational governments in different regions of Italy.[3] Although all these regional governments seemed identical on paper, their levels of effectiveness varied dramatically. Systematic inquiry showed that the quality of governance was determined by longstanding traditions of civic engagement (or its absence). Voter turnout, newspaper readership, membership in choral societies and football clubs—these were the hallmarks of a successful region. In fact, historical analysis suggested that these networks of organized reciprocity and civic solidarity, far from being an epiphenomenon of socioeconomic modernization, were a precondition for it.

No doubt the mechanisms through which civic engagement and social connectedness produce such results—better schools, faster economic development, lower crime, and more effective government—are multiple and complex. While these briefly recounted findings require further confirmation and perhaps qualification, the parallels across hundreds of empirical studies in a dozen disparate disciplines and subfields are striking. Social scientists in several fields have recently suggested a common framework for understanding these phenomena, a framework that rests on the concept of social capital.[4] By analogy with notions of physical capital and human capital—tools and training that enhance individual productivity—"social capital" refers to features of social organization such as networks, norms, and social trust that facilitate coordination and cooperation for mutual benefit.

For a variety of reasons, life is easier in a community blessed with a substantial stock of social capital. In the first place, networks of civic engagement foster sturdy norms of generalized reciprocity and encourage the emergence of social trust. Such networks facilitate coordination and communication, amplify reputations, and thus allow dilemmas of collective action to be resolved. When economic and political negotiation is embedded in dense networks of social interaction, incentives for opportunism are reduced. At the same time, networks of civic engagement embody past success at collaboration, which can serve as a cultural template for future collaboration. Finally, dense networks of interaction probably broaden the participants' sense of self, developing the "I" into the "we," or (in the language of rational-choice theorists) enhancing the participants' "taste" for collective benefits.

I do not intend here to survey (much less contribute to) the development of the theory of social capital. Instead, I use the central premise of that rapidly growing body of work—that social connections and civic engagement pervasively influence our public life, as well as our private prospects—as the starting point for an empirical survey of trends in social capital in contemporary America. I concentrate here entirely on the American case, although the developments I portray may in some measure characterize many contemporary societies.

Whatever Happened to Civic Engagement?

We begin with familiar evidence on changing patterns of political participation, not least because it is immediately relevant to issues of democracy in the narrow sense. Consider the well-known decline in turnout in national elections over the last three decades. From a relative high point in the early 1960s, voter turnout had by 1990 declined by nearly a quarter; tens of millions of Americans had forsaken their parents' habitual readiness to engage in the simplest act of citizenship. Broadly similar trends also characterize participation in state and local elections.

It is not just the voting booth that has been increasingly deserted by Americans. A series of identical questions posed by the Roper Organization to national samples ten times each year over the last two decades reveals that since 1973 the number of Americans who report that "in the past year" they have "attended a public meeting on town or school affairs" has fallen by more than a third (from 22 percent in 1973 to 13 percent in 1993). Similar (or even greater) relative declines are evident in responses to questions about attending a political rally or speech, serving on a committee of some local organization, and working for a political party. By almost every measure, Americans' direct engagement in politics and government has fallen steadily and sharply over the last generation, despite the fact that average levels of education—the best individual-level predictor of political participation—have risen sharply throughout this period. Every year over the last decade or two, millions more have withdrawn from the affairs of their communities.

Not coincidentally, Americans have also disengaged psychologically from politics and government over this era. The proportion of Americans who reply that they "trust the government in Washington" only "some of the time" or "almost never" has risen steadily from 30 percent in 1966 to 75 percent in 1992.

These trends are well known, of course, and taken by themselves would seem amenable to a strictly political explanation. Perhaps the long litany of political tragedies and scandals since the 1960s (assassinations, Vietnam, Watergate, Irangate, and so on) has triggered an understandable disgust for politics and government among Americans, and that in turn has motivated their withdrawal. I do not doubt that this common interpretation has some merit, but its limitations become plain when we examine trends in civic engagement of a wider sort.

Our survey of organizational membership among Americans can usefully begin with a glance at the aggregate results of the General Social Survey, a scientifically conducted, national-sample survey that has been repeated 14 times over the last two decades. Church-related groups constitute the most common type of organization joined by Americans; they are especially popular with women. Other types of organizations frequently joined by women include school-service groups (mostly parent-teacher associations), sports groups, professional societies, and literary societies. Among men, sports clubs, labor unions, professional societies, fraternal groups, veterans' groups, and service clubs are all relatively popular.

Religious affiliation is by far the most common associational membership among Americans. Indeed, by many measures America continues to be (even more than in Tocqueville's time) an astonishingly "churched" society. For example, the United States has more houses of worship per capita than any other nation on Earth. Yet religious sentiment in America seems to be becoming somewhat less tied to institutions and more self-defined.

How have these complex crosscurrents played out over the last three or four decades in terms of Americans' engagement with organized religion? The general pattern is clear: The 1960s witnessed a significant drop in reported weekly churchgoing—from roughly 48 percent in the late 1950s to roughly 41 percent in the early 1970s. Since then, it has stagnated or (according to some surveys) declined still further. Meanwhile, data from the General Social Survey show a modest decline in membership in all "church-related groups" over the last 20 years. It would seem, then, that net participation by Americans, both in religious services and in church-related groups, has declined modestly (by perhaps a sixth) since the 1960s.

For many years, labor unions provided one of the most common organizational affiliations among American workers. Yet union membership has been falling for nearly four decades, with the steepest decline occurring between 1975 and 1985. Since the mid-1950s, when union membership peaked, the unionized portion of the nonagricultural workforce in America has dropped by more than half, falling from 32.5 percent in 1953 to 15.8 percent in 1992. By now, virtually all of the explosive growth in union membership that was associated with the New Deal has been erased. The solidarity of union halls is now mostly a fading memory of aging men.[5]

The Parent-Teacher Association (PTA) has been an especially important form of civic engagement in twentieth-century America because parental involvement in the educational process represents a particularly productive form of social capital. It is, therefore, dismaying to discover that participation in parent-teacher organizations has dropped drastically over the last generation, from more than 12 million in 1964 to barely 5 million in 1982 before recovering to approximately 7 million now.

Next, we turn to evidence on membership in (and volunteering for) civic and fraternal organizations. These data show some striking patterns. First, membership in traditional women's groups has declined more or less steadily since the mid-1960s. For example, membership in the national Federation of Women's Clubs is down by more than half (59 percent) since 1964, while membership in the League of Women Voters (LWV) is off 42 percent since 1969.[6]

Similar reductions are apparent in the numbers of volunteers for mainline civic organizations, such as the Boy Scouts (off by 26 percent since 1970) and the Red Cross (off by 61 percent since 1970). But what about the possibility that volunteers have simply switched their loyalties to other organizations? Evidence on "regular" (as opposed to occasional or "drop-by") volunteering is available from the Labor Department's Current Population Surveys of 1974 and 1989. These estimates suggest that serious volunteering declined by roughly one-sixth over these 15 years, from 24 percent of adults in 1974 to 20 percent in 1989. The multitudes of Red Cross aides and Boy Scout troop leaders now missing in action have apparently not been offset by equal numbers of new recruits elsewhere.

Fraternal organizations have also witnessed a substantial drop in membership during the 1980s and 1990s. Membership is down significantly in such groups as the Lions (off 12 percent since 1983), the Elks (off 18 percent since 1979), the Shriners (off 27 percent since 1979), the Jaycees (off 44 percent since 1979), and the Masons (down 39 percent since 1959). In sum, after expanding steadily throughout most of this century, many major civic organizations have experienced a sudden, substantial, and nearly simultaneous decline in membership over the last decade or two.

The most whimsical yet discomfiting bit of evidence of social disengagement in contemporary America that I have discovered is this: more Americans are bowling today than ever before, but bowling in organized leagues has plummeted in the last decade or so. Between 1980 and 1993 the total number of bowlers in America increased by 10 percent, while league bowling decreased by 40 percent. (Lest this be thought a wholly trivial example, I should note that nearly 80 million Americans went bowling at least once during 1993, nearly a third more than voted in the 1994 congressional elections and roughly the same number as claim to attend church regularly. Even after the 1980s' plunge in league bowling, nearly 3 percent of American adults regularly bowl in leagues.) The rise of solo bowling threatens the livelihood of bowling-lane proprietors because those who bowl as members of leagues consume three times as much beer and pizza as solo bowlers, and the money in bowling is in the beer and pizza, not the balls and shoes. The broader social significance, however, lies in the social interaction and even occasionally civic conversations over beer and pizza that solo bowlers forgo. Whether or not bowling beats balloting in the eyes of most Americans, bowling teams illustrate yet another vanishing form of social capital.

Countertrends

At this point, however, we must confront a serious counterargument. Perhaps the traditional forms of civic organization whose decay we have been tracing have been replaced by vibrant new organizations. For example, national environmental organizations (like the Sierra Club) and feminist groups (like the National Organization for Women) grew rapidly during the 1970s and 1980s and now count hundreds of thousands of dues-paying members. An even more dramatic example is the American Association of Retired Persons (AARP), which grew exponentially from 400,000 card-carrying members in 1960 to 33 million in 1993, becoming (after the Catholic Church) the largest private organization in the world. The national administrators of these organizations are among the most feared lobbyists in Washington, in large part because of their massive mailing lists of presumably loyal members.

These new mass-membership organizations are plainly of great political importance. From the point of view of social connectedness, however, they are sufficiently different from classic "secondary associations" that we need to invent a new label— perhaps "tertiary associations." For the vast majority of their members, the only act of membership consists in writing a check for dues or perhaps occasionally reading a newsletter. Few ever attend any meetings of such organizations, and most are unlikely ever (knowingly) to encounter any other member. The bond between any two members of the Sierra Club is less like the bond between any two members of a gardening club and more like the bond between any two Red Sox fans (or perhaps any two devoted Honda owners): they root for the same team and they share some of the same interests, but they are unaware of each other's existence. Their ties, in short, are to common symbols, common leaders, and perhaps common ideals, but not to one another. The theory of social capital argues that associational membership should, for example, increase social trust, but this prediction is much less straightforward with regard to membership in tertiary associations. From the point of view of social connectedness, the

Environmental Defense Fund and a bowling league are just not in the same category.

If the growth of tertiary organizations represents one potential (but probably not real) counterexample to my thesis, a second countertrend is represented by the growing prominence of nonprofit organizations, especially nonprofit service agencies. This so-called third sector includes everything from Oxfam and the Metropolitan Museum of Art to the Ford Foundation and the Mayo Clinic. In other words, although most secondary associations are nonprofits, most nonprofit agencies are not secondary associations. To identify trends in the size of the nonprofit sector with trends in social connectedness would be another fundamental conceptual mistake.[7]

A third potential countertrend is much more relevant to an assessment of social capital and civic engagement. Some able researchers have argued that the last few decades have witnessed a rapid expansion in "support groups" of various sorts. Robert Wuthnow reports that fully 40 percent of all Americans claim to be "currently involved in [a] small group that meets regularly and provides support or caring for those who participate in it."[8] Many of these groups are religiously affiliated, but many others are not. For example, nearly 5 percent of Wuthnow's national sample claim to participate regularly in a "self-help" group, such as Alcoholics Anonymous, and nearly as many say they belong to book-discussion groups and hobby clubs.

The groups described by Wuthnow's respondents unquestionably represent an important form of social capital, and they need to be accounted for in any serious reckoning of trends in social connectedness. On the other hand, they do not typically play the same role as traditional civic associations. As Wuthnow emphasizes,

> Small groups may not be fostering community as effectively as many of their proponents would like. Some small groups merely provide occasions for individuals to focus on themselves in the presence of others. The social contract binding members together asserts only the weakest of obligations. Come if you have time. Talk if you feel like it. Respect everyone's opinion. Never criticize. Leave quietly if you become dissatisfied. . . . We can imagine that {these small groups} really substitute for families, neighborhoods, and broader community attachments that may demand lifelong commitments, when, in fact, they do not.[9]

All three of these potential countertrends—tertiary organizations, nonprofit organizations, and support groups—need somehow to be weighed against the erosion of conventional civic organizations. One way of doing so is to consult the General Social Survey.

Within all educational categories, total associational membership declined significantly between 1967 and 1993. Among the college-educated, the average number of group memberships per person fell from 2.8 to 2.0 (a 26-percent decline); among high-school graduates, the number fell from 1.8 to 1.2 (32 percent); and among those with fewer than 12 years of education, the number fell from 1.4 to 1.1 (25 percent). In other words, at all educational (and hence social) levels of American society, and counting all sorts of group memberships, the average number of associational memberships has fallen by about a fourth over the last quarter-century. Without controls for educational levels, the trend is not nearly so clear, but the central point is this: more Americans than ever before are in social circumstances that foster associational involvement (higher education, middle age, and so on), but nevertheless aggregate associational membership appears to be stagnant or declining.

Broken down by type of group, the downward trend is most marked for church-related groups, for labor unions, for fraternal and veterans' organizations, and for school-service groups. Conversely, membership in professional associations has risen over these years, although less than might have been predicted, given sharply rising educational and occupational levels. Essentially the same trends are evident for both men and women in the sample. In short, the available survey evidence confirms our earlier conclusion: American social capital in the form of civic associations has significantly eroded over the last generation.

Good Neighborliness and Social Trust

I noted earlier that most readily available quantitative evidence on trends in social connectedness involves formal settings, such as the voting booth, the union hall, or the PTA. One glaring exception is so widely discussed as to require little comment here: the most fundamental form of social capital is the family, and the massive evidence of the loosening of bonds within the family (both extended and nuclear) is well known. This trend, of course, is quite consistent with—and may help to explain—our theme of social decapitalization.

A second aspect of informal social capital on which we happen to have reasonably reliable time-series data involves neighborliness. In each General Social Survey since 1974 respondents have been asked, "How often do you spend a social evening with a neighbor?" The proportion of Americans who socialize with their neighbors more than once a year has slowly but steadily declined over the last two decades, from 72 percent in 1974 to 61 percent in 1993. (On the other hand, socializing with "friends who do not live in your neighborhood" appears to be on the increase, a trend that may reflect the growth of workplace-based social connections.)

Americans are also less trusting. The proportion of Americans saying that most people can be trusted fell by more than a third between 1960, when 58 percent chose that alternative, and 1993, when only 37 percent did. The same trend is apparent in all educational groups; indeed, because social trust is also correlated with education and because educational levels have risen sharply, the overall decrease in social trust is even more apparent if we control for education.

Our discussion of trends in social connectedness and civic engagement has tacitly assumed that all the forms of social capital that we have discussed are themselves coherently correlated across individuals. This is in fact true. Members of associations are much more likely than nonmembers to participate in politics, to spend time with neighbors, to express social trust, and so on.

The close correlation between social trust and associational membership is true not only across time and across individuals, but also across countries. Evidence from the 1991 World Values Survey demonstrates the following:[10]

1. Across the 35 countries in this survey, social trust and civic engagement are strongly correlated; the greater the density of associational membership in a society, the more trusting its citizens. Trust and engagement are two facets of the same underlying factor—social capital.
2. America still ranks relatively high by cross-national standards on both these dimensions of social capital. Even in the 1990s, after several decades' erosion,

Americans are more trusting and more engaged than people in most other countries of the world.

3. The trends of the past quarter-century, however, have apparently moved the United States significantly lower in the international rankings of social capital. The recent deterioration in American social capital has been sufficiently great that (if no other country changed its position in the meantime) another quarter-century of change at the same rate would bring the United States, roughly speaking, to the midpoint among all these countries, roughly equivalent to South Korea, Belgium, or Estonia today. Two generations' decline at the same rate would leave the United States at the level of today's Chile, Portugal, and Slovenia.

Why Is U.S. Social Capital Eroding?

As we have seen, something has happened in America in the last two decades to diminish civic engagement and social connectedness. What could that "something" be? Here are several possible explanations, along with some initial evidence on each.

The movement of women into the labor force. Over these same two or three decades, many millions of American women have moved out of the home into paid employment. This is the primary, though not the sole, reason why the weekly working hours of the average American have increased significantly during these years. It seems highly plausible that this social revolution should have reduced the time and energy available for building social capital. For certain organizations, such as the PTA, the League of Women Voters, the Federation of Women's Clubs, and the Red Cross, this is almost certainly an important part of the story. The sharpest decline in women's civic participation seems to have come in the 1970s; membership in such "women's" organizations as these has been virtually halved since the late 1960s. By contrast, most of the decline in participation in men's organizations occurred about ten years later; the total decline to date has been approximately 25 percent for the typical organization. On the other hand, the survey data imply that the aggregate declines for men are virtually as great as those for women. It is logically possible, of course, that the male declines might represent the knock-on effect of women's liberation, as dishwashing crowded out the lodge, but time-budget studies suggest that most husbands of working wives have assumed only a minor part of the housework. In short, something besides the women's revolution seems to lie behind the erosion of social capital.

Mobility: The "re-potting" hypothesis. Numerous studies of organizational involvement have shown that residential stability and such related phenomena as homeownership are clearly associated with greater civic engagement. Mobility, like frequent re-potting of plants, tends to disrupt root systems, and it takes time for an uprooted individual to put down new roots. It seems plausible that the automobile, suburbanization, and the movement to the Sun Belt have reduced the social rooted-ness of the average American, but one fundamental difficulty with this hypothesis is apparent: the best evidence shows that residential stability and homeownership in America have risen modestly since 1965, and are surely higher now than during the 1950s, when civic engagement and social connectedness by our measures was definitely higher.

Other demographic transformations. A range of additional changes have transformed the American family since the 1960s—fewer marriages, more divorces, fewer children, lower real wages, and so on. Each of these changes might account for some of the slackening of civic engagement, since married, middle-class parents are generally more socially involved than other people. Moreover, the changes in scale that have swept over the American economy in these years—illustrated by the replacement of the corner grocery by the supermarket and now perhaps of the supermarket by electronic shopping at home, or the replacement of community-based enterprises by outposts of distant multinational firms—may perhaps have undermined the material and even physical basis for civic engagement.

The technological transformation of leisure. There is reason to believe that deep-seated technological trends are radically "privatizing" or "individualizing" our use of leisure time and thus disrupting many opportunities for social-capital formation. The most obvious and probably the most powerful instrument of this revolution is television. Time-budget studies in the 1960s showed that the growth in time spent watching television dwarfed all other changes in the way Americans passed their days and nights. Television has made our communities (or, rather, what we experience as our communities) wider and shallower. In the language of economics, electronic technology enables individual tastes to be satisfied more fully, but at the cost of the positive social externalities associated with more primitive forms of entertainment. The same logic applies to the replacement of vaudeville by the movies and now of movies by the VCR. The new "virtual reality" helmets that we will soon don to be entertained in total isolation are merely the latest extension of this trend. Is technology thus driving a wedge between our individual interests and our collective interests? It is a question that seems worth exploring more systematically.

What Is to Be Done?

The last refuge of a social-scientific scoundrel is to call for more research. Nevertheless, I cannot forbear from suggesting some further lines of inquiry.

- We must sort out the dimension of social capital, which clearly is not a unidimensional concept, despite language (even in this essay) that implies the contrary. What types of organizations and networks most effectively embody— or generate—social capital, in the sense of mutual reciprocity, the resolution of dilemmas of collective action, and the broadening of social identities? In this essay I have emphasized the density of associational life. In earlier work I stressed the structure of networks, arguing that "horizontal" ties represented more productive social capital than vertical ties.[11]

- Another set of important issues involves macrosociological crosscurrents that might intersect with the trends described here. What will be the impact, for example, of electronic networks on social capital? My hunch is that meeting in an electronic forum is not the equivalent of meeting in a bowling alley—or even in a saloon—but hard empirical research is needed. What about the development of social capital in the workplace? Is it growing in counterpoint to decline of civic engagement, reflecting some social analogue of the first law of thermodynamics—social capital is neither created nor destroyed, merely redistributed? Or do the trends described in this essay represent a deadweight loss?

- A rounded assessment of changes in American social capital over the last quarter-century needs to count the costs as well as the benefits of community engagement. We must not romanticize small-town, middle-class civic life in the America of the 1950s. In addition to the deleterious trends emphasized in this essay, recent decades have witnessed a substantial decline in intolerance and probably also in overt discrimination, and those beneficent trends may be related in complex ways to the erosion of traditional social capital. Moreover, a balanced accounting of the social-capital books would need to reconcile the insights of this approach with the undoubted insights offered by Mancur Olson and others who stress that closely knit social, economic, and political organizations are prone to inefficient cartelization and to what political economists term "rent seeking" and ordinary men and women call corruption.[12]

- Finally, and perhaps most urgently, we need to explore creatively how public policy impinges on (or might impinge on) social-capital formation. In some well-known instances, public policy has destroyed highly effective social networks and norms. American slum-clearance policy of the 1950s and 1960s, for example, renovated physical capital, but at a very high cost to existing social capital. The consolidation of country post offices and small school districts has promised administrative and financial efficiencies, but full-cost accounting for the effects of these policies on social capital might produce a more negative verdict. On the other hand, such past initiatives as the county agricultural-agent system, community colleges, and tax deductions for charitable contributions illustrate that government can encourage social-capital formation. Even a recent proposal in San Luis Obispo, California, to require that all new houses have front porches illustrates the power of government to influence where and how networks are formed.

The concept of "civil society" has played a central role in the recent global debate about the preconditions for democracy and democratization. In the newer democracies this phrase has properly focused attention on the need to foster a vibrant civic life in soils traditionally inhospitable to self-government. In the established democracies, ironically growing numbers of citizens are questioning the effectiveness of their public institutions at the very moment when liberal democracy has swept the battlefield, both ideologically and geopolitically. In America, at least, there is reason to suspect that this democratic disarray may be linked to a broad and continuing erosion of civic engagement that began a quarter-century ago. High on our scholarly agenda should be the question of whether a comparable erosion of social capital may be under way in other advanced democracies, perhaps in different institutional and behavioral guises. High on America's agenda should be the question of how to reverse these adverse trends in social connectedness, thus restoring civic engagement and civic trust.

Note: Robert D. Putnam is Dillon Professor of International Affairs and director of the Center for International Affairs at Harvard University. His most recent books are *Double-Edged Diplomacy: International Bargaining and Domestic Politics* (1993) and *Making Democracy Work: Civic Traditions in Modern Italy* (1993). He is now completing a study of the revitalization of American democracy.

Endnotes

[1]Alexis de Tocqueville, *Democracy in America,* ed. J. P. Maier, trans. George Lawrence (Garden City, N.Y.: Anchor Books, 1969), 513–17.

[2]On social networks and economic growth in the developing world, see Milton J. Esman and Norman Uphoff, *Local Organizations: Intermediaries in Rural Development* (Ithaca: Cornell University Press, 1984), esp. 15–42 and 99–180; and Albert O. Hirschman, *Getting Ahead Collectively: Grassroots Experiences in Latin America* (Elmsford, N.Y.: Pergamon Press, 1984), esp. 42–77. On East Asia, see Gustav Papanek, "The New Asian Capitalism: An Economic Portrait," in Peter L. Berger and Hsin-Huang Hsiao, eds., *In Search of an East Asian Development Model* (New Brunswick, N.J.: Transaction, 1987), 27–80; Peter B. Evans, "The State as Problem and Solution: Predation, Embedded Autonomy and Structural Change," in Stephan Haggard and Robert R. Kaufman, eds., *The Politics of Economic Adjustment* (Princeton, N.J.: Princeton University Press, 1992), 139–81; and Gary G. Hamilton, William Zeile, and Wan-Jin Kim, "Network Structure of East Asian Economies," in Stewart R. Clegg and S. Gordon Redding, eds., *Capitalism in Contrasting Cultures* (Hawthorne, N.Y.: De Gruyter, 1990), 105–29. See also Gary G. Hamilton and Nicole Woolsey Biggart, "Market, Culture, and Authority: A Comparative Analysis of Management and Organization in the Far East," *American Journal of Sociology* (Supplement) 94 (1988): S52–S94; and Susan Greenhalgh, "Families and Networks in Taiwan's Economic Development," in Edwin Winckler and Susan Greenhalgh, eds., *Contending Approaches to the Political Economy of Taiwan* (Armonk, N.Y.: M. E. Sharpe, 1987), 224–45.

[3]Robert D. Putnam, *Making Democracy Work: Civic Traditions in Modern Italy* (Princeton, N.J.: Princeton University Press, 1993).

[4]James S. Coleman deserves primary credit for developing the "social capital" theoretical framework. See his "Social Capital in the Creation of Human Capital, *American Journal of Sociology* (Supplement) 94 (1988): S95–S120, as well as his *The Foundations of Social Theory* (Cambridge: Harvard University Press, 1990), 300–21. See also Mark Granovetter, "Economic Action and Social Structure: The Problem of Embeddedness," *American Journal of Sociology* 91 (1985): 481–510; Glenn C. Loury, "Why Should We Care About Group Inequality?" *Social Philosophy and Policy* 5 (1987): 249–71; and Robert D. Putnam, "The Prosperous Community: Social Capital and Public Life," *American Prospect* 13 (1993): 35–42. To my knowledge, the first scholar to use the term "social capital" in its current sense was Jane Jacobs, in *The Death and Life of Great American Cities* (New York: Random House, 1961), 138.

[5]Any simplistically political interpretation of the collapse of American unionism would need to confront the fact that the steepest decline began more than six years before the Reagan administration's attack on PATCO. Data from the General Social Survey show a roughly 40-percent decline in reported union membership between 1975 and 1991.

[6]Data for the LWV are available over a longer time span and show an interesting pattern: a sharp slump during the Depression, a strong and sustained rise after World War II that more than tripled membership between 1945 and 1969, and then the post-1969 decline, which has already erased virtually all the postwar gains and continues still. This same historical pattern applies to those men's fraternal organizations for which comparable data are available—steady increases for the first seven decades of the century, interrupted only by the Great Depression, followed by a collapse in the 1970s and 1980s that has already wiped out most of the postwar expansion and continues apace.

[7]Lester M. Salamon, "The Rise of the Nonprofit Sector," Foreign Affairs 73 (July–August 1994): 109–22. See also Salamon, "Partners in Public Service: The Scope and Theory of Government-Nonprofit Relations," in Walter W. Powell, ed., *The Nonprofit Sector: A Research Handbook*

(New Haven: Yale University Press, 1987), 99–117. Salamon's empirical evidence does not sustain his broad claims about a global "associational revolution" comparable in significance to the rise of the nation-state several centuries ago.

[8]Robert Wuthnow, *Sharing the Journey: Support Groups and America's New Quest for Community* (New York: The Free Press, 1994), 45.

[9]Ibid., 3–6.

[10]I am grateful to Ronald Inglehart, who directs this unique cross-national project, for sharing these highly useful data with me. See his "The Impact of Culture on Economic Development: Theory, Hypotheses, and Some Empirical Test" (unpublished manuscript, University of Michigan, 1994).

[11]See my *Making Democracy Work,* esp. ch. 6.

[12]See Mancur Olson, The Rise and Decline of Nations: Economic Growth, Stagflation, and Social Rigidities (New Haven, Conn.: Yale University Press, 1982), 2.

Appendix H

History–Social Science
and Service-Learning

History–social science presents many opportunities for students, teachers, and community partners to use the instructional method known as service-learning. Service-learning is a teaching and learning strategy whereby students learn the content standards through thoughtfully organized service to the community, the service providing the context for learning. The history–social science curriculum and standards call for students to engage in activities in which they use their knowledge to help define their present and future roles as active citizens, and one of the best ways of achieving such student engagement is through service-learning activities.

The *History–Social Science Framework* supports service-learning, stating, "This framework provides opportunities for students' participation in school and community service programs and activities." Service-learning has demonstrated effectiveness in improving student achievement. For example, the 1998 NAEP Civic Report Card for the Nation reports: "Twelfth-grade students who did volunteer work, whether through their school or on their own, had significantly higher civics assessment scale scores than students who did not participate in volunteer work." Furthermore, the richness of history, geography, economics, and civics provides the foundational knowledge and skills for community participation and civic engagement. Students who experience civic responsibility become responsible citizens.

Service-learning in California takes many forms. Project Citizen provides students in grade nine the opportunity to apply their analytical skills to a local need and present possible solutions. The project holds a statewide competition with the winner advancing to the competition's national level. Important to Project Citizen is not only students' spirit of civic engagement but also the demonstration of their research, analytical, and writing skills. Students must conduct an extensive investigation of an issue and examine it from multiple perspectives before providing possible solutions. Only with knowledge and skills acquired in the earlier grades are ninth-graders able to complete their projects successfully. In 1998 California students were able to demonstrate their academic prowess and their deep concern for their community, going on to win the national competition for Project Citizen.

An educational partnership between the Tehama County Museum and the Los Molinos Unified School District that began in 1996 provides a prime example of how students in service-learning programs can apply their understanding of the history–social science content and practical skills in their own community and gain a working and usable knowledge of the history–social science standards. Through this partnership high school students in the district's U.S. history class serve as weekend junior docents for the museum. Under the guidance of local historians, the student docents present their interpretations of local history based on oral histories as well as primary sources. Not only does a student's knowledge of the local history increase, but also the student's understanding of how national trends intersect with local changes. Key to a student's increasing knowledge and extending of service is the experience of working with other members of the community. Because much of the local history has been handed down orally rather than written, students must conduct interviews and receive guidance in the use of their community's primary historical sources. As one student explained, "The person's personal history or knowledge of the subject will live on through the person that was interviewing." The students further extend their service-learning by writing books on local history for third- and fourth-grade students. The museum, in turn, benefits from the students' displays and the youthful energy they bring to the museum. This example of service-learning demonstrates that students can indeed advance their knowledge and apply their skills to community service to the benefit of everyone involved.

City Works provides another example of combining the history–social science standards with service-learning. This program is designed for use as a component of California's grade-twelve U.S. government course. By addressing community problems through service-learning projects, teachers participating in this program help students understand the link between local, state, and national governments. The standards-based City Works program provides a structure for the development of research skills, including the assignment of a research paper, thus enriching and supporting the government curriculum in grade twelve.

R03-010 403-0004-04 1-05 20M

OSP 05 88157